THE REFLECTED FACE OF AFRICA

The Reflected Face of

Africa

DENIS MONTGOMERY

AFRICAN INSIGHT
in association with the Self Publishing Association

First published in 1988 by
AFRICAN INSIGHT
7 Brookdale, Belmont, Bolton,
Lancashire BL7 8BR, England

in association with
The Self Publishing Association Ltd
Lloyds Bank Chambers
Upton-upon-Severn
Worcestershire WR8 4HU
England

Typeset by Printit Now Ltd
in Palatino 10pt

Printed by Billings & Son Ltd., Worcester

Our party at Tamanrasset in the centre of the Sahara Desert in January 1986. The Long Safari was coming to an end.

Contents

Maps drawn by Sue Garlick and James Montgomery
Photographs by Denis Montgomery
Photograph of Gorilla (p. 163) by Katie Hale

List of Illustrations

INTRODUCTION

My family and I had lived in Africa for many years: firstly in Nigeria, then in South Africa. In that time our children had grown up and I had been engaged in career activities that by quirk of fate, or subconscious choice, had taken me about the Continent. Business had lured me in directions that were of intellectual interest and I had expanded these interests in the lands and peoples of Africa. In 1965 I had taken a year off to travel with a companion by Landrover through many countries in North, East and Southern Africa and that experience had trained me in the simple ways of going on safari in a Continent with vast wildernesses. Since then I had built on that experience and cultivated it; it had not atrophied.

Suddenly, on my birthday in 1985, twenty years after my first exciting traverse, I felt the drive to travel Africa again, roughly, camping all the way, a distance of more than fifteen thousand miles, before I lost the physical competence. More than the desire to travel, I also wanted to probe beyond the often simplistic history and distorted commentary that is commonly available on this massively complex Continent. In 1965, I had wanted to write a book about Africa, but had not completed it because I realised I did not know enough. Maybe I had now accumulated enough understanding of life to write something more than a light-hearted adventure story.

In 1985, I was not going to travel around in South Africa, for I had explored extensively in that great and complex country. I was going to take a grand safari in an Overland truck, with maybe twenty others, from Johannesburg to Nairobi in Kenya, then through the mysteries of Zaïre to the Sahel lands of West Africa, across the Sahara to the Mediterranean in Algeria and on home across the Straits of Gibraltar.

PART ONE:

SOUTH AFRICA

MOROCCO
TUNISIA
RIO DE ORO
ALGERIA
LIBYA
EGYPT
17
16
15
14
MAURETANIA
MALI
NIGER
CHAD
SUDAN
SENEGAL
GAMBIA
BIRKINO FASSO
13
12
NIGERIA
SIERRA LEONE
GUINEA
IVORY COAST
C.A.R.
11
10
ETHIOPIA
SOMALIA
LIBERIA
GHANA
BENIN
CAMEROON
8
TOGO
GABON
CONGO REP.
ZAIRE
9
UGANDA
KENYA
INDIAN OCEAN
TANZANIA
8
7
6
5
ATLANTIC OCEAN
ANGOLA
ZAMBIA
3
MOZAMBIQUE
KEY
Route
1 JOHANNESBURG
2 HARARE
3 LUSAKA
4 LILONGWE
5 DAR-ES-SALAAM
6 MOMBASA
7 MALINDI
8 NAIROBI
9 BUNIA
10 BANCASSOU
11 BANGUI
12 N'DJAMENA
13 NIAMEY
14 TAMANRASSET
15 GHARDAIA
16 CEUTA
17 GIBRALTAR
(a) RWANDA
(b) BURUNDI

NAMIBIA
BOTSWANA
2
MALAWI
ZIMBABWE
MADAGASCAR
SOUTH AFRICA
1
SWAZILAND
LESOTHO

N

0   150 300   600 MILES

MAP 1 : ROUTE OF TRANS-AFRICAN JOURNEY 1985 / 1986

CHAPTER ONE: *JOHANNESBURG, August 1985*

No, there is no going back;
and everything ahead
is earned with painful slowness.

> LOCUS. *Douglas Livingstone. [South African poet]*

Across the centre of the great brown-mottled bowl, a thin orange pencil stroke had been drawn. It went arrow straight, diverted around some dark markings, wandered for a short distance, then shot off directly to the fuzzy edge. My God! I thought, I must be mad to be doing it again. I was looking down on the Zambian bushveld from thirty thousand feet, and from my hissing eyrie I was seeing half a day's journey along that orange path with one eagle's glance. For a minute my mind was filled with heat and dust, my eyes watered from peering into the fire of the sunlight and I felt the clumsy lurches and thumps of a vehicle crawling on the rutted surface like a slow tortured beetle. I looked about me in the massive passenger deck of the British Airways Jumbo and saw the wakening dishevelment of my fellows, crossing Africa in twelve bored hours. Nobody was watching from the portholes. I turned to mine and stared downwards. Already the scratch marks on the brown bowl had changed dramatically and I could not see the faint streak of the road: it was all wilderness down there.

I do not know how many times I have flown into Jan Smuts airport outside Johannesburg, it's probably well over a hundred. I hate flying long distances. It is not any fear of flying in itself, it is dislike that is almost hatred for the instantaneous process of moving from one Continent to another, one climate to another, one culture to another, without any time to adjust physically or mentally. As I have often thought: my soul has been left behind.

Despite the mass of doom-filled news reports and media commentary on South Africa that I had observed with a chill in my heart for the last several months, Jan Smuts airport had an air of tranquillity. The crowded arrivals hall filled with the contents of two Jumbos was watched by two calm Black policemen, and the immigration officials were as courteous and efficient as I remembered them. My small suitcase (six months supply of toiletries, medicines and clothes) crawled around the luggage conveyor amongst the prestigious giants belonging to the businessmen and packaged tourists. My camp-bed had also arrived safely, veteran of many African expeditions for over twenty years. I had worried about bedding because I have never been happy sleeping on the ground, and I was determined that the expected physical hardships of the planned camping safari up the whole length of Africa should not be unnecessarily exaggerated by uncomfortable nights. It was there, with its bright orange 'special luggage' stickers that an amused porter had put on at Manchester airport: "A bit beyond all this, aren't you?" he had asked with a grin, looking me up and down. "Well, have a grand time, and this will arrive safe, don't you worry." Looking at it at Jan Smuts I had an instantaneous rush of warmth for home and my own people and a coincidental flash of apprehension at what I was about to do.

But, at the barrier there was the familiar wizened brown face of John, crinkled into a welcoming grin: "Hello, Mr Montgomery. You are welcome. Is it a business visit? We have not seen you for a long time." I laughed: "No, it's not business . . ." His friendly face changed my mood and I followed him to an Audi company pool-car and we were silent as we joined the streams of traffic on the motorway to Johannesburg. The forest of high-rise buildings in the city centre filled the windscreen. The sky was the pale blue, streaked by high cirrus, to be expected in the Highveld winter; the grass was dry and sere, the air chill and thin, the sun warm. I was in Africa, beloved Continent. The rapid transition by courtesy of the dreadful jet plane was over.

Fatigued after my long journey from Manchester, long in miles, less than twenty-four hours in time, I had to rouse myself to talk to John, whom I have known for several years. He is a Zulu, a slight bespectacled fellow, married with teen-aged children, living in Soweto, a serious church-going Methodist who has worked a long time in the head-office of a large South African based multi-national company. The friend at whose home I was going to spend my pre-departure week was the Chief Executive of John's division. We talked about the health of our children, bringing each other up to date with news of family and mutual acquaintances in his firm. I then asked him about the troubles in the Black townships, especially Soweto.

"Well," he said with his quiet, soft voice. "Things are not good there." He paused to sigh. "Where we live it is O.K., there have been no riots up till now because our neighbourhood is a bit far from the centres where these things start up. It's O.K. so far."

I waited for him to go on, but he didn't. "What about getting to work?" I asked.

"That is a problem." He showed some anger. "Those young people are always interfering with you, lecturing you, pushing pamphlets at you, shouting those revolutionary songs. They think we are ignorant. You know what I mean?" He glanced at me and I nodded. "I don't know, Mr Montgomery . . . You and I know the situation in South Africa. God knows we Blacks have suffered and we must have change now, but you will not change everything just with bloodshed. What is happening elsewhere tells any man this. We have to be patient because it is a very big problem and we all know how long it takes to make changes. Even the Government does not really know what to do next, you see. Killing is not the solution, there must be another way and burning schools will not make our people free." He shrugged. "Of course I have to be worried. I don't know when those people will come to my house and force my family to do something."

"How about your own children?"

"So far, not bad. My wife is a teacher, she helps them study at home."

"What do you think?"

He looked across at me briefly. "I am a Christian, as you know from our talking before. We must love our brothers. In South Africa, that is difficult, and we have to find a way for all the people. What can one do except to pray? Sometimes it is difficult to be patient." He sighed.

I sighed too, but I could not get angry, my head was filled with the cottonwool of my journey.

John dropped me off at my White friend's home in Bryanston, a commuting suburb about ten miles north of the Johannesburg city centre. Gratefully I slept that afternoon, and in the evening, after a good dinner, my friend and I talked well into the early hours as we always seem to do; mulling over the problems and infinite complexities of South African society, reviewing our personal ambitions, gossiping about acquaintances, enjoying each others company. One of the special pleasures of middle-age is that of old friendships. Tony left to join his family next day, and I was abandoned with the freedom of his home. It was time to make final preparations and face the reality of my latest trans-Africa journey.

Sitting in my friend's garden in Johannesburg, in between expeditions to supermarkets to get last-minute necessities, I thought about South Africa. It is a beautiful country which, together with its near neighbours, can provide a variety of scenery and geographical adventure which some would claim equals the whole of the rest of the Continent. The indigenous people range from 'Bushmen', some of whom were still hanging on to near Neolithic culture, at one end of the spectrum, through every degree of cultural evolution and change, within several tribal and language groups, to the largest middle-class, professional and commercial group of Black people in Africa, apart from Nigeria. The millions of people of Asiatic and European origin who have their home there have cultural roots as diverse as Malaya, India, China, Lebanon, Madagascar, Czecho-slovakia, Russia, Italy, Portugal, Holland and Scotland. The economic and social classes that these immigrants belong to almost exactly mirror similar society in Australia, the United States or Brazil. The political and social change that was occurring was massive and traumatic. These changes were being derided as 'cosmetic', but anyone with more than a superficial knowledge of the sub-Continent knew that there was a great social revolution in progress.

The problems facing South Africa now were not those of the old rules of social Apartheid. They were gone, or going. Now it was a matter of political power: who would hold the future of the richest and most highly developed sub-Saharan nation and, therefore, the whole geographical region.

What sickened me was that opportunists, smelling the blood of a wounded buffalo, had mounted a death-chase oblivious to the age-old African wisdom that he is the most dangerous animal in the bush. Before stability was reached in the post-Apartheid era, there were going to be a lot of new graves and thousands more mourners. Black people were already dying and being maimed because politicians jockeyed for positions in the new government they saw coming close to their grasps. The anarchy that inevitably follows the deliberate destruction of order by revolutionaries was being revealed in the Black townships. The thin police lines had been cast into the role of suppressors of political protest and had often abandoned their true task of maintaining the common law. Millions of people in South Africa's huge Black towns were at the mercy of lawless gangs and vigilantes. This could accelerate, the chase for power had started and many power seekers saw anarchy as a necessary ally. In Nigeria, another African state with comparable urban masses, autocratic governments had met this same problem of urban anarchy following abrupt political change by resorting to public hangings and firing squads on bathing beaches. Was this the freedom that Black South Africans had to look forward to?

I sat in the warm winter sunshine in the quiet garden, combating the gloom that filled my heart. The barbets, doves, Cape thrushes, yellow weavers and little house sparrows ate the fruit and seeds that were put out for them in winter time. I thought about the Africa I was about to traverse and the poverty and deprivation I would see. I knew I would also see happy people still living in simple peasant communities. But I wondered what had re-placed the White-man bogey that is alive and well in South Africa in those countries to the north. Or if the White-man bogey was still there in different guises? I was strongly aware of the conflicts of culture that had irrevocably damaged social structures in Africa so that populations were exploding, material and moral standards were lowering and many people could not see a clear path ahead. A destructive hopelessness infected many hearts.

I read some poetry and I found this piece by the South African, Achmat Dangor:

> Yet, I can write of hope,
> though the voice I hear
> in the icy dawn
> is still frail and tremulous,
> and the mists are a portend
> of a familiar and savage storm

THE VOICES THAT ARE DEAD

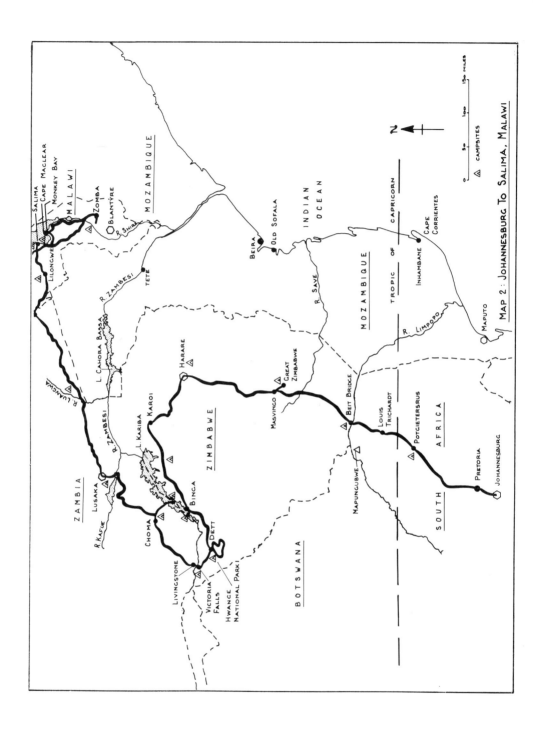

MAP 2 : JOHANNESBURG TO SALIMA, MALAWI

CHAPTER TWO: *THE GREAT NORTH ROAD*

The Gods of Africa regard me
From the edge of my suburban lawn.
They have the tall thick legs of tree-trunks,
And tiny white faces of the stars.
>   *DISTANCE. Anthony Delius [South African poet]*

The first of September, 1985: the day of departure.

I was delivered to the Chelsea Hotel in the heart of Hillbrow in Johannesburg. This was the most cosmopolitan part of the city, with gay clubs, single's bars, cabarets and non-racial restaurants; where you could buy marijuana or Kentucky Fried Chicken until late at night. The permanent multi-racial population lived in a jungle of high-rise apartments, one block claiming to be the biggest in the Southern Hemisphere. The sophistication of the style of Hillbrow made it appear to be on a different planet to anywhere else in Africa. Apart from the swinging night life, it was a sought-after tower-block residential area. TV news reporters never came here to mirror South African urban life. There were no graffiti on the buildings, no litter on the pavements, old ladies took their dogs out at ten o'clock at night. That made it different to many British city centres too.

From the Overland tour company's brochure, I knew what our truck would look like, and there it was parked beside the hotel. A cheerful fellow in his late forties with a Yorkshire accent came up to me with a grin. "Now don't you worry. Give me your things, I'll see them safe. Go into the hotel, up to the lounge; they'll be there." Thank God, I thought, there is somebody who understands the inevitable confusion at the beginning. In the lounge, smelling of stale cigarettes and beer, dark after the brilliant sunlight outside, there seemed to be a hundred silent people dressed trendily for a picnic. I was the only one wearing shorts and flipflops. I was looked over briefly by all those eyes. The silent tension was breathable. I had intended to give up smoking again that morning, but wondered if it would be possible.

A young man climbed onto a dais: "Well, we're all here now. I'm Charlie, your intrepid-fearless tour leader, if you didn't know me already." A ripple of nervous smiles and a giggle or two. "I'm going to give you a start-off briefing. I'll tell you about . . ." His voice faded in my head, I don't remember what he said. Suddenly it was happening, six months of tingling thought, changing to planning and then to action had brought me to this seedy lounge in a cheap hotel in Hillbrow. Wife and family were far away, but up until that morning I had still been cushioned by the familiar surrounding of my friend's home. Now I was launched into this mad venture with seventeen total strangers, in the hands of this bright young fellow. Not listening to his words, I heard his voice: he was like a subaltern in the 22nd Lancers telling the chaps about the expedition against the Fuzzy-Wuzzies; no, that wasn't right, we were being told how we would yomp across to get at the Argies. No, that wasn't right . . . People were filing past me, there was some talking, some tense laughter. I detected a loud Australian accent.

In the bright Highveld sunshine I trailed on the end of the queue climbing into the truck. It had comfortable seats like a coach back home, which surprised me, otherwise it looked sturdy and tough enough at first glance. There seemed to be only one seat left, right in the front next to a young girl with short cut black hair in a flowing white dress. She gave me a friendly grin as I sat next to her.

"Here we are," I said.

"Yes! Here we are," she agreed cheerily, and I discovered she was from Worcestershire. The engine started and we moved into Johannesburg traffic. Once onto the motorway system, Charlie asked me for directions to the North, he knew my background, and I asked him for a cigarette.

The Highveld was in winter clothes, frost-burnt dry khaki grasses, the few trees were black sticks, and the White-only suburbs on the Pretoria road were collections of dreary little boxes. During the Miners' Strike of 1984 British miners had emigrated to the Witwatersrand, no doubt lured by those TV commentators' descriptions of the White high-life amongst Black degradation. The miners were sadly disillusioned. Only the very wealthy five per cent live like the newsreels show, most Whites live in small houses with small backyards, just like anywhere else. And I suddenly realised something else the miners would not have liked: South Africa is so much quieter that Britain, as if everything is in slow-motion. It is a function of the huge space, common to all Africa, and the gradual interaction of Black and White cultures over many generations. This quiet is not true of supermarkets or downtown offices, but it is true of residential areas and the country. It is not the particular *mañana* style of the Mediterranean either. It is uniquely African, with fewer people moving slowly with no rush, the great sky dominating life. The Continental dimension infuses the minds of all its people with patience.

Steadily going up the ruler straight 'Great North Road' that was to reach Cairo in Cecil Rhodes' day, I began to relax. This was Africa and I had some understanding of it; arrogantly I felt that it was more mine than any of the others on the truck. I felt the inner support of knowledge.

At this point I should describe our vehicle and our party. The truck, as we were to call it, was a standard twelve ton Mercedes-Benz chassis with a turbo-charged engine on which was built a utilitarian aluminium body. Within were coach seats for twenty with room for four in the cab, which was cut away and joined to the body with a large flexible rubber seal, like two carriages of a train; thus the cab and body were one open space. Inside there were luggage shelves above the seats for cameras, small day-packs, medical kit and water-bottles. At the back was a large bin where food stocks, lubricating oil cans, odd spare parts and some luggage was stored with everyone's bedding on top. This amorphous pile grew as the journey progressed and precious souvenirs and private treasures were buried underneath where they would be safe. On some spare floor space at the rear a box of books, our library, and a large tin trunk for vegetables stood. There was also a picnic cool-box in which perishables were kept, not really because it kept anything cool, but because it had a tight fitting cover that defied ants, flies and cockroaches. It was known as the 'Eskay' because Australians call them that. Accessed from the outside, with fold-down flaps, were lockers in which a petrol stove, folding tables and camp stools, cooking equipment, plastic plates and cutlery, plastic containers of tea, coffee, sugar, cooking oil, condiments, peanut-butter and other foods in current use were kept. The vehicle maintenance tools and small spares were also kept on this side. On the other was a large locker which housed most of the suitcases (the size had been specified in the company's brochure) and the sleeping tents. There were two water tanks of about 200 litres each and two fuel tanks with a total capacity of about 500 litres (cruising range of about two thousand miles on reasonable roads). Jerry cans for emergency water and diesel fuel, petrol for the stove and engine oil lived in metal harnesses under the back of the body and there was a frame welded onto the back which carried massive sand tyres and the open-fire grilling grid. On the roof, there was a seat and holding-on rail for four people up front, with a hatch from the cab, and a large luggage rack on which was stored awkward sized suitcases and back-packs, the large cook-tent for rainy weather, spare sleeping tents, canned food and two to four spare tyres depending on the state of damage and replacement.

21

A huge, heavy gauge polythene blanket covered the roof luggage and there was an elaborate system for tying it all down. Mild-steel sandmats were slung on the sides and also stored on the roof. We had brooms for the endless task of sweeping sand and rubbish out of the inside, refuse and washing buckets and bowls, an axe for firewood, machetes (or pangas) for general cutting and chopping, a hoe and two shovels for digging the wheels out or for latrine and refuse holes. Indispensable for young people, we had a stereo cassette player with six speakers, and for night time there were two portable fluorescent lights.

As to our party, there were two of the company's staff: Charlie, the fearless-intrepid commander and driver, and Bob, the large jolly bearded-pirate mate and co-driver. The passengers (and hard-working crew) were divided in two: those who were going all the way to England and those who would leave or were to join at Nairobi. From Johannesburg there were two California girls in their thirties, a large jolly South African woman journalist with Australian passport, two New Zealand girls and an older New Zealand fellow who was on a busman's holiday from his Middle-East touring job, a lone Aussie nursing sister recently recovered from a bad motor cycle accident, a Canadian girl social worker, a bright young Geordie whose accent was difficult to decipher and who had a zoological degree in reptiles, the Worcestershire lass whom I sat next to on the first day, two young English technologists from the South, a veteran Overlanding lady of sixty and three middle-aged gentlemen: the helpful Yorkshireman (who had come down from Nairobi and was returning there), an instrument engineer living in Devon and myself. I was told that we were lucky to have such a good mix, a fair scattering of ages and almost equal sexes. It was an unusual group in that there were only four Antipodeans; there is usually a higher proportion. It was also unusual, as I was later told, in that there were a number of strong characters amongst us. Not one of us passengers had known any of the others before we came together in Johannesburg; we were all strangers.

We stopped early that first night in a rather civilised municipal campsite just outside the Transvaal town of Potgietersrust, founded by Piet Potgieter, one of the legendary leaders of the Afrikaner Great Trek into the interior in 1836. There were tiled ablution blocks with hot showers, barbecue grills and firewood already cut and ready. There was also 'The Great North Road' with thundering traffic all night long, an aspect of South African economic muscle that I would be pleased to lose as we went north. Charlie gave us a fuller briefing and this time I listened.

The general outline of our route was, of course, shown in the company's brochure which I had studied many times. We would go north into

Zimbabwe to Harare, then along the southern Zambesi River escarpment where Lake Kariba has been formed, to the Victoria Falls. Crossing into Zambia we would call at Lusaka before going east to Malawi, up the western side of Lake Malawi and into Tanzania. We would visit Dar-es-Salaam before spending time in the Serengeti and climb Mount Kilimanjaro (highest in Africa) if we wished. From there we terminated the first phase in Nairobi where the truck would be serviced, we would rest, and there would be a change-over of those passengers leaving and joining. After several weeks at Mombasa, the Kenya coast and Kenyan game reserves, we would go west around Lake Victoria to Rwanda and Zaïre, seeing gorillas and the lakes and mountains of the Western Rift Valley, before heading for Kisangani (formerly Stanleyville) on the Congo River in Zaïre for another rest. From Zaïre, we would travel north through the rain forest to Bangui in the Central African Republic (usually referred to as the C.A.R.) where we would have another break to recuperate and maintain the truck. We would leave the rain forest at Bangui and move into the Sahel in the Cameroons, passing Lake Chad and into Niger and there the trans-Sahara journey would begin. The Sahara route would be the conventional one, up the middle through Tamanrasset in Algeria to the Mediterranean at Algiers, thence along the coast into Morocco to see Fez and Marrakesh before crossing the Straits of Gibraltar and home to England, in February 1986. The intinerary was mostly to my liking though I would have preferred to spend more time on the Tanzanian coast, to visit Zanzibar and Kilwa (important early Arab colonies) but you can't have everything. I wondered how much time we would have on the Kenya coast because I wanted to get to Malindi to pursue my historical trail, but that was a long way off.

Charlie then demonstrated putting up the sleeping tents, described a normal day and the scheduling of jobs and chores, how the food 'kitty' worked and the buying and cooking routines, remarked on the need for hygiene and he described security precautions, emphasising how there would always have to be someone with the truck and valuables should never be left in tents or lying about. He or Bob would normally sleep in the truck at night. The important task with security was to ensure that no stranger ever got into the body of the truck. It seemed rather nebulous but it worked, although it worried me at the beginning. Charlie became very serious when describing the currency black-markets and how we could use them to our advantage. It meant smuggling cash into various countries with significant black-markets so that one had currency not declared on the official declaration forms to change with the illegal dealers.

The moment of truth in our briefing came with choosing sleeping partners and the allocation of chores. By a stroke of luck I was the odd man out, so I had my own tent, albeit an older one and a little more difficult to put up than those newly purchased for this round trip. Having my own tent throughout the trans-Africa journey contributed considerably to my peace of mind. Having some regard for my seniority in age, I was allocated the physically easy task of rubbish disposal. The young men were in charge of packing and unpacking the roof racks, the young women with cleaning the inside of the truck and keeping the various lockers in order. We cooked in rotation and the cooks planned, marketed, prepared and cooked the meals, washing up and clearing away afterwards. Cook-days were a serious nightmare for some and a much-disliked chore for all, which is a pity, but there is no alternative and all the jobs have to be done. I enjoy cooking, so I would have been happy to do more than my share if I could have been relieved of washing up and clearing away. In the end, I did cook more than anyone else.

After the briefing and when the tents had been pitched, we presented a sombre sight until dinner was served. The tents were mostly clean and new, pitched in a neat semi-circle around the camp fire and facing the truck. A silent inner ring of preoccupied travellers sat on the camp-stools in brand new clothes, some pretty trendy, all bright and fresh. I have a photograph of that first evening and the unease and tension is shown in the attitudes of everyone's bodies.

That first night I slept badly, waking frequently, various muscles ached and my shoulders became numb. I listened to the big articulated trucks roaring past on 'The Great North Road' a hundred yards away. I had my camp-bed in my own tent and I was miserable: I wondered how much worse it would have been if I had been sleeping on the ground, cramped with a strange bed-fellow. I kept thinking about my companions and whether we would be mutually tolerable. Three of the girls had jarringly loud nervous laughter and most of the young men and women had begun unconsciously jockeying for leadership and prestige, offering jokes and repeating stories of past travelling. This was to go on for days and I found it terribly tedious.

I was mentally exhausted the next day, my mind was dead and I left it that way most of the time. I desperately wanted to observe closely the departure from South Africa and the first days in 'Black' Africa, but I also wanted this settling in period of our party of strangers to be over. The latter would take days, the former happened all too quickly. We stopped to fuel at a big service station on the bypass around Louis Trichard, an old Afrikaner settler town at the foot of the Soutpansberg mountain range. A white church with its tall dark spire stood out against the emerald of the sunlit mountain slopes, still a beacon in the great loneliness that its builders had intended a century before. A large, well dressed Black man came up to me. He was of the Venda tribe.

"I don't recognise the number-plate of your bus, where are you from?" he asked. We were to be asked this same question a hundred times in a hundred places. It was always good for starting a conversation if you wanted one.

"The truck is from England," I said. "But we have joined it in Jo'burg and are travelling back to Europe."

"To Europe! To England!" He rubbed his face and crinkled his eyes, visualising the enormity of it. He laughed and looked me over. "I suppose you know what you are going to do. Those countries up there can be very rough, not like our country."

I nodded. "I know. But we will be careful."

"I wish you luck," he said, and shook my hand.

We stopped on the crest of the Soutpansberg mountains to have lunch of salads and fresh wholewheat rolls and I was glad. The Soutpansberg is a strange, great line of folded rock, a couple of hundred miles long, like a straight French bread stick laid precisely east-west on the map. To the south there is endless flat plain that used to be grassland and is now intensely cultivated agriculture as far as you can see. It is called the Springbok Flats because hundreds of thousands of those pretty antelope lived there at one time. I stood for a while looking south, my eye following the ruler straight grey line of the 'Great North Road' to where it met the pale blue sky. Here, the system and method of the European way that has created abundance out of wilderness at the cost of indigenous life was clearly seen. Here was the reflection of the rolling cultivation of Holland or Germany under an African sky, and here too was the established order that had been used to transplant that disciplined food machine. I stared for many minutes, implanting that view strongly into my mind, for I knew it would become an important reference in the months ahead.

On the other side of the Soutpansberg, like fantasyland hidden behind a stage curtain, tropical Africa started.

"Baobab trees!" I exulted aloud as we drove past the first group of the wide-girthed, pink-purple skinned, ugly-beautiful monsters with bare arms uplifted to heaven. I pointed one of them out to Ted, whom I had discovered was deeply interested in everything. Ted, who lived in Devon, was one of my contemporaries and we became fast friends in the next five months. "They are very solitary and they walk in the night to mate with their partners," I told him. "According to legend, the baobab is the link between the upper world and the underworld. If you have the Power, you can enter the right tree and be taken down below. You can also squeeze liquid from the flesh if you are dying of thirst and they yield cream-of-tartar to ferment beer or raise bread." Ted smiled, but he stored the information away.

South Africa is the most conservation minded country in Africa, every baobab tree on the road north of Louis Trichard was numbered and it was an offence to damage them. To me baobabs are the great symbol of the tropical thornbush, because although their companions the acacia family of thorn trees are more widespread, you will strangely never find baobabs outside the exact latitudes of the tropics, nor do they like altitude. When I see a baobab I am warm and I can feel the dust between my toes.

The South African customs post was a large, utilitarian complex built many years ago when there was great movement of people between South Africa and the Rhodesias. There were empty waiting rooms, large echoing toilets and rest rooms, a long counter inside the main hall for officials in well pressed tropical white shorts and shirts with British style navy epaulettes and gold rings of rank. The officials were White, and I was transported in time. The Empire was still alive and well. The bland courtesy and correct procedures were familiar, and if one needed a symbol to punctuate our leaving of the so-called White South, then this customs post was it. Ironically, the majority of people crossing the border were Black immigrants formed in a long quiet line of poorly dressed men clutching tattered identity documents and carefully tied small bundles of possessions, desperately seeking employment in the racist state to the south. I sighed with despair at the complexity of Africa and the reality of ordinary survival. Beyond the barrier, on the Zimbabwe side, a forlorn group of women stood unmoving and silent, projecting their sadness and uncertainty over the months of parting that lay ahead.

We clattered across the iron girder bridge over the Limpopo and, looking down at its winter emptiness, I was glad to see it conformed to Kipling's description.

"It does look grey and greasy," Ted said. "But no crocodiles." I was beginning to like Ted very much.

"Crocodiles later," I replied and we smiled.

PART TWO:

CENTRAL AFRICA

CHAPTER THREE: *GREAT ZIMBABWE*

The warrior will lie there, solemn
in his impregnable casket.
His proud widow and children will say,
    "Weep not for him,
    He was a brave warrior;
    Let him rest on the buffalo-hide bed,
    where his forefathers repose."

                    WEEP NOT FOR A WARRIOR.
                    Oswald Mitshali [South African poet]

Charlie was nervous at the Zimbabwean customs post: here was our first tangle with the 'BM', the currency black market. We had stopped in between the border posts to organise it in a performance that was to grow routine. This time, I was not personally interested for I had a sufficient quantity of South African currency notes that were not significantly black-marketable. It was U.S. dollar and British pound notes that had a high premium. We were especially warned about discussing smuggling in front of officials. Maybe because African officials are Black and frequently casually dressed and behaved, White travellers can do strangely colour-blind things, like the girl who spoke up with a clear, English accent demanding to know the BM rates in a crowded Tanzanian customs shed, to the horror of her companions and the unconcealed amusement of the officials.

My currency was counted against my 'dec' form, but there was no great delay. One advantage in travelling in a group throughout Africa is that although you may have to wait a while, once the officials have reconciled themselves to the sudden appearance of a mass of White foreigners, they will often process you all together. Provided that the first few in the group are faultless in their documentation and behaviour, the rest get handled with increasing despatch as boredom sets in. Charlie took advantage of this as the safari got into its stride by preparing a passenger 'manifest' with relevant passport details. The more conservative of us headed the list and dozens of photo-copies were made to distribute at the increasingly numerous police and military check-points in Central and West Africa. I benefited because I headed the list so was always through first, but I wondered if I should feel flattered.

We passed into Zimbabwe and drove a short distance out of the dusty little town of Beit Bridge for firewood gathering. The mopani trees looked dead because it was the end of the dry season, but they were not. Being so close to town, most dead sticks and tree trunks had long been collected by the local people. We got some, however, and it was part of our early training for without firewood and water, food is useless. Dragging a dead branch back to the truck I smelled the dust I was kicking up, my arms and legs were dry and powdered, the air was balm; we were in the tropics at the best time for Southern African travelling. No rain had fallen for months but the magic of springtime was forcing the flowering bush-trees and shrubs to bloom in predominantly reds, pinks and oranges. The certainty of continuing fine weather and the physical ease of dry warmth elated me. A field of pale maize stalks stood from the last harvest and a troop of baboons crossed the road some distance away.

The official camping site was an acre of hard brown earth, well scoured by daily sweeping, beneath a scattering of mopani trees. The ablution block had taps, showers and toilets that worked, but the faded limewash of the building had a dried muddy skirt all round that indicated several rainy seasons since it had been last painted. It was empty but for a battered caravan with the settled domesticity of washing lines and worn household furniture sheltering under a tarpaulin. It belonged to a Coloured couple who had come to work in the town, seemingly semi-permanently. They had a Black domestic servant to do their chores and tend the small children during the day. I was disturbed by these people, neither fish nor fowl, too superior to live in an African hut, not able to get a job paying enough to rent a 'European' bungalow.

A strange deaf-mute boy adopted us, a continual smile on his little monkey-face, eagerly anticipating work for his small hands on stick-like arms, helping to unpack our kitchen from the truck. He seemed more used to our gear than we did. Our group gently teased him, which he enjoyed, like a stray puppy. He shared our dinner and was with us until we went to sleep, but I do not know where he lived.

Again, a neat semi-circle of blue tents grew facing the truck with an inner circle of camp stools. Because there was time, the girls produced a blossoming of laundry on lines strung between the mopani. I particularly remember these early camps for the laundry; at every stop there were long multi-coloured strings of shirts, blouses, slacks, socks and panties as the girls invariably changed after the day's travel when they had a shower or wash. The young men were not so busy with changing and washing, but they wore clean clothes most days. This was in sharp contrast to our camps in later months. After pitching my solitary tent, still clumsily, resulting in sweat running from me, I stood under a luke warm shower from the cold tap, water cascading from an old fashioned rose the size of a pudding plate, and in ten minutes my body was dry without using a towel. Wonderful Africa!

The slow process of getting to know each other continued that evening. The extroverts had emerged with confident role-playing, or was it role-playing to cover lack of confidence? I am not sure that anybody is confident in these situations. It is a matter of those who are driven, or need, to establish their personality early as opposed to those who find it easier to wait, or easier still not to try at all. I found myself pushed back on memories of school and especially of joining the Navy many years ago. It was surprising how close I found those memories. It was the loud, forced laughter that seemed to be the most obvious symptom of this process, especially from a distance when I could not hear the conversation that accompanied the guffaws and giggles. Where I had lately been thrust into similar situations of meeting a group of strangers it had been in the rather different conditions of business or academic seminars where everyone has some level of status or rank to support their personality. In those first evenings around the camp fires in Africa, we all had to establish these things from raw beginnings, where the only marks were our physical appearance, our clothing and our behaviour. Nick, the New Zealander who had led adventure tours in Egypt, began to stand out. He was twenty-eight, with dark good looks and a neat and controlled manner of handling himself and a macho way of dressing: well worn sheepskin jacket and military trousers, tooled leather belt, neckerchief at times, heavy leather boots which were well looked after. Inevitably, he was to clash with other strong personalities but I learned early on that his often abrasive bravado concealed a complex and sensitive character. His ego was quite fragile and I often supported him because I saw that it would be best for harmony.

I woke at six next morning after sleeping comparatively well, pleased that my bed was working. The dawn chorus woke me, as it was to do for most of the safari. I timed my ability to attend to natural functions, shave and pack up my bed and tent: fifteen minutes for ablutions, fifteen minutes to pack up, on that first reasonably normal morning. Whether the tent was wet from dew, or whether termites had made a nest under the integral ground sheet, determined speed. Tents, during most of our time, served the purpose of providing privacy rather than protection from weather, and during the early days everybody pitched tents.

The two New Zealand girls cooked breakfast that morning, a delicious great mess of scrambled eggs and toast. There was some left over and somebody made a comment on this.

"Well, we thought that we would make a good quantity," Adie said, innocently. "We used three dozen eggs."

"Three dozen eggs!" roared Bob, in his piratical role. "Well, me darlings, we'll do well with you as cooks! But will the money last?"

"Three dozen eggs!" Nick came in on cue. "Three dozen eggs!" He shook his head dramatically. "What are you two doing to our reputation? We Kiwis have got to stick together. Three dozen eggs . . ." He wandered off, telling everybody: "Do you know what? They used three dozen eggs!" So do catch phrases get born and for a while we kept inventing them.

Before we left we went to the bank to change money. This was another regular and much disliked chore whenever we passed through the far-apart commercially sophisticated towns in Black Africa. Barclays Bank at Beit Bridge was the reminder to me of what lay ahead: the delays and waiting while documents are checked two and three times, the initialling by senior staff, the moving from counter to counter that is endemic from Zimbabwe to Niger. At least, here we were attended to by an attractive and efficient Black girl in smart uniform. When we crowded in, she literally cleared her desk for action and called for assistance.

"Disturbed your morning," I said apologetically.

She gave me a grin. "It makes a change. And you all speak English, don't you?" I remembered the significance of that twist when we encountered the inevitable blank faces and language problems in Franco-phone countries.

Just outside Beit Bridge Charlie stopped to pick up a hitch-hiker. He had to sit next to me because the seat was vacant. He was a confident young man, freckled and prematurely balding, slim and compact, tough looking. I watched the mopani bush pass on the endlessly straight smoothly tarmacked road towards Masvingo, which was called Fort Victoria in colonial days. Inevitably, we exchanged remarks and when he was reassured that I could be friendly to a White person in Southern Africa, for many have sadly grown large chips on their shoulders in recent years, he talked.

"I know this country well," he told me. "I was an assistant in the veterinary service in this area for years. Most of the time I was in the bush. Just me and a couple of Blacks with our Landrover. You learn to love the bush and to fit in with the wilderness." His job was to supervise the destruction of diseased stock or the quarantining and moving of herds about. He left Zimbabwe after the official Independence in 1981 because unqualified Whites were being replaced by unqualified but less experienced Blacks. He did not resent this, it was inevitable he thought, but he was bitter because he was certain that standards had to drop whatever the skin colour of the newly promoted men.

"Why?" I asked.

"Because they don't have the old Rhodesian Civil Service traditions to back them up, you see. I would say: 'Now look, you know that I'm just doing my job, and I have to do it.' There were no arguments."

I listened to his description of his life in South Africa, savouring his typical accent and his simply told stories. He had gone to Cape Town because there were not so many 'Kaffirs' and at that time he had been bitter about them. They were good days to look back on, but not his way of life.

"You see. Shit! In the end I knew I had to come back to Rhodesia." He was staring out the window and his voice strangled. *"I missed it terribly."*

The transfer of feeling was instantaneous and there was a tightness in my throat too as I sat quietly with this apparently hard man who could make such a simple statement, full of emotion.

At Masvingo, we had lunch in a café by a garage. I had my last hamburger for months, a great meal of the junkiest of food; oily fried onions, greasy fried egg, roughly spiced hamburger, limp lettuce leaf, tomato ketchup and all. The Coca-Cola was ice-cold. But the toilets in the garage were locked, one of the girls told me, and we went over to the petrol attendant.

"Have you got the key to the toilet?" I asked him in Zulu.

He thrust his hand into his pocket and pulled out a cent piece. He took my hand and pressed the coin into it and said dramatically: "That is the key." We grinned at each other.

At the Lunde River, granite domes and hills begin some miles short of Masvingo. This is the start of the Great Zimbabwe country. From the British colonial town, symbolised by the closed and sadly shuttered, colonaded red-brick Victoria Hotel and its ghostly echoes, we drove into ruined Great Zimbabwe: old capital of Bantu Africa's greatest urban state. Zimbabwe is the name given to the empire created by a series of descending dynasties, which occupied much of the modern independant country of that name. Assuming that it is almost mandatory for African countries to re-name themselves after Independence, Zimbabwe is a happy choice although it is a Portuguese corruption of a local word used to describe chiefs' kraals and nobody knows what the original Zimbabweans called themselves.

The story of old Zimbabwe and its place in African pre-history is one of my passions and that evening I gave our group a potted story round the fire surrounded by the brooding ruins of the ancient stone town. There was a full moon and the velvet sky and still air provided a special magic.

Old Zimbabwe was an empire of a small section of the Bantu people, a cultural group of tribes who originated in Central Africa probably two thousand years ago and whose origins I wished to review when we got there. Shortly after the beginning of our Christian era a quite rapid expansion of the Bantu peoples moved into Southern Africa, diffusing their cultural and tribal cohesion as it spread. The lands from the Equator to the Cape were already occupied by the Khoisan race who were Neolithic hunter-gatherers and herders, subtly different to the Central African Negro race. The migrating Blacks with their iron and agricultural technologies absorbed the Khoisan except in the desert and semi-deserts of south-west Africa. In the 10th century, the healthiest of the rich coastal lands were south of the Tropic of Capricorn, today's Southern Mozambique and Natal, where populations grew to the maximum limit imposed by geography and culture. These people were aware that a gold and copper trade had started between Arab traders on the Mozambique coast and the mineral rich Central African plateau and an invasion by an elite tribe probably occurred northwards to colonise the Limpopo Valley. This area has copper, iron and some gold and they joined the Arab trade, through coastal middlemen, and steadily developed a feudal system over the local tribespeople. The Arabs increased their African trading acitivity, fuelled by the machine of Islamic Civilisation and gold became increasingly important as a medium of exchange from India to Britain. Much gold existed in surface deposits all over Zimbabwe so a new, more advanced feudal empire was established with its capital at Great Zimbabwe, and the poorer territory along the Limpopo declined in importance. For more than three hundred years this empire flourished, smaller provincial stone towns grew, agriculture was developed to feed expanding populations, extensive trench mining along surface reefs took place and ore was processed to produce gold. Trade with surrounding interior areas took place, especially copper rich Katanga where another strong Bantu kingdom grew. Arab chroniclers described this gold trade based on their port of Sofala in Mozambique.

After my talk, some of us walked among the ruins. I stopped in the great elliptical stone enclosure, now identified by Professor Tom Huffman as the Palace of the Queens, and listened to the night silence. In retrospect, I should have slept there that night, and will do so if the opportunity comes again. It is one of the most magical places in Africa, similar to the great Zulu royal valley, Emakhosini, on the Indian Ocean coast in Natal, and walking about slowly, I sensed the strange links that I believed exist between them. In the moonlight I felt the tug of ancient ghosts.

I got up before dawn the next morning and climbed to the stone Palace of the Kings on the granite hill overlooking the city complex. Some of our group took photographs in the pearly light and then I was alone for an hour or two, missing breakfast. I was grateful for the solitude and the quiet; it was another still clear day.

CHAPTER FOUR: *ZAMBESI*

Elephant
Tall-topped acacia, you, full of branches,
Ebony-tree with the big spreading leaves

ANIMAL SONGS: ELEPHANT.
Hottentot Fables and Tales: Bleek

Next day we were in Harare and camped for two days in the spick-and-span municipal camp site. It was to be the last really 'civilised' camping with tiled ablutions, instant hot water, paper in the loos and daily refuse collection. Harare is a city not unlike Nairobi in size and character and I knew it from previous visits. I stayed in the camp site, guarding our tents, reading and thinking, while the others went to town to shop and Charlie did some company business. I was still withdrawn in a private world, getting used to travelling in a group, especially one that did not seem to share many of my particular enthusiasms and interests. It was to be two or three weeks before I adjusted myself and was able to both join in and retain a private mind. I was not capable of the posturing and competitive joking, and I was in this mood when we started north again in our truck from Harare.

Before leaving home, I had read Quentin Crewe's travel book, *In Search of the Sahara*, in which he makes several scathing remarks about 'Overlanders', describing how they travel in their vehicular bubbles, playing loud music, scattering litter, shitting in monumental ruins, asking inane questions and poking cameras into the faces of gentle aborigines. I had read these remarks with some apprehension, since I was going to be an 'Overlander', but thought that he was being rather patronising. After all, he was travelling with his companions about Africa, his photographer photographed the locals, he asked a lot of questions and he was presumably shitting somewhere in the wilderness too. Of course, I understood what he meant: it was all a question of style. On the road north from Harare, I was reminded too powerfully of Quentin Crewe for a different mood infused several of my companions: they were leaving 'civilisation', they were going into real Black Africa. That night we were going to have our first bush camp. We were all looking forward to it, but there was a touch of hysteria in our truck with uncertainty at its root. The six stereo speakers played rock music at top volume and in the back, Cape wine was being used to dilute vodka. Katie, a sensitive Californian, who was sitting next to me in the front, shut herself off with her Walkman after saying: "I cannot *believe* that we are going to party all the way up Africa." I too was filled with dismay and a sick feeling lay in my stomach. Great Zimbabwe and the great feudal kings from coastal Natal disappeared into the past like those technical tricks they play in TV documentaries.

Later, Charlie put on a cassette of South African folk-pop music by a racially mixed group called 'Juluka' and turned the volume down. In the back the laughter had become more subdued as vodka worked its anaesthesia. We were travelling through country that I suddenly found to be quite exquisitely painful in its beauty. The sun was lowering and cast a golden light across level sere grassland with little islands of dark deciduous bush with *msasa* trees and feathery palms in their centres. A few stray cattle moved slowly. I saw a couple of isolated wild antelope. Amongst some of the islands, the strange golden light caused the scarlet blooms of flame trees to appear to ignite. The air, on the high plateau, was dry and balmy: that unmistakable balm of tropical air when the sun begins to go down. Dear God! It was beautiful! I felt that extraordinary exhaltation that can come to one sometimes, a peak of emotion that in its vividness is a mental orgasm that affects the whole body. I lounged back in my seat, hardly hearing the music, my eyes wet behind my closed lids, my arms goose-pimpled.

Katie touched my arm, "Are you alright?"

I opened my eyes and gestured at the golden plain.

She looked out. "I see it," she said.

We left the main road at Karoi, a rough town with an air of the wild frontier. Young men hung about the petrol station where we stopped to get water and they had a tough, menacing look with dirty shirts hanging unbuttoned over tight jeans. They eyed us through dark glasses and passed seemingly scornful comments between themselves, combined with lascivious interest in our girls. It was a disturbing town, strident and tense. During the Rhodesian War this area had been busy militarily because of the constant movement of guerrillas across from Zambia.

The Zambesi valley is filled here with the waters of Lake Kariba which is formed by a giant dam. The southern escarpment along which we travelled for two days is an area of endless, thick mopani scrub, dry and leafless at that time, with occasional startling patches of colour from other indigenous trees in spring bloom. The land undulated, our road crossed many valleys of rivers leading to the Zambesi. At one of these rivers, the Senyati, there was a big army camp for the soldiers who guard the bridge against rebel commando attack. Shortly after, we pulled off the road into one of the few spaces in the bush that could accommodate our truck and there was an old fire-place that Charlie recognised from a previous expedition. Our tents were pitched, for the first time, in a haphazard way, scattered through the thick mopani, wherever space could be found.

Val and I were cooking partners as far as Nairobi where she was to break away from us. Val was sixty-one I believe, a veteran traveller from London. That day we were cooking for the first time and I had bought a long rope of *boerwors*, a traditional South African spicy sausage, which I was to barbecue. The concentration on cooking for the first time in a bush camp with half our number well inebriated, was good for me, because it returned me to the necessity of accepting that mode of travelling which I had chosen with long deliberation. My mood of solitude and mysticism was broken. I was able to continue to look and think, but I was not so resentful of my companions who had their own adjustments to our mammoth safari to pursue. A firewood expedition had no difficulties here: there were no kraals for miles and the bush was virginal. I soon had a great roaring beast of a fire going which gradually died to produce a bed of coals on which to grill my boerwors. I was anxious to do it right and was soon dripping with sweat, smelling of mopani wood-smoke and my feet and legs were baptised with scratches from stumbling about in the flickering illumination on the rocky ground scattered with sharp tree branches. But it was a success. People talked about my grilled sausage months later, and I slept that night with an easy mind.

In contrast to the town of Karoi, the scattered and isolated Shona *kraals* we passed next morning were friendly, lively and cheerful. We stopped at two of them to take photographs and the headmen welcomed us. There was the natural behaviour of people with the mutual interest and lack of self-consciousness that I had expected in Africa. At one kraal an old woman, the grannie of the family, was preparing the day's supply of beer from a fermenting sorghum soup and I was delighted to see scattered around her a set of cooking utensils culled from a range of time. There were several sun-dried and lightly fired pots in traditional shapes with ancient decorations in diagonal hatching around their upper circumferences. Quite unrehearsed, there were also a three-legged cast-iron kaffir pot of traditional South African manufacture from some time in the first half of the 20th century, a plain shiny metal plate, probably aluminium, chipped enamel bowls, a galvanised iron bucket and, inevitably, a plastic detergent container. There were not only pots: wooden spoons made from local materials were in use together with store-bought machetes and kitchen knives, and to complete the cultural ensemble, the grain was being pounded in a deep, hollowed tree trunk with a giant wooden mortar wielded by young women and children.

A Shona woman with her cooking utensils, Zimbabwe.

I use the South African word *kraal* because it is difficult to substitute. Whether one is describing a Zulu king's kraal, housing fifteen hundred people, or that of a poor young man with two or three huts, one is referring to the particular African collection of buildings that house a family group. Because Europeans have no recent social history of extended families living together, there is no common word in everyday use to describe it. Village or homestead is a poor substitute. Like all peasant constructions anywhere, the huts that make up a kraal are built with local materials: timber, withies, grass, palm fronds, mud, cow dung, clay and, more rarely, stone. But, they are usually round, and where they are squared off you know that Arab or European influence has been at work. A kraal, in Bantu Africa, ideally consists of a hut for the head of the family, a hut for each married woman, huts for other senior males and females, huts for the unmarried girls and young men. If the extended family is poor in resources or people, the number of huts is reduced and sharing takes place. A natural order and tradition governs these matters, prolonged resentments and conflict would be unthinkable. In some places, where tribes have lived in favourable environments for generations, villages or towns develop; but these large population groups are collections of kraals. The massive and sophisticated construction of Great Zimbabwe, a town of probably twenty-five thousand people, conforms to this pattern.

Within fifty miles or so, the Zambesi Valley kraals changed from walls of wattle and daub to wooden poles and back again. The same variations for material reasons can be seen as far away as the northern side of the Congo Basin, on the edge of the Sahel, and the change can be equally abrupt. Where poles are used as opposed to a wattle frame, it is usual to put up the roof first, supported by several sturdier poles, then the house walls are constructed within the roof, thus giving the building a verandah. Even when houses are rectangular, with corrugated iron roofs, this is still a common practice; very practical and pleasant. Tribal identity is found in the decoration of huts, and these can be fine examples of primitive art reflecting the cultural experience of the people. The formal variation proceeds from uniform simplicity to highly individualised complex designs; the colours depend on the availability of local clay and mineral washes.

Elaborate hut decoration in the Zambesi Valley, Zimbabwe.

We turned off the road down to the shores of Lake Kariba at Binga at the foot of an escarpment overlooking a colonial style hotel, still bravely kept in good condition, with a hot mineral spring gushing from the mountain side into a swimming pool. It did not take us long to pitch camp in a rough meadow and move up to the hotel. Nick, Marie (the Aussie nurse), Katie and Jaime (the other California girl), Bob and I sat on a deserted terrace by the hot pool and drank iced Castle lagers as the sun slowly sank over the lake. In the gardens of the hotel there were several varieties of bougainvillaea in full bloom; pink, orange, scarlet and purple; frangipani with their powerful scent, brilliant canna lilies and red blossomed giant spathodea trees. A hadeda ibis flew over, calling its raucous cry, one of the great sounds of Africa, and I was so content in our privileged isolation.

"'Government ink never dries'," Katie quoted, looking at the view.

"What on earth do you mean?" I asked her, lazily.

She folded a U.S. dollar bill she had ready to pay for more beers. "Give me that packet of cigarettes."

I passed the cardboard box to her. She rubbed the bill across it, and it left a faint green mark. "See. 'Government ink never dries'. That's how you tell if U.S. money is real." She gestured at the scene before us. "This is honest, it's real."

I nodded, understanding.

After dinner, most of us went up to the hot pool again and wallowed in its clean, faintly sulphuric water, watching the moon. We had beers. There was easy talking and Bob told a long, involved nonsense story. Our group was coming together.

The next day we drove to the Hwange National Park. On the way we had stopped at another kraal, which Charlie had first approached to get permission for us to photograph. There was a herd of long horned cattle in good condition grazing amongst the dry maize stalks planted about it. These people were Ndebele and I greeted the head man in Zulu as he sat on an elaborately carved stool. He responded, but his replies were dull and disinterested. His people were dispirited and although quite friendly to us, they were strangely indifferent. The women were dressed in tattered European style dresses, and they were dirty; also strange. I asked how things were and I was told that the drought was bad, things were bad. The headman shrugged, he clearly did not want to talk. I looked into the raised grain stores, and there was still a stock of maize cobs although it was the end of the dry season. We stopped in the village of Dett to buy food in a store and again there was a bad atmosphere. There were people about, but they were lounging listlessly, there was no loud African chatter, we were examined with uncharacteristic disinterest. The store was poorly stocked and the other shops had a long-deserted air. Broken down buses and jeeps lay in a garage yard. This was a remarkable difference to the rough vitality of Karoi at the other end of the northern frontier along the Zambesi.

The main camp at Hwange was built to accommodate several hundred visitors in pleasant small bungalows and well serviced camping areas. In other days, before the war, it was booked up during school holidays and always busy. But our lively truck arriving was like the coming of a carnival to a dying town.

In the afternoon we drove to a waterhole and after seeing giraffe, kudu, waterbuck, baboon, ostrich, impala, lechwe, steenbuck, zebra and wildebeest, I was delighted with a great herd of more than five hundred Cape buffalo. They came to the water in an endless single file, drank in a ever-changing group of not more than a dozen, and went off steadily in a different direction. We watched them for about an hour. A fish eagle screamed repeatedly from its observation post on a dead tree and I saw a bateleur eagle. I love the African fish eagle, it has an extraordinarily evocative call. There were black-backed jackals but no other predators.

In the evening Charlie drove us to the nearby Lodge, a three-star hotel run by a South African chain with international efficiency and style. We had only been travelling and camping for little over a week, but I felt the alienness of this humming, air-conditioned presence in the bush; more so than I did later at the lodges in Kenya for some reason. Perhaps I was more sensitive at that time to the intrusion of its smooth urbanity: the well-trained staff, the contrived decor, subdued lighting in the lounge glowing on comfortable furniture, the bland taped music playing softly, the well-groomed guests in smartly casual evening clothes. (I was intrigued by my heightened awareness of the smell of toilet soap and perfume). Katie asked me to have a drink with her, and we settled on a settee in the lounge overlooked by a complete stuffed elephant's head. She was unhappy and had thought of leaving the safari: she wondered if she could survive the constant rock music on the truck, the joking and forced laughter of our group as they manouevred for compatibility, the lack of sensitivity others appeared to have for the real Africa we were passing through. I had instant sympathy, for I had travelled that emotional path a few days ago. I talked and I think I reassured her somewhat, for she stayed on. We missed a herd of elephants that walked through the grounds of the lodge causing much excitement. Debbie put her bag down to watch and it was stolen: the price of civilisation in the bush.

The next day we drove about the park. We observed many more animals and I was glad to see a small herd of the endangered sable antelope with several young. We made breakfast in a picnic area with round, thatched shelters and barbecue pits. There was a middle-aged fellow in charge, and after he had collected fire-wood for our cooking, I was able to have a long conversation with him. He was Ndebele so we spoke in an easy mixture of Zulu and English.

"I do not see many people here at Hwange," I remarked.

"Few people come here these days. Before, there were many South Africans and those from overseas, but they don't come now." He sighed and shrugged. "It is two weeks since any tourists visited this picnic place."

"My word," I said, surprised. "But you keep it tidy and well prepared."

He smiled. "That is my work. Anyway there is nothing else to do."

"How do you feel, living with wild animals?" I asked. "It must be different to living with the cows and goats in a kraal?"

He answered seriously. "It is different because they are not my animals to decide about. I have to think of them, for they are in my care especially from poachers, but they do not need me, they have their own ways and they have not been changed by us like cattle or goats which have to be looked after like small children. It is the White men of authority that like to treat them like cattle."

"You mean by tagging them and counting them and so on?"

"More than that. Everything they do is more complicated. They have to look for many reasons, when the reasons are simple. And they are *culling.*" He used the English word with distaste.

"They are culling elephants here?" I asked, knowing it to be happening from a report in a nature programme on TV back in England.

"Many animals." His arm moved widely. "And elephants, of course." There was contempt in his voice. "When they cull elephants, there are many tusks to sell. We are told that Hwange has thousands too many and it is the fault of the war because there was no proper control in those years." He looked at me with a sideways smile, then his voice changed. "They shoot from helicopters with machine guns. The war is now with the elephants."

This was a subject on which I have strong views. "I have seen many young animals in the last two days. I supposed this was because there has been a drought. But, if they also cull heavily, the breeding will increase faster as the animals naturally make up the difference. Then there are more animals to cull. It is a wheel that always turns faster."

He nodded as I spoke. "You know, then, what I mean. That is the way of wild animals. They know what to do. But cattle and goats will also

43

breed faster if they are healthy and many have died or have been slaughtered."

"People too," I said.

"People too," he agreed. "That is life."

We paused for thought

"If they don't cull, what is your answer?" I asked.

He gestured. "Before the White experts came, there were animals. They knew what to do. The numbers will be more or less according to how their land is. That is the way it has been." His statement was final.

I changed the subject. "We passed some kraals of the Ndebele coming here from Kariba. The people were very quiet, but the cattle looked strong and there were *mielies* in the stores."

He looked at me closely. "You have heard of the Korean Fifth Brigade?" I nodded. "That is why," he said.

"But the Government can't have fighting, it has to be stopped."

He made a sound of disgust. "Smith [the White Rhodesian Government] never used a Fifth Brigade," he said. "We Ndebele have a name for the new Prime Minister, Mugabe. We say he is *Dabulabantu* [Killer of people]."

He was looking at the horizon.

"Will you stay here in Hwange?" I asked, politely. It was time to go.

His answer surprised me. "I want to go to South Africa. I want a change and I hear many good things about there. My father worked in Johannesburg for many years. There are many *mpahlas* [manufactured goods] there." He grinned impishly at me.

At Hwange I shared a little bungalow with Paul, the young Geordie with a zoology degree specialising in reptiles. He was shy, serious about the pursuit of his interests and usually kept apart from the general social *melée*. On our last morning, we had several cups of coffee together as the sun rose, talking of the wilderness of Africa and its wild life. I told him of my discussion with the game-guard at the picnic place and we had a lively conversation on culling. His first reaction was the conventional one, that having interfered irrevocably with the wilderness, therefore creating imbalances, conservation authorities had to be continually redressing them even if the methods were often drastic. I argued that culling in the name of conservation was merely compounding the interference.

A herd of buffalo at Hwange National Park, Zimbabwe.

45

We watched the cheeky hornbills and fed them bits of bread. With a little patience, they would have been taking titbits from our fingers. I saw a woodpecker and we watched long-tailed shrikes courting, playing together and touching each other like love-struck teen-agers. The 'go-away' birds, grey louries that hunters disliked because they provide an efficient bush warning system, were about in numbers too. There 'gwe e e e eh' sound is another great bushveld call. Before our camp livened up, the birds were everywhere. Ted joined us and we talked about the huge herd of buffalo we had watched coming down to the water hole to drink, in perfect bovine order without rushing and stumbling over each other, in contrast to people who crowd each other pushing and shoving. Paul had noticed that other species drank at the same time, but each took its own place and none interfered with another.

"Do you remember the crocodiles and the hippos?" I asked.

Ted's eyes lit up. "Of course. The crocodiles were there, not hiding themselves and the antelope were watching them, but it did not change anything."

"And the baby hippo?"

"Yes." Paul grinned with delight. "Fantastic, it was!"

As the buffalo drank in their ponderous order, there was a baby hippo that played near them for adventurous pleasure and experience, to test itself and learn about these large animals that used its habitat for drinking. The baby hippo splashed about in the shallow water beyond their reach, bouncing around like a dog chasing sticks in a pond. The buffalo took no notice at all. After a while, the baby hippo began making mock charges and still there was no reaction, the great solid beasts with their heavy heads and horns bowed to the water, drank until satisfied, then wandered off to be replaced by others. The mock charges became bolder and spray showered about as the baby dashed in and retreated. Eventually an old bull buffalo raised his head, water dripping from his chops, and stared at the nuisance. Others followed his example and the drinking ceased. The baby loved this attention. Across the water, a hundred yards away there was a sudden upheaval, as a large shape surfaced. "Unh! Unh! unh-unh!" the great grunting noise echoed around in the dusk. The baby hippo instantly turned and swam back to its mother.

"I'll never forget it," said Ted.

"There's a theory that all behaviour is specific, all animal play has clear learning capability and that animals, naturally, have no imagination. Animals don't inter-react with other species unless there is biological purpose," mused Paul. "I suppose that baby hippo was learning, but it looked like a lot of fun to me."

46

"I wish all children were so obedient," said Ted. "How did she know, when she wasn't even watching? The buffaloes didn't call out to her: 'Hey, your son is being a bloody nuisance!'."

We laughed. Then, "It has to be telepathy," Paul said seriously.

I told them of a report I had read in a South African magazine, supported by a series of photographs. An impala antelope was seized by a crocodile at a crowded river bank, but he did not get a good grip and the impala pulled free. The crocodile came out of the water and again seized the impala which struggled wildly. Suddenly, a hippo charged the crocodile very aggressively, the impala was released, and the two large animals faced each other until the crocodile retreated to the water.

"What about that?" I asked Paul.

"It's not supposed to happen. In theory anyway."

"Yes," I agreed. "Of course, there probably were hippo young about that influenced its behaviour. But lower animals are not supposed to make judgements and think imaginatively. The writer stated that after the crocodile had gone back to the water, the hippo went over to the impala and nudged it to see if it was all right, because it was lying on the ground. The impala got up after a while and stumbled away."

Paul was very intent. "It showed compassion," he said.

"Aye," I said. I had long ago concluded that there is considerably less division between species, and between man and other animals, than is usually accepted. Communication and sympathy between different species, let along between animals within a species, has never seemed strange to me. Surely intellect is a matter of degree, rather than of exclusivity?

I first visited the Victoria Falls in October 1965, with my Aussie friend Barbie on my previous trans-Africa safari and we had been travelling in dry, arid country for weeks. The only running water we had been close to all the way from Mombasa had been when we camped at a small waterfall eleven hundred miles away near Mbeya on the Tanzania-Zambia border. I remembered clearly how enchanted we had been with the Zambesi and the awesomeness of the Victoria Falls, so that we had difficulty tearing ourselves away to continue our journey. It had not been only the sight of the great Zambesi, it had been its *presence*. The road on either side passes endlessly through the scrub and the view is restricted to the eternal bush. There is a faint roaring, a tremor in the air that grows gradually. Ahead, a whisp of cloud seems to drift over the trees and, without foreknowledge, the traveller could believe that he was coming to a furious bush-fire. Suddenly there is this giant of a river, filled with clean blue water and white foam, slipping majestically past its shallow banks and numerous palm clad islands to thunder into the mile wide cleft of the Falls.

David Livingstone, the first Briton to visit the Falls, approached it by canoe, down river on 16 November 1855. He was accompanied by Sekeletu, his friend, chief of the local Kololo tribe, and they landed on one of the islands on the brink of the falls. From the cliff edge of Livingstone's Island, one gazes straight down at the surging floor of the falls, within its narrow canyon, three hundred and fifty feet below, while water thunders down on each side, exploding into the spray that surges into the sky in rainbow painted clouds.

The trees and shrubs were richly decorated, bougainvillaea and flame trees seeming to have exploded in reds, oranges and purples everywhere, contrasting with the bright yellow cassias and mauve jacarandas which were also in full bloom. It was the dry season, but nature compensated with its painted trees. I walked with Ted the length of Falls on the first day, enjoying his fascination and feeling for the marvel more than my own renewed pleasure at being there. The water was lower than I had ever seen it, the whole centre section was dry and the great cliffs were black and baking in the sun.

The tourist town was practically deserted and I was amazed at the contrast with earlier visits. Even in 1976, when the Rhodesian War was nearing its peak, there had been more activity. Several of us went in the truck to a Lodge up river and enjoyed the quiet of its tropical garden. The Zambian shore on the other side with riverine forest was small with distance. I could imagine Livingstone in the tribal canoes as they paddled gently to keep in the stream and dodge the hippos. As lunchtime approached, a bunch of young soldiers emerged in camouflage jackets carrying automatic rifles and fanned out across the garden followed by business-suited men and a couple of smartly dressed women. The delicious aroma of a barbecue floated by.

I turned to Karen, our Canadian girl, with a sigh. "I thought the quiet might have lasted . . ."

"Yes," she said. "One of the waiters told me that it is a Tourism Promotion Conference." She laughed. "Do you think that explains the soldiers and guns?"

That evening I walked alone in moonlight to the Victoria Falls Hotel. I had stayed there in 1976 and my mother and grandparents had been guests fifty years earlier. It had been one of the grand colonial hotels of

Southern Africa in those days, so I was afraid that I might be sadly disappointed, but I was not. The great buildings surrounding a courtyard with immaculately groomed tropical plants were freshly painted. The high, Cape-Dutch style windows sparkled within their richly oiled teak frames. I had forgotten how big it was. In the courtyard I found, preserved, a small-gauge rail trolley-car complete with gay canvas roof awning and I instantly remembered a picture of my mother posing in it with a self-conscious smile on her face and a parasol in her hand. I wandered about looking into the public rooms, hearing the voices of the past in my imagination, smelling the cigar smoke, listening to the tinkle of a piano and the sigh of a violin. On the front terrace, leading off an elegantly appointed dining-room I joined a group of my companions finishing their Zimbabwe currency. Our mixture of accents, our unpressed clothes and the unkempt hair of our girls caused interested looks from the well-groomed South African tourists around us. When we walked back later I saw the Southern Cross, low down, for the last time until we were in the Sahara.

Victoria Falls, Zimbabwe.

CHAPTER FIVE: *KARIBA*

You can play some kind of tune on the white keys only.
You can play some kind of tune on the black keys only.
But for real music with full rich harmony,
You must use both the black and white keys.

Kwegyir Aggrey – Ghanain writer.
[Marie reminded me of this quotation]

"EVERY DAY GETS BETTER AND BETTER" – my diary, 10 September 1985.

Victoria Falls was a romantic place because two 'couples' formed. One was to result in a serious marriage engagement, the other lasted all the way to England, off and on. Some might think that because we were about equally matched in numbers and because of the nature of the experience, there would be automatic sexual pairing off and maybe considerable promiscurity. This was not the case. The people whom I travelled with had not undertaken the very tough adventure of travelling across Africa for sexual excitement. I am sure that there is more drive for casual sex on a two or three week holiday at a Mediterranean resort than there could ever be on a five month safari in Africa. Talking with many Overlanders on the journey confirmed that our group was no different to others. After the difficult settling-in period, I was delighted by the normal behaviour and reasonable harmony, considering our varied backgrounds and our situation. When the going became really rough and people were ill or injured, there was a group spirit that I recall with emotional pride.

Charlie arranged for some of us to take a white-water rafting run on big rubber boats down the Zambesi gorge below the Falls when we crossed over to Zambia. We stopped at the Intercontinental Hotel sited near the Eastern Cataract, and a couple of athletic young Americans were waiting to take charge. Their organisation operated white-water rafting on the Colorado River and many other places and they reckoned that the Zambesi was one of the most spectacular of all. Eight went (at $US70.00 a head) but I turned it down because I am not at home in wild water. I was an enthusiastic voyeur, however, and Katie, who was rafting, asked me to photograph the start, so I followed them down the path to the floor of the gorge below the Victoria Falls. This was itself an unforgettable experience. The path was steep and we scrambled down the cliff face through the thick riverine bush, clambering over huge boulders that had fallen from the heights above. Gradually the roaring of the river came closer and the smell and sense of sharply increased humidity became clear in my nostrils. I kept sneezing. Vervet monkeys swung over our heads in the tree tops, clutching lianas. The whole expedition seemed to be a dreamlike TV documentary into which I was strangely plunged. Coming abruptly out into the bright sunlight I stood almost breathless from the confrontation with majestic nature. Despite the low river, the power and rage of the whole Zambesi pouring through the narrow gorge between four hundred foot cliffs was beyond any experience I had had. The air seemed to vibrate with contained energy.

I found a vantage point and waited, sitting with Paul, immersed in the spectacle. When the two large rubber rafts swept into view from the launching place around a corner with their orange life-jacketed crews, they looked small and vulnerable, like bright water spiders cast into a rushing mountain stream. In the viewfinder of Katie's camera they were coloured dots on the blue and white running stream with chocolate ice-cream walls rearing out of sight. They were gone around the next corner in a minute. We climbed back up, dripping with sweat, to the dry dust of the bushveld, the thunder of water subdued to a gentle drone. We waited at the hotel, a sleazy run-down example of a British international chain, where a Scandinavian Aid organisation was having a conference, accompanied by sun-tanned, blonde girls. While we were there, a strange dusty cloud mass crept across the sky, which was to last for days. Gone was the clear blue sky of South Africa.

As soon as the rafters returned full of exhilaration and excitement (Adie had been washed out of her raft, but had been pulled on again without incident), we were off, into Zambia. I remembered the town of Livingstone being a busy colonial market in 1965, but it was now a dreary place with abandoned suburban bungalows, rusting advertising signs and pot holed streets. The strange light from the dust in the sky made the scene particularly dismal. At the railway station there was a remarkable steam locomotive graveyard; dozens of tired old juggernauts were lying in a shunting yard, rusty paint flaking off boilers streaked with the stains of several rainy seasons and brass forever dulled. Somehow I was particularly appalled by that dying town. It was the first of many I was to see on our safari and I suppose that it was the suddenness of confronting Zambian regression that struck me. Twenty years ago, ex-colonial Africa had such optimistic visions of progress after throwing off imperial yokes. I pondered my emotional reaction to the visible decay of Livingstone town and wondering what other shocks awaited me further north.

We arrived at our destination well after dark, but it was not too late for a proper dinner by a roaring camp fire. Our site was beneath tall, old eucalyptus trees in the farm-yard of a friend of Charlie's, who provided the camping facilities and had arranged an expedition on Lake Kariba. Charlie had been giving us a trailer of this adventure for days. It was natural enough, this trailing of future events, and amused me. No sooner were we at one 'marvellous' place than we were told about the next one, which was always better.

We pitched tents in the dark and Val and I cooked, so we were busy about the fire when Charlie and his friend, Jack, sat and talked. Every now and then, Charlie would include me by saying: "Listen to this, Denis." It was interesting. Jack had lived in Zambia for many years, he owned a large farm and was deeply and sincerely concerned about the country and his own situation. Especially, he was critical of the agricultural policy of the government, which had entered a destructive cycle, sadly common in the Third World, as I well knew. The most politically sophisticated people are those who live in the urban areas and start revolutions, he explained. Therefore, governments keep essential consumer costs down and food prices are fixed relative to the pain threshhold of the urban dwellers. Costs of fuel, machinery and fertiliser to farmers, contrarily, have to vary according to the international market and the government controlled value of the local currency. With massive foreign debts, incurred irresponsibly, the tendency is for governments to permit a slide in official currency values with consequent massive inflation. The squeeze between fixed, or even lowered, food prices and increasing costs results in reduced food production. The downward spiral steepens until food Aid is provided by the international community. This props up desperate or cynical governments who continue to maintain this disastrous course.

"Are you not talking about large commercial farmers like yourself who may be obsolete in this environment?" I asked Jack, to provoke him.

He laughed. "You're telling me that smallholdings run by the locals can produce cheaper than I can with five thousand hectares? Long term, that's complete bullshit, but there's a specious point to that argument in the short term. In this country there are schemes being run by government with advice from various agencies, and some are being run directly by foreign Aid people. They always seem to take off well because the start-up expenses are funded from outside and infrastructure is created for the local farmers. All seems good and crops are produced. You would imagine that with low overheads they could compete easily with myself, especially as they are not paying any wages. In terms of price, they can compete, if you can call it that. All they are doing is producing maize or vegetables and selling to the government at the government's fixed price which is determined by what the urban market can pay.

"The smallholders are feeding themselves from their own land, as they have done forever, and they spend whatever money they have to on clothes and suchlike. That's fine. But what about next year, when they are short of cash? They buy less fertiliser, they don't replace tools and implements, they plant and harvest less, so less food is produced."

He paused to look around, then jabbed his finger at me. "It's your taxes and voluntary contributions to Aid schemes back in UK that are propping up this government, you know. And the terrible thing is that government ministers and top officials have all got their Swiss bank accounts. Oh, yes! Be sure about that!"

"Come on, Jack," Charlie teased, with a sideways smile at me. "You're just jealous because your Swiss bank account isn't as big."

But Jack would not laugh. "No, Charlie, I'm being very serious. My life is here, on this land. I'm not a pirate, I'm a farmer. At the time of Independence, Zambia fed itself. To-day we live on food Aid and the maize that comes up from South Africa. All our copper exports have to go down the railway to be shipped from East London. I suppose they've made some secret deal with the South Africans, but how long can they keep it up? They're calling for sanctions against South Africa, but South African goods and fuel are keeping us going. How will they earn any foreign exchange if their exports are stopped by Pretoria? It's a bloody mess, I tell you."

"So how do you manage?" I asked.

He poked at the fire, then looked up at me. "Three-quarters of my farm is idle. Would you believe it? I can't plant year after year knowing that every acre will show a loss. I haven't got the money anyway, and the commercial banking system is all buggered up. I do some ranching, I've got a small garage business in town, I've got a village butchery, I've got an interest in fishing. I do what I can to make a reasonable living and keep my work-people in employment. But I'm worried about health, I'm not getting younger and the local hospital has no drugs any longer and the equipment is worn out or going missing." He shrugged.

That night after dinner when we were all assembled, Jack told some of the expected tales of old Africa. He had done a lot of hunting in his day, but gave it up because the wild animal populations had declined so drastically. Many years ago he had asked a witch-doctor to help him with his hunting, more or less as a joke. The witch-doctor had prepared a complicated spell and blessed an elephant's hair bracelet that he wore. The witch-doctor said that the spell would give protection from fifty elephants. Jack used to keep a tally and when he got up to fifty, he had, despite his commonsense, become apprehensive. The fifty-first elephant was walking in the bush and Jack tracked it for some distance. As he came round a small hillock with thick scrub about it, he had a strong feeling of danger and so moved with increased caution. It was well that he did, because the elephant was waiting for him. He aimed for it confidently and squeezed the trigger, but there were no bullets in the gun. Incredible! The elephant charged and he swiftly climbed a tree.

"Did you shoot it?" someone asked.

"No. I left it alone, and after about an hour it calmed down and walked away."

"What about the witch-doctor?"

"I went back to him," Jack said. "And I paid him to give me more protection. I was all right after that. You can make what you like of that story."

"What happened after the next fifty elephants?"

Jack laughed. "I never counted after that and I paid him for a more powerful protection. I wasn't going to take a chance either way. But I've shot about three hundred elephants in my life."

"So you believe in native medicine?" Charlie asked.

"Let's say that I don't disbelieve. You can't live in Africa without accepting that there's something to it. Let's say that I believe in mind over matter."

The next morning we changed our money with a black marketeer. The official rate was three Kwachas to the pound, similar to the South African exchange for the Rand. On the B.M. we got eight Kwachas to the pound.

Visiting a kraal near Choma, Zambia.

We went shopping in Choma on our way down to Lake Kariba where we were to spend the next couple of days. We had been warned that due to the shortage of foreign exchange to buy wheat, there was no bread to be had in the country, but somebody was told by a shopkeeper that there was some in a Government Co-op store. A big crowd jammed the store, waiting patiently, so Nick and Jaime, the cooks for the day, went in to see what they could get. The crowd saw that they had come from our truck and with typical African courtesy and friendliness towards foreigners, they were ushered through to the head of the line. They got their bread and in the excitement and the clamour did not realise until we had driven off that they had been given too much change. Jaime was quite upset by this and to my surprise, she launched a strident attack on British colonialism and White people in general. "Those poor people," she said. "They're so used to being ripped off all the time by Europeans, they let us come to the front of the line. They even sold the bread to us at a cheap price. It's just too amazing! It just proves how much they got ripped off by the British. Those poor people!" She was nearly in tears and could not get over it. She kept talking about the incident and her extraordinary conclusions in her soft Californian accent. So are strange legends born and I could imagine her re-telling the story back home and her sad misinterpretation being accepted as doctrine by her circle of friends.

We arrived at the lakeside in mid afternoon. Charlie had arranged, through Jack, with a local fishing company that we would spend a night on an island followed by a day's sightseeing. The fishing company, together with several others from both the Zambian and Zimbabwean sides, used floating platforms like small oilrigs to dredge for *kapenta*, a silvery freshwater fish about the size of a sardine that swarmed in shoals. Nets were let down from booms at night and a powerful light lowered into the centre of the net. After about half an hour, the nets were raised full of kapenta that had been attracted by the light. The average catch each night from the five rigs the company operated was about one and a half tons, worth about five thousand Kwachas. But we were told that catches were beginning to fall and there was no control over the industry with companies working with cynical competitiveness out of both neighbouring countries.

"What will happen when the resource is reduced to uneconomic levels?" I asked Jan, the young manager.

"We'll simply close down. We've already amortised our equipment and we have no fixed assets of any value."

In the current economic climate of Zambia and with no attempt by governments to control the fishing, they would not consider investing in any sophisticated processing plant and all the operators were working hard to make as much money as they could while there were still fish in the lake. If Jaime was interested in a 'rip-off' of Africa, this was a real one.

The fishing camp was on a bluff overlooking the pale blue of the great artificial lake covered by the silver sky, still coloured by the fine dust from the strange storm that had passed over the day before. The lake had retreated more than a mile from its planned level at the foot of the bluff due to the droughts of the last few years, and we had to be carried by Landrovers to a rickety temporary jetty built of mopani poles where a workboat awaited us. It was not running well, the engine belched smoke and the coxswain nursed it along at half speed. I did not mind because it was beautiful on the lake. The air was still, the water a mirror and the milky sky became infused with palest pastel golds merging into delicate pinks. As the sun descended further and later as it set, the pastels gently changed to pinky mauves with purple rising from the eastern horizon. The air was balm. We passed between islands, some little more than sandbanks that would be covered by the lake at its normal level, others had patches of grey leafless scrub and lumpy boulders peering through the mesh of dry branches. The shadow of the earth climbed the eastern sky and the dust haze became a deep blue. Lights appeared, twinkling across the water, and soon we moved in blackness towards the points of artificial life. The evening had stolen on us with that effortless tropical speed and it had been a particular experience that all of us would remember. Suddenly in the black dark of a starless, dust-filled sky we were all vulnerable, feeling naked there in the middle of Africa.

The rash of kapenta rigs swooped around our coughing boat, for the world seemed to be moving; we were stationery in our noisy, smelly vessel. And then we were alongside one of them. An old Lister generator hammered away, powering the harsh lights. Half a dozen sweating men, wearing torn and filthy jeans manned the rig, and they greeted us with grins and friendly chatter. They spent days on the rig until relieved for a break on shore. A headman showed us the gear and tea was brewing on an open fire burning in a split oil drum. We watched as a catch was landed. Cables descended from booms that had been swung over the side. On one of the cables the light to attract the fish was suspended and there was a misty luminescence in the green water. Floodlights shone onto the rig and the water and a million insects were attracted in a frenzy to the lights themselves and the shiny surface of the water, but there were no insects near us. An ancient Ford tractor engine was used to lift the catch and it sat on the deck complete with gear lever, clutch and accelerator pedals. Its grinning operator was perched on the tractor's seat which was welded into position. The net was hauled in and swung over the catch box and the silver shower of fish released in a cascade. It appeared to me to be a small quantity of fish as reward for all this old farm machinery bellowing away and the shouts and excitement of the crew, but we had already been told that the catches were declining. I looked around into the African night at the dozen or so other brightly lit rigs in a radius of a mile from us within the great zone of black wilderness inhabited by crocodiles, hippos and elephants. Man is a remarkable creature, I thought.

We camped that night on an island in the middle of the blackness and three fires cooked our food, gave us light and kept the crocodiles away. Jan cruised the shore to look out for them and the crack of a shot rang out and thrilled us. "Just frightening a couple away," Jan told us. I suspected that it was part of the service to create a bit of authenticity, but the others were impressed. Most of the sleeping bags were spread out carefully between the fires.

After dinner, Jan spoke about his fears and disillusion under Kaunda's 'humanitarian' regime, which made South Africa appear to be a Utopia. He also expounded on the follies of economic mismanagement, repeating much that Jack had said the night before.

"What about you personally?" somebody asked.

He smiled rather sadly in the firelight. "I was born in Zambia. I'm a Zambian citizen. I've got nowhere to go, so I'll battle on. Kaunda himself is sincere and I believe he's honourable. It's the raw corruption beneath him that is the trouble. We've thought of everything. I'm ready to try anything. Tourism was a good idea ten years ago, but where are the tourists going to come from? The hope was South Africa, but South Africans aren't actually encouraged these days . . ." He got up. "I've got to catch some fish. See you in the morning."

I lay in my sleeping bag, looking up at the naked sky, thinking.

I slept very soundly, but others had been up guarding us against the crocodiles. Nick had kept the fires going and the smell of their smoke made me think of coffee immediately I awoke. A pale pink wash touched the mackerel structures of the high clouds and behind the dust there was a hint of blue. I got up and after dressing, I walked about our sandbank in the quiet before the others. There were no crocodile tracks, but there were two fish eagles on their perches. The nearer one screamed as I came close and lazily flew across to dead trees on the far side of the islet. I had a tremendous feeling walking about, alone. No boat moved on the lake, away from the camp there was no sight of man, and the lake itself, so vast in the centre of the surrounding wilderness of scrub bush, affected me with a great sensation of space and freedom within that space.

We went explorating in the workboat with Jan to guide us. The sun grew into a silver furnace directly overhead as noon approached and we cruised alongside several islands. We went ashore on one where a herd of about a hundred elephant lived. Jan told us about this herd and I listened carefully to what he had to say. The island covered an area of about five thousand acres, mostly thick bush that had been undisturbed since the dam had been built and the lake had formed twenty-five years ago. Many animals had been chased and ferried off the islands as they were created by the rising water, but this herd of elephants had either been missed or the game rangers had thought that they could fend for themselves. After all, elephants can swim and a herd of a hundred should have been numerous enough to be able to know what to do. They had stayed on the island and in the many years since had established perfect stability. Their numbers varied little and the bush was not damaged by over feeding. There was no poaching because of the location of the island in the middle of the lake. So elephants can live in a constricted territory without destroying their habitat, and maybe they do practice sub-conscious birth control. Culling was unnecessary.

We landed and walked about warily, sensing the fear and the stimulation of a gentle flow of adrenalin that the presence of these great animals created. Although they were not hunted, the special circumstances of living on an island had made them shy and nervous, and nervous animals are unpredictable. There were plenty of tracks and droppings, but the elephants were away in another part: we saw about ten moving on the edge of some trees about one kilometre away. I would have liked to stay there for days, to savour the feeling of sharing the island with the elephants, but we had to move on to the mainland and our camp back on Jack's farm.

The next night we camped in the grounds of a house twenty miles west of Lusaka. Our hosts were Sally and Tim, a pleasant young English couple, who, like everybody else, were glad to have a contribution of hard currency from us for the use of their garden and bathroom. Tim was a vet employed by a group of ranches owned by the South African multinational, Anglo-American Corporation. Their house was a modern bungalow, badly in need of decoration, sited on a hill overlooking a great scrub-bush plain that disappeared into the dusty haze of far distance. There was a stained swimming pool with water coloured a deep green with algae (there were no chemicals available in Zambia) and broken garden furniture. The lawn stretching to where the bush began was unkempt: there were no spares for the mower. It was hardly the dream of expatriate luxury that they had probably expected when signing up for the exciting two years overseas contract. Because Tim was frequently out at all hours, they were deeply concerned about Sally's physical safety in the lonely bush bungalow. Daily there were stories of robbery and violence. They had dogs, but dogs can be poisoned or shot. Going into Lusaka next day I remembered what Tim and Sally had said about security when we passed through a residential suburb surrounded by high walls topped by broken glass. Guards sat in shelters by the gates.

Barbie and I had been quite impressed by Lusaka twenty years before. The city is colonial, like Nairobi and Harare, and there is no traditional reason for its existence. When we came through in 1965, we were struck by the wide main boulevard with cheerful flower beds and green grass between the carriageways; the city centre had been clean and neat with a mixture of older colonial buildings and modern office blocks. There had been businesslike bustle and the people were well dressed. The suburbs, industrial and residential, seemed to have that spark of progress: bright paint, tidy street, an air of purpose.

Ted and I walked about and Lusaka was not the same. Gone was the purposefulness and in its place was a kind of watchful apathy with shabby young people hanging about on street corners. I was accosted by a drunk or drugged young Black man with safety pins in his ears and a ragged cocks-comb haircut, he had discovered punk and wanted rock music cassettes. The islands down the middle of the boulevard were red earth, bare of grass or flowers. The streets were potholed. There was litter drifting and the buildings were streaked with the mould of past rainy seasons. We looked over a curioshop, but it was filled with expensive Zimbabwe-made junky copper souvenirs, and there were no customers. I wanted to buy postcards and after walking up and down and asking directions, we found a bookshop which had some finger-marked greeting cards for birthdays and even Christmas, but no picture postcards. There were few books, those that were on display were dusty and dog-eared; an incongruous mixture of United Nations pamphlets, Communist dogma printed in Russia and Czechoslovakia, English anti-Apartheid literature, out-of-date school textbooks that had probably been in stock for twenty years and poorly printed government statistical reports. I felt sudden, awful despair.

Youngsters in Lusaka, Zambia.

Charlie drove us to the five star Padmodze Hotel near the principal government buildings and embassies in a leafy suburb. This was the Lusaka of the visiting Aid missions, international salesmen, the diplomats and the South African A.N.C. 'freedom fighters' in exile. I strolled about the plush public rooms feeling uncomfortable in my Overlander clothes listening to snatches of earnest clichéd conversations which sauvely rolled out the transparent politics and confident sales patter. I eyed the politicians in their tailored safari-suits, shiny shoes, Paisley cravats and expensive spectacles, and returned their stares. Ted and I sat down for a beer in the bar. This show-case hotel only served imported beer because the local brew was notoriously bad: cloudy and with what a barman had called, 'floaters'. Katie joined us there in some distress. She had gone with Steve to the central police station to report the loss of some documents and while waiting they had heard a Black man being flogged and screaming for mercy. He was a petty thief apparently, being softened up for a confession. There had also been a White boy in the police station, held for possessing marijuana that was being peddled openly on street corners. He had been in shock, not knowing what lay before him.

I was glad to get out of Lusaka.

That night we had a party for Bob's birthday at Sally and Tim's bungalow in the bush. We built a long fire and barbecued the finest porterhouse steaks I had eaten in a long time. There was nothing wrong with Zambian meat and there had been plenty in the supermarket that the cooks had patronised. The prices had been reasonable, at the value of our BM currency. But there were hardly any manufactured goods: whole shelves had perhaps one case of Vim or Omo stretched out like guardsmen in open order.

The party went well with lots of beer which we had bought at a roadside tavern filled with drunken men and women, each bottle turned upside down carefully to check for the dreaded 'floaters'. Karen and I had a long discussion about the care of handicapped people in Canada and South Africa: it seemed incongruous where we were. Later, Charlie led Scottish reels and 'The Dashing White Sergeant' and out on the lawn confronting the invisible bushveld plain to relieve myself, African style, I listened to the music and laughter. I was suddenly assaulted with sharp nostalgia for similar nights in Nigeria nearly thirty years before that seemed so immediate and familiar. I compared the two cultural islands I had experienced that day: the bar lounge of the five star hotel with murmured, knowing conversations, and the bare bungalow with the wailing cassettes of Scottish music and whooping stumbling dancers. The birthday party was honest, and that was important to me.

It was two days to Lilongwe, capital of Malawi, along the colonial 'Great East Road' which runs along the northern side of the Zambian border with Mozambique. We camped en route in a gravel pit, the first of a great many on our safari, shortly after crossing a fine suspension bridge over the Luangwa River heavily guarded by the Zambian army. The country is comprised of endless mopani bushveld forest for most of the way and the few kraals were similar to those in Zimbabwe on the road running along the southern side of Lake Kariba. But many of the kraals were abandoned and falling into ruin. It was depressing country and the sky was still hazed. After the Luangwa River, there was some flat land with enlarged villages and a few abandoned mud-brick stores with rusted advertising signs. There had been cultivation, but from observing the size of the patches of grass, encroaching secondary scrub and the termite mounds in the fields, I could conclude that crops had not been grown for a least one or two rainy seasons. What had happened to this country? It was as if the people had given up on life.

The brown arms of the mothering plateau
Seem to restrain me here against a fall
Into the lambent sea of bush, below
This high blue cleft in the escarpment wall,
From which slow-rolling waves of febrile heat
Swirl up, to daze the mind with vertigo
And race the pulse with metronomic beat
THE LOWVELD. *Charles Eglington. [South African poet]*

Many contemporary writers on Africa write unfavourably of Malawi in a political way. There is an 'old guard' of presidents in Africa who are praised and written about with affection no matter how harmful their ideologies have been to their people or corrupt their regimes have proved to be. They seem to be able to do no wrong. Their mistakes are blamed on the legacies of imperial powers, failure of their ministers and advisers, world economics or their pure idealism that has been undermined by this or that unfortunate circumstance. Kamuza Banda of Malawi is an exception because Banda is austere, conservative and has adopted an openly realistic policy towards South Africa. He is accused of being authoritarian and intolerant of political opposition, and this is true. However, he holds those traits in common with many African leaders. If he was a hypocrite and proclaimed his regime to be some form of socialist peoples' state and banned all contact with South Africa, while trading under the counter, he would be able to join the club of 'progressive' leaders. It is clear that he knows this, for he has said so in public many times.

I had enjoyed Malawi on my way overland to visit Mozambique Island in June 1970, so I was especially pleased to return. I knew that I was favourably biased in advance, but I was ready for unpleasant changes if they had occurred. My dismay at the crumbled façade of Zambia had prepared me.

Having passed through the hands of the casual Zambian border officials in their unkempt and shabby buildings with dusty litter scattered around outside, Charlie warned us to expect a hard time at the entrance to Malawi. He had gone into his 'border crossing mode' and had changed to a long-sleeved shirt and tie. We were warned about respectful behaviour and the girls were told to ensure that their knees were covered.

65

In Malawi, mini-skirts and female shorts are banned in public by Presidential decree. We were also warned that the truck might be searched for the first time since leaving Johannesburg because girly magazines and Marxist propaganda were also banned, as was one of the Overlanders' bibles, *Africa on a Shoestring*, because it contained trendy-leftist comment and is critical of Malawi. I was therefore a little nervous when we drove up to the Malawi border.

At first sight, I imagined that I was back in South Africa. The neat buildings were freshly painted and surrounded by a carefully tended flower garden contained in a border of whitewashed stones. Trees shaded the gates and buildings, bougainvillaea provided livid colour. There were benches to sit on and refuse bins for litter. The girls reported that their loo was clean, always a critical matter. We stood about for a while waiting for Charlie to check on the routine. He returned, smiling, with printed forms for us to fill in and said that the formalities would be done as a group. We did not have to be involved.

"How about that?" I said to Bob.

"It proves something simple to me," he said, then gestured at the flower beds and the tidy compound. "These people are very proud of their country. They like to show it off and they enjoy being efficient."

There was a commercial lorry park on the other side of the border post where a long, orderly queue of articulated trucks waited: ocean container carriers, fuel tankers, refrigerated trucks, Bob pointed at them and said, "From South Africa. There's probably more consumer goods and fuel passing through customs here this afternoon than there was in the whole of Lusaka when we were there." Bob was always outspoken: "Zambia's totally fucked up . . ."

We weren't searched. A small, slim uniformed man poked his head in at the door and smiled at us. "Anything to declare? Any 'Shoestringies'?" His smile widened at the negative chorus. He glanced over the girls who had wrapped their legs in bright printed cloths that they had bought for that purpose in Choma market, then waved us off. Charlie looked over his shoulder from the front with a grin: 'You can get out the 'Shoestringies' again." There was a surge of relieved laughter.

Immediately after the border, a change was obvious. The road itself was in good repair, the road signs were new, the first village had a cheerful little store plastered with advertising posters. The people by the side of the road waved and smiled and the children shouted greetings: always a highly significant indication of a country's morale when travelling in Africa.

That night we camped at the Lilongwe Golf Club where the Secretary, a South African, was helpful, exchanging some money for us and making us all temporary members. Apart from the night on the crocodile island in Lake Kariba, I had pitched my tent every night but in Malawi I did not bother and enjoyed the freedom and almost indefinable psychic pleasure that sleeping in the open gives you. This is especially so in Africa, where that pleasure can be quite acute in the wilderness. Whereas the tent gives you a feeling of security and snugness, sleeping without is something akin to bathing naked in a warm ocean and running on a deserted beach. It was the dry season and in Zimbabwe and Zambia I had not noticed any mosquitoes, so that first night in Lilongwe I did not bother with a net and was not attacked. I hardly used a net at all throughout our safari when I slept without a tent, except in the rain forests, where my concern was less with mosquitoes than with spiders. The most uncomfortable thing about sleeping under the stars is the dew: it is unpleasant having to get into a damp sleeping bag and to eliminate that problem I would always put my bed under a tree, which helps. It is another pleasure to be close to a tree in the quiet of the night. We tend to take the strong, slow friendship of trees, the most passive and gentle of our living companions on Earth, for granted.

Charlie had a camp-fire discussion with us about a change in plans. He had warned us at Potgietersrust that Tanzania had recently massively increased the entrance fees to all its National Parks, including Mount Kilimanjaro. He had been worrying, and his proposal was that we should spend an extra week in Malawi and arrange more time in the Kenya Game Parks. There was disappointment and some angry comment about the short-sightedness of the Tanzanian Govenment, but Charlie's plan was accepted.

How does one describe an idyll without endlessly repeating superlatives? Despite rigorous reflection and careful thought with my diary in front of me, I cannot seem to find a blemish on the next seven days. There were blemishes on the experiences of others in our group, but I had none. From Lilongwe we drove east along a flat plain on a good road until quite suddenly, we were at the edge of the Great Rift Valley escarpment and I asked for a break. While it was useful for most as a loo stop, I walked a short way along a small ridge and stared ahead and downwards, with a special excitement, for the Rift Valley is Africa's greatest geographical feature. Africa is unique in being bisected by the Equator with remarkable uniformity of climatic zones to north and south. Its vastness is overpowering and after days in the endless traverse of apparently unchanging landscape it can become dull. But the Rift Valley takes the place of the Andes or Himalayas in providing relief from the ennui of bushveld plains. It runs from the Dead Sea in Palestine to Mozambique in Southern Africa. It forms the Red Sea and the Gulf of Aquaba. In Central Africa it divides in two to provide chains of great lakes in Kenya in the east and along the borders of Uganda, Zaïre, Rwanda, Burundi and Tanzania in the west, joining up again in Malawi. These lakes drew Livingstone, Grant, Speke, Burton and Stanley, our great Victorian British explorers, and before them, Egyptians, Romans and many unknown Arabs. Volcanoes stud the lengths and fringes of both the Central African branches, and these mountains are the highest in Africa. On both sides of the valley there are escarpments, thousands of miles in length, sometimes puny, but usually forming cliffs one or two thousand feet high that disappear in both directions into the haze of distance. The Rift Valleys shelter the earliest known remains of mankind on Earth. We were to cross and recross the Great Rift Valley on our safari, but that stop near Lilongwe was the first time we gazed into it.

When we descended to the bottom, the character of the vegetation changed. The mopani and cleared agricultural fields gave way abruptly with lower altitude to acacia thornbush. As we moved on across the flat valley bottom, there was intensive cultivation, broken by tall deciduous trees that had been thankfully left to stand sentinel like giant scarecrows. We passed a low range of folded hills then into a flood plain; an area of uninhabited parkland, the short grass, quite green for a change, sheltered by yellow-boled fever trees. The pink-purple bulk of a baobab loomed here and there. In the late afternoon, we came over a gentle rise in the land and there was Lake Malawi; a pale pastel blue in the golden light with the shadowy hint of the high escarpment on the other side, in Mozambique.

We headed for Cape Maclear which was much changed since 1970 when I visited Malawi previously. In place of the thick forest that ran down to the water's edge there was a great bowl of ploughed lands between the volcanic hills and the Lake. Cape Maclear was the first mission on the Lake founded by David Livingstone's Scottish colleagues on his urgings to 'civilise' Central Africa to try and beat the Arab slave trade. On my previous visit in 1970 I had been struck by the loneliness of the small collection of graves of some of those first missionaries that are preserved there: so far from the Victorian order and the cold, clean climate of Dundee or Aberdeen. The graves were still preserved, but they seemed even more remote and lost, surrounded by the new cultivated lands. Fever had driven the missionaries away from the Lake up to the Nyika Plateau to found the colonial village of Livingstonia, remote from most of the population. Livingstone would not have approved, he was a stern uncompromising man.

At the lakeside there was a rim of undisturbed bush beyond the dried stalks of last year's maize crop standing alongside fields of manioc, beans and green vegetables, and we nosed our way into it following the track past the back-yards of holiday cottages. The hotel that we had been directed to by a pretty girl in the American Express office in Lilongwe was at the end of the track and Bob backed our truck carefully underneath the trees at the side. The hotel was no longer taking guests, but it functioned as a bar, occasional restaurant and a base for camping. It had been a substantial private home with wide verandahs in old colonial style and rooms were added around a courtyard: I have seen so many hotels of this character in Africa and have always loved them and deplored their substitution by purpose-built, economical and functionally efficient creatures with little atmosphere. I looked about at the carefully raked grounds, breathed the scent of the mature frangipani trees and noted the bougainvillaea in bloom, admired the tall palmyra palms standing in the clean sand by the gently lapping Lake that stretched to the horizon. The enthusiastic calls of my companions as they explored, confirmed that we would be enjoying the idyll here.

I erected my camp-bed under the spread of a gnarled old bougainvillaea and that night I slept dreamlessly without waking. There were no mosquitoes.

EXTRACTS FROM MY DIARY: 20 September 1985. CAPE MACLEAR

Woken at 5 a.m. by the very loud scream of a fish-eagle, just as I was on the first morning by this Lake at Palm Beach fifteen years ago. What an extraordinarily good omen. Beautiful dawn: pastel mauves, pinks and palest blue in sky and reflected on the water. Walked along the waterfront past several week-end cottages and caravans, some occupied. Dave's company cottage must be one of them. Fishing boats are out, dug-out canoes, a larger boat ferrying people along the coast, their shouts of conversation carrying across the water above the noise of the engine. It's still paradise . . .

Washed clothes and bedsheet, shampooed hair in the Lake. The biggest bathroom in Africa! Spent the day slowly exploring and absorbing. What an incredibly fine place. The Lake is in complete ecological balance and free of bilharzia — I keep splashing the water because it SMELLS so clean, full of oxygen, like a mountain stream. Charlie went snorkeling and reported lots of varicoloured tropical fish off the rocks at the point. We had been warned about hippos, but they were at the islands. The fish were so tame, Charlie kept saying. I observed a cormorant from six feet away. A bulbul sits three feet above my head as I lie on my bed dozing off and on: we watch each other . . .

At Otter Point in the afternoon, observed three fish-eagles and saw their high nests. There were many rock-rabbits scurrying about and stopping to look at us. A ground squirrel bounds about our camp. A hammerkop fishes at the lake's edge, wagtails very close. Walked down the beach with Charlie and Ted in the evening, looking for another hotel I visited fifteen years ago. Saw Steve's Place, a kind of motel, and were directed further on to the African village where we found a rough bar with a paraffin freezer and cold beers. The village catches kapenta fish and dries them on matting racks, just like at Kariba, but here it is a communal activity, not a big commercial venture. I love to see the village doing it gently without the disastrous effects of those power rigs. (Pray they will never come here). Ted and I took pictures of the sun setting on the water, naked Black girls washing at the edge in silhouette.

Three huge Lake fish, potato chips and fresh salads for dinner. I ate well. Brandy with Bob afterwards on the verandah, talking slowly . . .

Our local barman, George, told me about the hotel that I remembered so well from last time. He calls it the 'Aeroplane Hotel' because it was built to service the B.O.A.C. flying boats that used to ply up and down to South Africa just after W.W.II. I didn't know that. The hotel has now gone. "It was taken away, right to the foundation . . ." I asked George what had happened to his own hotel. He told me that there used to be a European 'Madam' but she had sold up and gone to South Africa. Since then, when something broke down, it's not replaced. First went the lighting plant, then the freezer, (but they have a new one because of the beers), then the plumbing to the bathrooms, and finally the old diesel pump that sent up water from the Lake. Oh Africa! But it is all still so clean and tidy, even if nothing works. I told George that, and he smiled shyly . . .

From Cape Maclear we went into Monkey Bay for supplies, a small town and port for the two Lake steamers that ply a regular service up and down. The market was busy and cheerful and the bright little supermarket of the state owned rural trading-store chain was open for business although it was a Sunday. Throughout our safari, I used country stores, markets and city shops as a crude measure of the prosperity of the particular countries we were in. It was not the value of individual items that interested me so much as the quality, variety and appropriateness of the goods, as well as the atmosphere: the 'buzz' as a professional retailer might call it. Monkey Bay's soul was cheerful and alive, the supermarket was full of a good variety of sensible household merchandise, two or three brands of most necessities to enable the consumer to choose, but no obviously useless luxuries. Our group were glad to stock up on washing powder, toilet paper (suddenly become a critical matter because of an epidemic of diarrhoea), cooking oil, South African jam and peanut butter, and excellent local tea. I was glad to find torch batteries which I had not been able to get in Zambia.

A young man came up and talked to me while I waited by the truck. He began by using me as an informal geography teacher, asking intelligently about conditions in England: the climate, what our farms were like, how did the farmers sell their produce, what were the cities really like. He wanted my address so that he could correspond: "To improve my written English."

"Are you still at school?" I asked.

"Oh yes. I am in standard nine. I hope to write Senior Certificate next year, if my father can let me stay on. I have to help him, because I am the eldest."

"What does your father do?"

"He is a carpenter."

"What do you want to do?" I asked him.

"If I have chance to finish my schooling, I will go to South Africa." South Africa, always the mecca of Central Africa. If only they knew what socio-political struggles that country was engaged in.

"What would you do if you got to South Africa?" I asked before saying good-bye.

His eyes lit. "I would attend a technical college and learn about television, then work with it and make some money. One day we will get TV in Malawi and I could have a very good start."

That was different. "Good luck!" I told him with sudden emotion. We clasped hands for a moment.

South of Monkey Bay is the Club Makakolo and we called to see if we could change travellers' cheques, which the polite and efficient Malawian manager agreed to do. A South African-based multinational's executive twelve seater plane was at its airstrip, a 'sport and health centre' was in construction (squash, sauna baths and massages for tired executives), there were neat rows of chalets and poolside bedrooms giving

71

off their characteristic roar of air-conditioners converting fresh balm into humming refrigeration, new turf sparkled under hissing sprinklers covering the patio area around the giant swimming pool a few yards from the only healthy great natural lake in Africa. I saw a group of smooth-faced, round-stomached men wearing sunglasses and Company T-shirts sitting about in morning ennui: the contents of the company plane up here for a 'think-tank', away from the fourteenth floor in Cape Town or Johannesburg, two or three thousand miles away. 'Brut' and 'Fauberge' wafted to me.

Strolling on the immaculate lawn with its few exotic shrubs and baby coconut palms, cocooned in little thatch shelters, replacing the twisted giants of the bush that had been hauled away by bulldozers, I was suddenly struck intensely by the message shouted at me. This alien creature that had been put here was obviously well-managed and employed a number of trained local people, it was approved 'development'. The presence of the hung-over executive group, sipping iced beer and the first Bloody Mary of the day, showed that it was being well marketed. But was this not inappropriate development for Africa? We had just left the ramshackle old colonial hotel tucked into a cranny of the rugged bay at Cape Maclear, surrounded by granite hills, nestling amongst old trees, struggling for existence after the old white 'Madam' had given up and gone to retirement in South Africa. A tenth of the money that had been lavished on the Club Makakolo would have revitalised it and it had an aesthetic appeal vastly superior to that of the multi-million dollar technological beast down the coast with its two hundred air-conditioners poised to break down and its fragile computerised accounting system awaiting bureaucratic disaster. Later I was told that the financial partners of that hotel had pressed for a casino license, but that President Banda had personally vetoed it. To me, that told a significant story about Malawi.

We spent a day on the Zomba Plateau, a volcanic ecological island in the middle of the Rift Valley, before proceeding northwards along the Lake on a good road to Nkhota Khota, which I had been interested in visiting for years. This town had seen hundreds of thousands of slaves from the Kazembe kingdom in Northern Zambia corralled in compounds, after being collected by Arab and Swahili slave dealers, before being sent down to Bagamoyo and Zanzibar. Many went on from there to Arabia and Egypt. The slaves were shackled by the neck to forked poles, one at each end, so that they became Siamese twins for months on end until they were eventually auctioned off to their final masters. David Livingstone visited Nkhota Khota for the second time on 10 September 1863 and sat down under a giant African fig tree to negotiate with the local chief, Jumbe, trying to enlist opposition to the Arab slavers. The tree still stands next to the mission church and is marked with a plaque. I wanted to see these places and Bob, who was driving that morning, agreed to try and find them: neither he nor Charlie were aware of the significance of the place. Approaching Nkhota Khota, the escarpment retreated away from the Lake and there was a wide alluvial plain, cultivated with manioc, groundnuts, beans and green vegetables. Everywhere there were mango trees. Ted had commented on the fact that as we went north, mangoes seemed to have become the dominant trees. They were everywhere on that plain; big mature trees, with their rich dark foliage, standing out like giant green tumbleweeds scattered by endless winds. I was puzzled for a while, wondering how such a great number of exotic fruit trees had become established so widely without any evidence of formal planting. They were too random and widespread to have been a British colonial project. Then I remembered reading that it was the normal practice for Arabs to introduce mangoes from India wherever they settled for any time. It was an interesting symbolic exchange for the slaves they removed.

We drove along a wide natural causeway and stopped on a bridge to watch men and boys fishing from dug-out canoes in the clear surging water as it poured out of a ten mile long lagoon into the Lake. They were using fine nets attached to two slim poles, like wands, which were dipped into the stream by the man in the bow while his mate at the stern kept the canoe steady with skilled paddling. I watched a small harvest of kapenta being brought in on the nets. Further on, the causeway widened until we were on a broad promontory, and the town appeared with a long yellow sandbank paralleling its shore. This was an old, untidy town with winding dusty streets and a mix of mud huts with thatched roofs and neat cement block houses and shops. Children ran in the streets and waved to us. Old mangoes, palms and giant indigenous spathodeas, figs and acacias were everywhere so that it was difficult to make out the structure of the town. It was clear that it was founded long before the orderly British had arrived: it was an old Arab town and a hundred years ago it was the only town for many hundreds of miles. I was excited by it, despite its awful reason for being there.

The fishermen of Nkhota Khota, Malawi.

A rough sign pointed the way to 'Livingstone's Memorial' and we arrived at a quiet compound with a long church built of rough bricks and rusting corrugated iron roof to one side and an old monster of a fig tree at the far corner. We all got out and wandered about, the usual chatter and laughter of our group muted. Some years ago I had made a pilgrimage to Kuruman in the Northern Cape Province of South Africa, where Robert Moffat, whose daughter Mary married Livingstone, founded the base for the penetration to the north in 1824. The two churches were of the same style, so I carefully took a photograph from the same angle as I visualised my picture of Kuruman, surrounded there by old syringa trees. In the neglected garden at Kuruman with its irrigation channels for the vegetables that sustained the pioneers, there was the dead stump of an almond tree under which Livingstone is supposed to have proposed to Mary Moffat. They were married there on 9th January 1845. Mary Livingstone died and is buried on the lower reaches of the Zambesi in Mozambique.

I could see why the Arabs had established their base at Nkota Khota. It was almost an island, to the south was a narrow sandy causeway, to the north were marshes and the offshore sandbank provided shelter for many canoes. Near the town is an unusual conical hill which must have been a good landmark from far out on the Lake as their lateen-rigged dhows sailed over from the northeast.

The road north became rough gravel and we crawled along past a big sugar estate and then up the escarpment to Mzuzu, a town that President Banda was visiting for a Malawi Congress Party conference. Ted counted 1,356 flagpoles with the national flag flying on the road out to the airstrip where two helicopter-gunships rested beside the Presidential plane.

We stopped at Nkhata Bay, a port for the Lake-steamers which I found delightful. The colonial town with dusty corrugated-iron roofs nestled around a rocky point that forms a sweeping sandy bay with fishing canoes drawn up on the beach. Coconut palms, casuarinas and mangoes shaded the streets and the market square. Nick, Marie and I sat on the verandah of a store drinking cold fresh milk and chatted with a bunch of local lads idling the afternoon away. One of them told me that there were Ngoni people living around Nkhata Bay which interested me: the Ngoni were invaders from faraway Natal led by the Zulu chieftain-general, Zwangendaba, whose army had ravaged as far north as Lake Victoria before returning to set up a colony hereabouts. When Livingstone had been in this area the Ngoni were still butchering the local tribes, attempting to establish a feudal state.

That night we camped at the Lakeside on a bush track, near a village below the Nyika Plateau. The villagers returned at dusk, the men from fishing and the women from the vegetable gardens, amazed to find us cooking dinner on the way to their homes. The men walked through the bush in a wide circle around us, but the women huddled shyly in the pathway, too polite to barge through. I suggested to Katie and Karen that they should escort the women, which they did. I sat by our fire that evening, listening to the drums pounding loudly near by and the excited talking and calling, undoubtedly caused by our unexpected presence. Charlie and a few of the others took some beer to the village to apologise and joined the dancing. I went to sleep with the magic of African singing in my ears.

Before leaving Malawi we camped on the beach at Karonga, for we were too late to tackle the difficult border crossing into Tanzania that day. All day we had passed villages and kraals becoming increasingly primitive with people ever more friendly. The children ran out onto the road screaming with delight, clasping their hands above their heads, their black faces split by wide white grins. Children's greetings change as you traverse Black Africa, here they were pure scream.

There was a young Italian man already camping at Karonga beach with a rather dishy Malawian girl. He came over to offer us some local *pombé*, of which he had already had plenty. It wasn't actually pombé, which is usually fermented palm or sugar cane juice, it was a distilled version and blindingly strong and I thought it wise to stick to beer. He told us his insurmountable problem. He had been working in Botswana for the government and at the end of his contract he had bought a powerful Yamaha cross-country motorbike to ride home to Italy. Concerned about carrying large amounts of cash or travellers cheques, he prudently transferred most of his funds to a bank in Dar-es-Salaam, Tanzania, where he could make new arrangements for the next stage. When he got to the Tanzanian border, however, he had been turned back because he had South African transit stamps in his passport. He pointed out that he had been working for the Botswana government on an U.N. Aid contract and had papers to prove it. But the Tanzanian officials had been adamant.

"What are you going to do?" somebody asked.

"What am I doing?" He laughed and waved his glass. "I'm drunk. That's what I am doing." He hugged his smiling girl-friend. "And she helps me."

76

"But what will you do?"

"When I have finished the money we have, we will go to Blantyre, I will try to sell my beautiful motorbike, and I will buy a ticket to Rome. Maybe, one day I shall get my savings out of Dar-es-Salaam, if God wills."

PART THREE:

EAST AFRICA

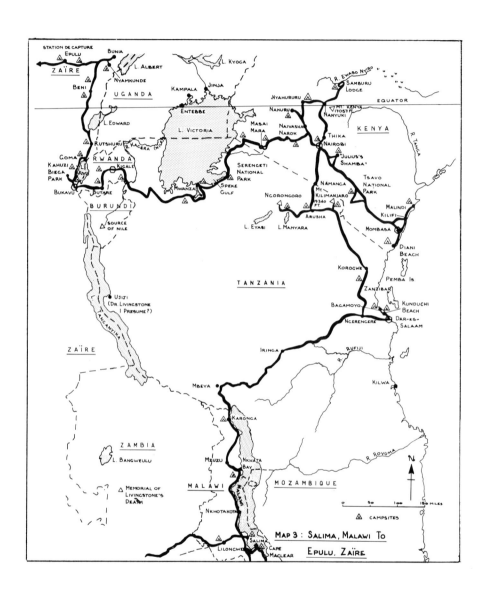

STATION DE CAPTURE
EPULU • BUNIA
Z AÏRE
NYAMKUNDE
BENI
UGANDA
L. ALBERT
L. KYOGA
KAMPALA JINJA
ENTEBBE
L. EDWARD
L. VICTORIA
R. EWASO NYIRO
SAMBURU LODGE
EQUATOR
NYAHURURU
NAKURU
MT. KENYA 17057 FT.
NANYUKI
KENYA
R. TANA
RUTSHURU
KAGERA (NILE)
MASAI MARA
NAIVASHA
NAROK
THIKA
NAIROBI
"JULIUS'S SHAMBA"
GOMA
KAHUZI BIEGA PARK
KIVU
KIGALE
RWANDA
MWANZA
SPEKE GULF
SERENGETI NATIONAL PARK
NAMANGA
MT. KILIMANJARO 19340 FT.
TSAVO NATIONAL PARK
MALINDI
KILIFI
BUKAVU
BUTARE
NGORONGORO
ARUSHA
MOMBASA
BURUNDI
SOURCE OF NILE
L. EYASI
L. MANYARA
DIANI BEACH
TANZANIA
KOROGWE
PEMBA Is.
UJIJI (DR. LIVINGSTONE I PRESUME?)
ZANZIBAR
KUNDUCHI BEACH
BAGAMOYO
NGERENGERE
DAR-ES-SALAAM
ZAÏRE
IRINGA
RUFIJI
MBEYA
KILWA
R. ROVUMA
KARONGA
N
ZAMBIA
L. BANGWEULU
MZUZU
NKHATA BAY
MOZAMBIQUE
0   50   100   150 MILES
MEMORIAL OF LIVINGSTONE'S DEATH
MALAWI
CAMPSITES
NKHOTAKOTA
MAP 3: SALIMA, MALAWI TO
LILONGWE
SALIMA
CAPE MACLEAR
EPULU, ZAÏRE

CHAPTER SEVEN: 'LAY DOWN YOUR HEARTS'

Before him, like a blood-red flag,
The bright flamingoes flew;
From morn till night he followed their flight,
O'er plains where the tamarind grew,
Till he saw the roofs of Caffre huts,
And the ocean rose to view.

He did not feel the driver's whip,
Nor the burning heat of day;
For Death had illumined the Land of Sleep,
And his lifeless body lay
A worn-out fetter, that the soul
Had broken and thrown away!

THE SLAVE'S DREAM. H.W. Longfellow

"I am heartsore, and sick of human blood."

David Livingstone, 20 March 1871

I was up early and bathed with several naked men in the Lake, modestly washing all over with plenty of soap. (Women were doing the same about a hundred yards further along). The sun rose in a dark red ball, the sky was mauve-pink-eggshell blue, reflected on gentle waves, in the centre of a scarlet rippling trail from the sun. Gorgeous! Fisherfolk were getting their boats ready.

In Karonga market place, I saw an ocean shipping container full of canned pilchards from Namibia. Labels showed that the last two ports were Walvis Bay and Durban. The romance of trade lived anew with containers which penetrate the heart of Africa . . . We travelled on a road not marked on maps, crossing the Songwe River into Tanzania, where the border post was manned by one grinning officer who sent us on to his "head office". Suddenly, Malawi was gone: mango trees gone, screaming happy children missing. But the land was lush and well cultivated: bananas, cashew-nuts, coconut palms, manioc, maize, citrus fruits, avocados, groundnuts and beans: all growing together. I was greatly impressed by this system, it seemed a very natural and sensible method of tropical peasant agriculture, the various trees and crops complementing each other, protecting one another from wind and heavy rains, guarding the soil from erosion. Was this a traditional system or taught by experts? I believe it was traditional, with a little help and encouragement.

After a long drawn out ordeal with slow officials checking currency at the official border post, we started to climb the hills as we rose out of the Rift Valley and the scenery was rather fine. Tea plantations, then *shambas* with tea mixed with bananas, maize. The land was green and rich, but the tea very patchy and neglected and I wondered if it was still cropped. Tukuya which was once a prosperous town with many country stores, and a discernible town centre, had gone to seed with rusting roofs, buildings unpainted for years, several shops abandoned. The road had deep ruts and trash lay in ditches. A tall gum tree avenue and pines showed evidence of White colonists of the past and I saw patches of arum lilies and hydrangeas in the middle of the town. The decay of Tanzania was a particular shock to me because I had always regarded it as a more prosperous land than Malawi, and although I was prepared for failures of authoritarian socialism, which is a particularly virulent form of cultural neo-colonialism, I had not expected such instant comparisons with post-Independence conservative Malawi.

Suddenly, we were over the crest of the divide and greenness was gone. Harsh eroded grassland spread to the horizon, dust blowing, no trees. Where are the trees I saw here twenty years ago? Irregular patches of badly ploughed bare earth seemed the only attempt to grow food. Approaching the main road junction near Mbeya we entered ribbon development; an endless village on both sides of the road for miles and miles, with bare open land beyond with no evidence of life. Square grey mudbrick houses with rusted corrugated iron roofs, others roofless and already abandoned. Cold dust was blowing, the sun going down, all brown and grey. Some of us got out to take a photograph when we saw an eating house but we were forced to retreat by ragged threatening people, a young man threw stones. Rude and aggressive hawkers came, but we drove off. There were wrecked and broken-down buses and pick-up trucks by the side of the road. What miserable unhappy people.

The endless village went on and on into the night. No lights! No cooking fires! Was this a land of zombies? What had happened since I was here twenty years ago? Where were the scattered acacia trees on good grass savannah and well-spaced kraals with decorated huts? I fretted about it as we drove onwards, thumping into great pot-holes in the broken blacktop road.

EXTRACT FROM MY 1965 DIARY: IRINGA TO MBEYA, TANZANIA

24 October 1965: Up very early (6.30) and off in cool air. Past several small 'shambas' with the huts painted with patterns and neatly thatched roofs. People out cultivating their maize patches. Children waved. Acacia thick in places and baobabs looming. Drove over escarpment out of Rift Valley to Southern Highlands. Saw bundles in trees and asked about them: people still 'bury' their dead in trees . . .

Bad road, but grand scenery. Over many small bridges, very dusty, so stopped at a 'tourist site' at 3.30! Waterfall with sparkling water, washed clothes, cooked slowly on brushwood fire. Some Indians stopped and had tea, told us how they were going to Kenya "on business". Later some Africans came and smiled and greeted, but could not speak English...

25 October 1965. Drove through pleasant countryside with scattered 'shambas' on open country with acacia. Little villages again had painted huts and all had pawpaws and mangoes growing around their maize and vegetable patches. Children lined up for a photograph when we stopped to buy fruit. Reached Mbeya before lunch and went round the shops. Had a huge samousa in an Indian 'duka' owned by a Sikh . . .

On to Zambia!

Because of this rural slum that has spread like a malevolent cancer from Iringa to Mbeya, the fruit of Julius Nyerere's grand ideology of 'African Socialism', Charlie would not stop to camp and we drove on through the night towards Dar-es-Salaam. After Iringa, the road descended the escarpment down the spectacular Ruaha River gorge and we stopped on the lowland plain in the Mikumi game park at dawn for breakfast, a rest for the drivers and to clean up. I talked to Bob about the shock I had received; he had not known it to be any different, of course.

"We always drive through at night," he said. "The people living there give all the Overland trucks a bad time, throwing stones, shouting abuse, and there's hardly any traffic on this road if you have trouble.

"But this road was built with foreign Aid, hundreds of millions it must have cost from Dar-es-Salaam to Lusaka. It was going to open up Tanzania and give Zambia an outlet to the sea independent of South Africa." Bob laughed, but not with his usual hearty roar. "How many trucks have we met, maybe two or three? Wait till you see Dar-es-Salaam harbour. Nothing works. As for development, you've seen Zambia. Tanzania's also totally fucked. I can't wait to get out of this country, I can tell you. We'll be lucky to get diesel, and God help us if we break something . . ."

It was a grey morning, high sheet-like stratus clouds were a blanket in the sky, a silver patch showing where the tropical sun was blazing away. I reckoned that we were on about the siderial Equator then, the sun was directly overhead at mid-day; as we moved north, the sun was moving south. The great plain backed by misty hulks of mountains had a grand and sombre majesty. It was another face of Africa; grey, empty, brooding: a giant colourless landscape on a massive African scale. I shuddered, not from fear for it seemed to have a neutral, almost benign nature, but rather from the sudden sense of personification I received. Africa was a god that morning at Mikumi; not the trees, the earth, the volcanic hills, certainly not the absent people. Africa itself was the god. I sense it again as I write this.

Dar-es-Salaam was originally a colonial creation. The Omani Arabs and later the Germans founded it because it had a fine natural harbour on a coastline of hundreds of miles of straight, shallow coral-sand beaches. A hundred years ago, the harbour was satisfactory, to-day it would need huge quantities of money to make it a modern port suitable for the giant computer driven monsters of the deep. It is a sprawling, dirty city where the buildings are all older than twenty years, apart from a few in the centre. Dar-es-Salaam physically stopped growing at Independence, but who knows how much the population has grown? It is crowded, clamourous and vital with constant movement of people and it has the style of the Indian Ocean Swahili culture.

"Reminds me a little of Cairo," Nick said thoughtfully as we drove through on the way to the beach resort where we were to camp. "A suburb of Cairo, of course."

"What on earth do all these people do?" asked Ted. "There can't be much regular work for them."

In the city centre the degradation was too obvious. Tenements had mouldy walls, most windows were broken. The Technical College had cannibalised Landrovers lying about in the grounds and the lecture-rooms were derelict – that was bad. Litter blew everywhere. The streets were potholed, old light standards had long lost their lights, wires sagged on drunken poles. Nothing had been painted for years. There were no advertising signs, people squatted at the entrances to shops with empty shelves. We parked near the Kilimanjaro Hotel, the international five star hotel designed by an old friend of mine for the heady days of Independance celebrations. Letters of its name on the central tower were damaged, black mould streaked the façade, the girls reported that the toilets were a mess. Charlie went off to change money, a hazardous business because of pimps and police informers, but he got 120 shillings to the pound on the BM with the official rate at 23 shillings.

We camped alongside the old Silversands Hotel at Kunduchi Beach. I was told that it had been taken over by the University and so was in reasonable repair and kept clean. We paid to have the use of toilets and their water supply, but there was no water. We were beginning to learn that water is probably the most critical element affecting ordinary life in Black Africa. Urban water supplies operate with machines, consume relatively massive amounts of power and need purifying chemicals, which are all vulnerable in a climate of economic failure and social decay. Distribution often fails, and frequently we saw precious water gushing and flooding streets where pipes had burst or steadily leaked. Dependent on the same sources as the local people as we camped our way across Africa, we obtained first-hand experience of the hardship and the unending daily effort needed to acquire domestic water.

We arrived on a Sunday and the verandah and beach in front of the hotel were packed with a great variety of people. Some were obviously strict Moslems, the women well covered with richly coloured robes or enveloping black cloth and the men wearing embroidered white caps, but most were in casual Western dress; slacks, blue jeans, T-shirts with logos and slogans obviously originating from the U.S., bright blouses and shirts. Nobody was swimming. A barbecue stand was selling snacks and sweating waiters tried to keep the crowd of a couple of hundred supplied with beers and soft drinks. Music was blaring from loudspeakers. We were the only Whites present and were greeted with friendliness; I was told that the local 'expats' never went anywhere other than their own yacht club. (The natural Apartheid of modern Black Africa.) I enjoyed the crowd, thankful for evidence that dull socialistic ideology cannot suppress natural African exuberence. A professional photographer plied his trade, posing self-conscious family groups against backgrounds of the ocean or coconut palms sprouting from old coral outcrops. Hawkers were selling cheap jewellery and local carvings, a black market in cigarettes and local rum operated in the reception office.

That evening, the people changed, the afternoon leisure seekers were replaced by disco-goers. Several of us danced till midnight to scratchy records and tapes of the powerfully repetitive rhythms of African pop music. In Tanzania it was called 'boogie', and our group called any local music and the dancing that goes with it 'boogie' from then on. Shuffling and jumping away in the mesmerised crowd, few people dancing with partners, I was happy. I was reminded of endless dancing in big crowds to the samba in Brazil. Taking a rest in the cool by the sea, I was engaged in conversation by a group of young men. They were friendly and well-spoken and fears that I was going to have to deal with aggressive peddlers evaporated. They wanted to change some twenty dollar bills, but I explained that we had just arrived and would change the other way round. They told me that they were 'beachy boys'; that was their profession. There was a four star tourist hotel further along where they did their business: girls of various specialities, teen-age boys, curios, booze, car hire, dhow trips, deep-sea fishing, marijuana, they had anything that tourists wanted. The only problem they had was the lack of tourists recently. They liked to talk to the Overlanders they occasionally met at our campsite because we spoke plainly and did not look down on them.

As in most places in Africa there was a nightwatchman; they are called *Askari*, Swahili for soldier, in East Africa. Ours was a young professional supplied by the Tanzanian Army complete with Russian AK47 assault rifle. I slept in the open and I heard him scrunching his boots and clearing his throat in the night.

In the morning most of us went into town after washing in the milky warm sea beside a row of abandoned beach cottages from the British colonial era. The dawn-reflecting sea was a bright golden colour with the silhouettes of lateen-sailed fishing boats and dug-out canoes with outriggers riding on it: evidence of ancient contacts across the Indian Ocean.

Charlie and Bob took the truck to one of the central petrol stations to join the blocks-long queue for fuel. Apparently, whenever a tanker arrived off the port, the word was passed and as fuel was transported to the filling stations it was pumped straight into the vehicles. I was also told that the country had been in such dire straights the previous year that they acquired a load of aviation kerosene from South Africa to be able to keep international air communiations going. When the news leaked, there was high scandal. We left our truck parked next to another Overlander truck sandwiched in the line with resigned drivers quietly waiting their turn. The other Overlanders told us that they had been delayed five days waiting for diesel.

Kunduchi Beach, Tanzania.

I wandered alone all morning through the city. It was a Western city that had visibly regressed a hundred years and I found it fascinating that day. Once one had blinkered the eyes against the dirt and decay and only looked at the people, there was excitement at the anthill activity. It was a huge African village living in the concrete structures of the Dar-es-Salaam of 1960. I imagined that Kilwa, Mozambique Island or Mombasa would have had the same atmosphere on a smaller scale half a millenium ago. The shops, as we had seen from the truck, were mostly empty, but the streets had become the bazaar. Office buildings had faded or defaced name plates where attorneys, doctors, architects, shipping agents, surveyors, wholesale merchants or the Chamber of Commerce once worked. They were long gone. On the sidewalks and intruding onto the roadways where few cars passed, covered stalls and tables piled with assorted merchandise flourished. If you knew where to go, you could buy most things: transistor radios, native medicines, modern drugs, hair straightener, washing powder in little plastic bags, toothbrushes, digital watch batteries, second-hand T-shirts, little pyramids of spices and curry power, Communist literature from the Eastern bloc and even rare cigarettes hiding in a bag at the seller's feet (a few loose cigarettes lying on a table was the advertising sign). I marvelled at it, and the irony of it. Here at the heart of doctrinaire African socialism where Nyerere's spirit of *N'Jamaah* and the renunciation of private wealth was proclaimed to the world, Margaret Thatcher's creed of small capitalism was burgeoning.

I wandered the waterfront, walking the once-elegant boulevard whose bordering lawns had become a rough country field heaped with refuse smelling of excrement and laced with curving African footpaths. I bought an orange, elaborately peeled by a smiling stall keeper, and sat looking over the pale blue expanse of the harbour with feathery coconut palms around its far shore. Five rusted wrecks of old coasting steamers were beached in front of me. One had rather fine lines and a slim, well-proportioned funnel left there to die. Walking past an old German colonial building from 1900, I spied a sea-going dhow and hurried down onto the sandbank where it was beached. It was a real dhow and in working order: rigging tautly set, sails bent onto the long main spar, a thatched shelter in the stern. Two lads were lazing in the shade and I talked to them. Yes, they still carried cargo up and down the coast to Tanga and Kilwa, sometimes to Mombasa. But no, they did not know Mozambique Island although they had heard of it. I admired this remnant of the great Arab Indian Ocean trading system and photographed it. There are few enough left. There were few remnants of the great European Indian Ocean trading system either, I thought wryly, as I turned to the rusted steamers and photographed them too.

I had lunch in the Agip Motel. Italy provides a lot of Aid to Tanzania, so I supposed that it was reasonable that Italian companies could be exempt from socialist constraints. I sat at a table eating a passable chicken curry and was joined by two 'expats' and we had a lively conversation. One was a young Danish dentist who said he was trying to teach young people with two or three years of high school education how to be dentists in six months. He admired the keenness and honest dedication of his students but thought that extractions were all they would be able to accomplish and effective painkillers were scarce. He and his wife lived in Tanga, by the beach, and it was pleasant, but it was a very artificial existence in a well-guarded high-walled compound with other foreign Aid workers.

The other man was my age and an old Africa hand, having spent some years of his civil engineering career in Sierra Leone. He was on a sabbatical from Coventry Polytechnic, doing a survey on roads in tropical Africa. Coincidentally, a Canadian consultancy was preparing a project report at vast expense for a trans-Africa highway from Cairo to Gaberones. (Gaberones is the dusty little capital of Botswana: it would be ideologically unsound to build a highway that connected with Johannesburg or Cape Town! What farce!) He told me that he had long since reached his conclusions, he was merely collecting corroboratory figures and trying to have fun driving about Africa examining great holes in tarred roads in the bush. There was hardly any traffic on the roads of East and Central Africa except in the Kenya Highlands and Coast, and the billions that were spent on prestigious highways were a criminal waste. These foreign Aid roads were not maintained by the recipient countries and broke up after five years from the action of the weather. A fraction of the money should be spent on adequate gravel roads and on keeping district work gangs in employment to repair the ravages of each rainy season.

"Just like in colonial times," I said with a smile.

He paused then nodded thoughtfully. "Yes, exactly . . . Like in colonial times."

I met up with Ted after lunch and we went into a bar to buy a cold beer and maybe talk to some locals, but ran into colour prejudice. Despite the beers standing in front of the customers, we were told that there were none. Ted was shocked. "We're wicked White imperialists," I explained to him.

By late afternoon our truck had finally got to the front of the queue and fuelled up at economical cost by courtesy of BM money. We could go through to Zaïre now if it was necessary, so Charlie was in cheerful mood as we drove around looking for water, our stereo system pounding out a boogie tape that somebody had bought. Eventually, on the way back to Kunduchi near the Tanzanian army headquarters with hundreds of derelict vehicles lying in dusty rows, we found a house under construction. Charlie slammed on the breaks, crying: "There's a hose-pipe!" Five minutes of joking and chatting with the foreman followed until he agreed to let us fill our tanks. The hose pipe led out of the bathroom of a double-storied luxury villa next door, over the ten foot high, broken-glass topped wall, along the roadside and into our truck. Every now and then, the hose had to go back to feeding a cement mixer, so it all took a little while.

Back at Kunduchi Beach, Pete had bought fourteen fine live crayfish which had us all excited. They lay in a gently scrabbling bundle of wet sacking. Nobody seemed sure what to do with such a great mass of living luxury food and the cooks of the day refused to take the responsibility.

At length, Charlie caught the grin on my face. "Come on, Denis! I'm officially delegating you. I know you must have done this before."

"Two conditions, Charlie," I said. "I have as many helpers as I need and somebody keeps me supplied with beer."

"It's a deal!" was the general cry.

Pete and Paul built a roaring monster of a fire on the beach with driftwood and old palm thatch from an abandoned shelter. I borrowed metal buckets from the hotel, filled them with sea water and boiled the crayfish. Bob and Nick peeled them. Ted brought me beer. The girls chopped a mountain of garlic, onions, aubergines, green and red peppers, fresh coconut meat, pineapple and tomatoes and I fried it in coconut oil and some tumeric and coriander seeds. There was a great pot of steaming rice. We ate to satiation, drank beer, talked and sang next to the swish and splash of the Indian Ocean. I think it was the best campfire dinner of the whole long five months. None of us forgot it.

Early in the safari, Charlie knew from chatting with me that I was particularly interested in visiting as many historical places as were practical. I had given a potted history of Zimbabwe to our group and I did the same on the Tanzanian coast, pointing out that Europeans and Americans had little knowledge of the ancient Indian Ocean trading systems. The Atlantic, which usually dominates our knowledge of maritime history, was little used by anybody except rugged, unsung fishermen until the 16th century. But the Indian Ocean was criss-crossed by traders well before the birth of Christ. The great civilised empires of Egypt, Sabea, Persia, Rome and India sailed ships in the northwest; Indian, Chinese, Indo-Chinese and Indonesians travelled in the northeast. Goods moved between China and the Mediterranean along the Indian Ocean route. East Africa, because of the monsoon winds, was also touched by these sailors. A trickle of slaves, ivory and curios reached India, Arabia, Persia, Egypt and the Mediterranean as the centuries rolled on. But it was the Islamic Revolution in the 7th century which combined the scattered energies of Middle-Eastern Arabs and Egyptians, resulting in the permanent colonisation of East Africa and the founding of the chain of trading ports and cities from Somalia to Mozambique. From Africa was carried ivory, rhinoceros horn, slaves and Zimbabwean gold; to Africa was brought cloth, metal artifacts and, greatest contribution, technology and culture. Over centuries, the distinct Swahili culture, a mix of Moslem Arab and Bantu African, was established and flourished. The first Persian and Arab ruling dynasties established their principal colonial capitals on islands for security. As generations passed and these dynasties became a settler élite and then aristocratic communities of the distinct Swahili culture, the island cities remained the centres of power. The 19th century Swahili rulers retained their power-bases on Mombasa and Zanzibar. It was in the 19th century that the Arab and Swahili slave trade reached its height, because slaves were no longer sought only for domestic service, the stocking of harems and the strengthening of armies. African slaves became exploited for plantation work on Zanzibar, in Egypt and Arabia, just as they had been in Brazil, the Caribbean and the United States a century before.

Bagamoyo was the mainland port that had serviced Zanzibar and we went there from Dar-es-Salaam, camping again in the grounds of a beach hotel. Hundreds of thousands of slaves brought down in long pitiable streams from the inland depots at Nkhota Khota on Lake Malawi and Ujiji on Lake Tanganyika were stockaded there before being shipped out. Bagamoyo is translated as 'Crushing of the Heart', or more usually as 'Lay down your Heart'. That is what the slaves called it. It was the base from which the famous British explorers of Central Africa ventured forth: Livingstone, Burton, Speke, Grant and Stanley. It was also where the Alsation Order of the Holy Ghost founded their first mission in East Africa, coincident to the British missions in Malawi. So it was another visit I was particularly excited about.

Alan Moorehead in his classic, *The White Nile*, writes: ' . . . *it is a beautiful place, with a line of rustling coconut palms on the shore and beyond them, at the right season, one of the loveliest sights of Africa: the flamboyant trees that spread like chestnuts and blaze with the brightest shades of scarlet, flame and orange.*

'*The Indian Ocean here has the texture, and no doubt the specific gravity, of warm, very salty soup and is infested with a thousand slimy things, broken fronds of seaweed, livid jellyfish, perhaps an empty coconut floating by. There is no harbour, but a coral reef breaks the force of the waves and the beach slopes very gently inland. At low tide the sea receded for a quarter of a mile or more and all the debris of the shore lies stranded on a wet grey plain. In the old days it was customary for the Zanzibar dhows to run in as far as possible on the full tide . . . Then at low-tide the boat was propped up on either side by mango poles and lines of slaves came slopping out through the shallows to unload her.*'

I did not see any sign of the coral reef. From the beach, which is not as noisome as he describes it, the sea runs clear to the horizon where Zanzibar lies, about twenty miles away, out of sight because it is low lying. The coconut palms were there, however, and the flamboyant trees, and the old town which delighted me. Charlie warned us that the inhabitants were difficult and suspicious, security of the camp and ourselves needed care and we should not take photographs. There was not much law and order. I was reminded of Nkhota-Khota for Bagamoyo was an Arab and Swahili town with very little European influence. The buildings in the centre were all old, but substantial, and the narrow sandy streets with mature shade trees wandered crookedly. The houses were built of coral rock, some whitewashed, most a bit crumbly, but the doors were carved and the windows were wooden shutters. The absence of advertising in Tanzania suited this place and it did not indicate lack of commercial enterprise. The market was an excellent one, abounding with produce from the coastal shambas: fresh and dried coconut meat, coconut oil, coarse crystals of evaporated salt, brown lumps of locally produced sugar, cassava roots and bundles of cassava leaves, okra, onions, tomatoes, fresh and dried sea fish, good long-grain rice, fresh ginger and many ground spices. I saw one quite well stocked shop with manufactured goods: milk powder, soap, torch batteries and kitchen utensils.

The people were mostly Swahili, the Arab-Negro mix was clear, but the Arab genes seemed dominant: straight hair, greeny-grey eyes, aquiline noses and thin lips. Some men squatted in doorways wrapped in long cotton robes, some women had their heads well covered and black was their favoured colour. We were in the 19th century. They seemed friendly towards us, but reserved, and we observed each other with mutual curiosity. I wished I could have taken many photographs, but when I raised my camera in the market there were shaking heads and negatively waving fingers.

A few miles north of the old town of Bagamoyo lies the mission of the Order of the Holy Ghost. It stands in a vast, orderly palm plantation. There is a multi-storied hospice, numerous workshops and stores and two churches, (the smaller dated 1868), all built in the 19th century. The buildings are pleasantly spread about a well kept garden of lawns, religious statuary and old trees. Hibiscus, flamboyants and frangipani provided colour and perfume, and we strolled in this European cultural oasis. Interestingly, the Sultan of Zanzibar did not obstruct the founding of the mission despite knowing that one of its principal objects was to combat the slave trade which was the main pillar of his national economy. There is a small museum which houses old correspondence, relics of the first missionaries, Arab and local artifacts and a special section devoted to David Livingstone.

Livingstone began his African explorations as a young man based on Moffat's mission at Kuruman in the Cape Province of South Africa. In Bagamoyo that day I stood before the old church where his mummified body lay before being shipped back to England and the high honour of burial in Westminster Abbey. After he died at Chitamba's Kraal just to the south of Lake Bangweulu in Zambia, his body finally struck down by decades of malaria and dysentery, his three servants decided that he was a man of such great respect that they had to return his body to his own people. So they cut out his heart and liver and buried them under an *mpundu* tree before salting and drying the corpse to be able to carry it on the long trek back to the coast. It is recorded that when Chuma, one of the faithful servants, arrived at Bagamoyo after nine months he reported simply: "Our father is dead".

That afternoon I sat in the palm-thatched shelters of our small hotel on the beach facing Zanzibar Island. Later, I walked on the beach before the town where there were outrigger canoes and fishing boats anchored offshore and I decided, in my imagination, in which of the waterfront houses Livingstone may have boarded before setting off on his last expedition to find the sources of the Nile. I felt that I had done something important in my life that day. Even in the later 20th century it is a long way from Kuruman to the Victoria Falls, Nkhota Khota and Bagamoyo.

Mission Church at Bagamoyo, Tanzania.

94

Kilimanjaro was about four hundred miles from Bagamoyo and we seldom stopped. We progressed on endlessly straight, damaged roads. The patches of remaining tar were a hindrance for they had become raised islands in a corrugated laterite track and our driver was constantly slowing and accelerating and, when he misjudged, the truck would crash into a tar island or lurch off it. The bush was monotonous but in good condition, new green leaf showing after the rains that had started there. We saw the first Masai herding cattle to the coastal markets, but this land is tsetse fly country and almost unpopulated, there are few roadside villages. The horizon always seemed to have one or two old volcanoes breaking the monotony with their perfect cones. I had forgotten how volcanic East Africa is. Baobabs reappeared. Passing through a gap between two volcanoes, directly ahead a mass of cloud was spread like a small cyclonic storm and I watched it for a while puzzled that it did not tower into the stratosphere with an anvil head. Suddenly I realised it was Mount Kilimanjaro and we had come further than I thought.

"That's Kilimanjaro?" I asked Charlie and he grinned: "I wondered who would work it out. We're still about sixty miles away."

Around Kilimanjaro, which we did not climb because of the newly exhorbitant fees levied by the Tanzanian authority, we passed through Arusha and on the way there was an aesthetically attractive agricultural mix, taking advantage of the perennial rains harvested from the moist high airstreams by the 19,000 foot bulk of Kilimanjaro itself and its grey, conical volcanic partner, Meru, looming 14,000 feet above Arusha town. Bananas, coffee, sugar-cane, maize, beans, vegetables: all flourished in rich mixture amongst avocadoes, mangoes and other shady trees. This style of African peasant farming which I had noticed in Southern Tanzania seemed to make a great deal of sense. The people who are responsible for this island of concerted agriculture around the great mountains are of the Bantu culture and are quite different to the Nilotic Masai who live on the arid plains where their increasing numbers are steadily converting savannah to desert.

We stopped in Arusha, which I remembered well from twenty years before. Again, I was shocked by urban deterioration. The long, potholed main street was flanked by lines of late colonial era shops and *dukas* but it seemed that none had felt the swish of a paint brush in all that time. Many broken windows were boarded up. Most were displaying reconditioned tools, poor local leatherware, cheap clothing and what we would consider to be useless second-hand junk. Dull people hung around. Dates set into concrete facades were mostly of the 1950s when there had obviously been a commercial boom, there were even a few from the 1930s with characteristically elaborate plaster decoration, but none since Independence.

Onwards, the wide plains of the Masai Steppes flowed away out of sight. I remembered typical savannah, a great grassy plain dotted with acacia; but the trees were gone and the grass was short cropped with many bare patches. Population pressure was evident. I was horrified later to be told that the Masai were being persuaded to grow maize and other crops around permanent kraals (*manyattas*), which seemed the last thing that should be done on this grassland where months of drought are followed by heavy tropical thunderstorms. When grass cover and scrub bush goes, desert will follow unless there is careful and intensive husbandry. The Masai were herders with no knowledge of agriculture: were there enough dedicated experts to train hundreds of thousands of people to look after the land with new, reluctantly accepted technique when they were already degrading it with their traditional lifestyle? In South Africa where similar activity has occurred on the highveld, disastrous erosion often followed, and I understood that similar misuse had caused some of the problems of Ethiopia. Whatever solution was eventually found to prevent famine amongst the Masai, turning savannah into desert could only be the short-sighted desperation that follows hopelessness. I thought of the thousands of square miles of empty acacia bush to the south. Cattle were in danger there because of sickness carried by the tsetse fly, but traditional nomadic herding culture would flourish if the tsetse could be eradicated. Concerted international cooperation to remove the tsetse from East and Central Africa would surely be a most important revolution that should be attempted. South Africa had achieved it as early as the 1930s as a national priority and strides were being made in Zimbabwe. But would these regimes, forever squabbling over ideology and blaming the West for their failures, ever cooperate? In Ethiopia and the Sahel, the emphasis was on settlement and pressure to convert herders to agriculture including forcible movement of entire tribes.

The next day we had lunch on the plain west of Kilimanjaro on the road to Nairobi. The mountain was in clear view, fifty miles away due east, and it presented a fascinating sight. Up to about the 12,000 foot level, moist air from the oceanic trade wind system was blowing north-westward creating a comet-tail of cumulus clouds that streamed off before evaporating. In the lee of the mountain beautiful skeins of turbulence curled up to about 25,000 feet from where a ghostly silver plume blew away to the southeast, back towards the ocean.

Where we stopped, there was dry thorn scrub standing in a heavy carpet of white sand. I was reminded of the Kalahari Desert in

Botswana. There was not a blade of grass, but wherever I looked there were the trails of cattle and goats. A huge flock of goats herded by Masai boys came by in a fog of fine dust. They were followed by some children carrying coloured balloons . . . I couldn't fathom that phenomenon until I guessed that other Overlanders must have been ahead of us.

The Tanzania-Kenya border at Namanga epitomised the difference between the economic philosophies of the two countries. For once, reality was more vivid than any devised propaganda. On the Tanzanian side, there were unpainted, weather-battered, wooden shacks with crudely handlettered signs. Chickens scratched amongst blowing dust and litter. Ragged, unsmiling people lounged about. On the Kenya side, a row of shops ranged along the road with neat grass verges selling a variety of goods we had not seen since the Dar-es-Salaam city centre bazaar. Every duka was bright with fresh paint. Cheerful touts called and joked, and grinned when they were turned away. A well-organised open-air curio market displayed battalions of wood carvings. Three petrol stations were open for business. On our truck the atmosphere was like school being let out.

CHAPTER EIGHT: *THE SWAHILI COAST*

This isle lay to the Continent so neer
That a small chanel onely ran between:
In front thereof a City did appeer
Upon the Margent of the OCEAN green:
Fair and Majestical the Buildings were,
At a far distance plainly to be seen:
    Rul'd by an aged King. MOMBASSA, all
    The Isle; the Town too they MOMBASSA call.
    OS LUSIADAS, canto I : 103. Luis de Camões [pub. 1572]

I had begun to build up some tension as we approached Nairobi for several reasons. Debbie was down with a serious bout of fever, my leg was badly inflamed and obviously quite seriously infected by a graze from coral rock in the 'soup' sea of Bagamoyo. There was the partial breaking up of our now compact social group as some were leaving at Nairobi and suddenly we were all aware that major changes were imminent. Charlie announced that he would be going home for a much-needed rest from Bangui, in the Central African Republic, and Bob would carry on as leader without a professional assistant. This caused some comment. Bob had not led a major Overland journey and there was some trackless desert country in Chad to go through that neither he nor Charlie had tackled before. In any case, we would all miss Charlie.

Before going down to the coast at Mombasa, we stayed some days at the Youth Hostel in Nairobi which is a modern caravanserai. Overlanders of all types stop there to recuperate, plan the next stage of their personal odyssey and to use it as a base for travelling in East Africa. It is not a hostel for the young in calendar age and we met people from eighteen years of age to sixty-five. What everybody had in common was the youthful philosophy of Overlanding: travelling the world cheaply which therefore means travelling as ordinary local people do, local buses and trains, hitch-hiking, sleeping in flop-houses or in tents. Many travel alone and this especially requires courage, for loneliness becomes an enemy. Others travel with companions from the beginning of each odyssey or make friends on the way. Others travel in organised groups as we were doing.

The Nairobi Youth Hostel, at an African crossroads, was a good place to observe Overlanders. One thing that was obvious from the first evening was the independent spirit, the self-confidence and the internationalism of the breed. It was also obvious that here were many generally ordinary people doing something quite extraordinary and unique to our time – a mass movement of explorers without wealth or material goals going out into the Third World just to see and experience. Unstated, there was an air of pride in themselves and their achievements. They were quiet people mostly, neat and careful of their possessions and they spent a lot of time washing themselves and their clothes when they first arrived. Although they covered the age-spectrum, most were in the middle to late twenties, and they were about equally balanced sexually. They came from all over Europe, North America, the developed Far East and the Antipodes (the First World). There were very few Black Africans; and no South Africans of course, which is bad because unless young people are permitted to travel and meet one another there can never be understanding and respect.

In the lounge area, amongst the discarded paper-back books and travel folders, there was a book in which Overlanders wrote their remarks and stories. It was fascinating reading. Advice and experiences from a whole range of traveller types were in it, some bright and witty, some laborious and sensible, some long, rambling and poignant, obviously put down during lonely hours, maybe during a sleepless night. From those pages you could learn who the best BM currency operators in Dar-es-Salaam might be and how to watch out for plain-clothes police in Arusha, what essentials to buy in Nairobi, how to climb Kilimanjaro on the cheap, how to get to Lamu or Zanzibar and a list of the honest boarding-house keepers, which were the practical routes to take through Zaïre. Problems with visas to watch for, where it was safe to buy grass and where hard-drugs pushers were dangerous. What was not in the book were offers of contacts or travelling companions; self-sufficiency was a discernible thread through the dozens of scrawled anecdotes.

Nairobi has many new high-rise buildings and bustling streets as well as vast shanty-town squalor behind the scenes which is 'no-go' for tourists. Inevitably, I compared it with Harare, which it superficially resembles. There were a great number of well-stocked shops of various categories but Ted and I searched in vain for a department store or large general supermarket and I was interested in our irritated reaction to this. Because the city has all the surface hall-marks of modernity, we assumed that we would find the retail industry that had become second nature to us. Ted had gone shopping in Johannesburg before we left and was surprised that there was nothing like the huge hypermarket chains that sprout everywhere in South Africa. "There was easier shopping in that country town in the Northern Transvaal," he complained. It took time to buy toothpaste, Kodachrome film, toilet paper, biro pens, envelopes, picture postcards, a new pair of sandals and a replacement day-bag; not because they were unavailable, but they all seemed to be in different shops. It forced us to walk about, however, and pick up some of the ambience of this strange city stranded on an empty African plain.

Nairobi was founded as a railhead during the construction of the Uganda Railway. The goal of British colonisation in East Africa was threefold: to subdue the Arab slave-trade on the coast and in the Sudan and Central Africa under pressure from missionaries and their political allies; to exploit the riches of Uganda which had been described by the influential late Victorian explorers of the sources of the Nile, particularly Stanley and Baker; and to forestall their rivals, the French, Belgians and Germans, from gaining control of the upper Nile.

The Egyptian and Roman Empires had sought control of the whole of the Nile but it had eluded them. Either strong Sudanese kingdoms or the great swamps of the Sudd in southern Sudan had prevented Egyptian pharoahs or Roman emperors from conquering the Nile, but the British had finally succeeded in establishing fortified outposts along its length by the late 1870s. Sophisticated kingdoms were situated to the north of Lake Victoria in a fertile land of agricultural wealth and great potential, but the lines of communication from Alexandria were too long to support conquest or a negotiated protectorate over powerful and well-organised native states. The vulnerability of a four thousand mile long river transport system was proved by the capture of Khartoum and the death of Gordon, the hero, in January 1885. The way to Uganda was by rail, through the useless wilderness that Kenya was seen to be, and not by travelling up the Nile. But Uganda was not suitable for general White settlement, there were no empty lands to parcel out, so the Kenya Highlands, sparcely populated in those days, became the centre of European agro-industry in East Africa and Nairobi grew to be its commercial hub. It is also a great tourist centre and the banks were efficient. American Express issued travellers cheques against my home bank in England without hesitation. Ted and I spent an hour in the finest African curio store I have come across with the best cull of wood and ivory carvings, purpose manufactured tourist goods and an enormous collection of traditional masks, drums, stools and other artifacts from all over Central and West Africa.

Julius joined us in Nairobi for our trip to the coast and for the tour of the

100

Kenya Game Reserves that Charlie was planning. Julius was a Kamba from the Machakos area, a tall slim man in his thirties with a charming smile and an easy-going temperament. His body made me think of a serpent, his limbs relaxed into amazing postures that a modern dancer would try hard to achieve. He spoke quietly and his fluent English was made enchanting sometimes with quaint yet strangely apt misuse of common words and phrases. He was employed by Charlie to help out with the food marketing and washing up when we camped and to assist generally with the refurbishing of the truck and its gear. He took on this kind of casual employment with a number of Overland companies. What he wanted to do was work regularly as an assistant and co-driver on the trucks that go up and down Africa, but his first hurdle was to get a passport which is not easy for a Kenyan, requiring endorsements from influential people in the KANU party machine and suitable bribes or favours for officials. He had been busy on his passport problem for months. Julius was knowledgeable on local pre-history and traditional lore and we had many long discussions in the following month.

The Mombasa highway is wide, fast and mainly in good repair. We travelled quickly through the grasslands of the high plateau and as we gradually lost altitude patches of thornscrub appeared in the shallow valleys. Beyond the turn-off to Machakos there were cultivated fields; Julius told me that the usual crops were beans, maize, native sorghum, sugar-cane, pumpkins, arrowroot, cabbages, onions and tomatoes. It was a list similar to that of the Zulus of Natal who live in similar country. He told me that the Masai had come from the north in the old days and had tried to occupy the Kamba lands, but had failed. The Kamba had fought with large shields and poisoned arrows which the Masai could not combat with their small shields and long spears with heavy blades which were designed for battling the lions that menaced their beloved cattle, so the Masai were chased south to the drier country around Kilimanjaro. The Kamba viewed the Masai as traditional enemies and did not have much respect for them: they were primitive people who were unable to learn from experience. Following evolutionary theory they were a doomed society.

Julius also told me on this journey about the colours used in contemporary bead jewellery in East Africa. The favoured colours by both the Kamba and the Masai are the paler shades of green, yellow and pink;

pastel colours. He said that these colours were favoured to-day because those were the colours that had been introduced by the Arab and Indian traders long before the White man came. It was an example of a cultural preference being established by what was available in a new product rather than by any existing fashion. I found this interesting and told him how the Zulus were famed in South Africa for their beadwork in predominantly red, white, bright green, black and blue. Beads had first been introduced to them by the Portuguese much later, and those colours were no doubt what were being made in Europe at that time. Julius agreed with this and I wondered what colours the Shona people of Zimbabwe favoured to-day, and whether this thought had been pursued by archaeologists investigating Great Zimbabwe where old glass beads had been dug up. It would be an interesting line of investigation into pre-British colonial trade.

Baobabs were seen one hundred and eighty miles from the coast and we were into the acacia bush. At Mtito Andei, which I remembered well from twenty years before, we turned off into the Tsavo West Park and we were enclosed in the magic of wilderness again.

I asked Charlie if he would divert to the Roaring Rocks, a spectacular vantage point. The parking place was at the foot of a low rocky hill that is approached over a wide plain and when the summit is climbed, a vast panorama suddenly spreads out to the south, because on that side there is a 500 foot cliff. I was particularly glad to be there again because one of my most treasured photographs from my 1965 visit was taken there, the frame filled with thornbush retreating outwards between old volcanic hills into the dusty distance of Africa. Whenever I had projected that slide to others it had usually been greeted by indrawn breath. That afternoon, I was back to see it again in reality. I sat for a long while transfixed by the marvel of utter stability, as some of our group clambered on the rocks and others also sat gazing at the great Heart of Africa; for that is how I had seen this view all those twenty years. I took its picture again, with the same lens, and so immaculately had the original photograph been printed on my memory that when I eventually compared the two, they were identically composed. The twenty year gap was hardly noticeable: in the foreground where there was the path of a river, some large trees had grown larger and others had died and gone. Otherwise, the bush was unchanged through the intervening periods of droughts and storms. The African Heart beats on, unchanged within its rhythms. For a short time there I could immerse myself in the wonder of stability and feel the healing power of a sense of endless time. I could understand something of the soul of the African people who have been attached to this great slow-pulsing heart by psychic arteries for aeons. After all, it was here that mankind evolved.

We camped that night some distance from the Kilaguni Lodge at an official site. It was a small, unfenced area with a water stand pipe, pit latrines and a couple of tattered thatch shelters. Val and I cooked a huge stew and rice on a slow fire of brushwood coals. It was a still evening and despite the need to be busy for minutes at a time, the magic persisted as the quick tropic dusk fell. Birds were calling as the dark approached, I heard a group of hadeda ibis scream, winging home from their feeding grounds. Then it was silent as all the wilderness settled for the night. With joy I saw fireflies, so rare nowadays in cultivated lands. Later, there was the fearful thrill of the deep grunt of a lion, not far away.

Bob said we should sleep in tents and most did, but I could not in that place that night. In the small hours I woke when a wind blew for a while, flapping the nearby tents and ruffling my hair, and I lay on my back with my eyes roving over the incredible wheel of the southern Milky Way. Throughout our journey so far the night sky had gradually slipped as we changed latitude and a bright planet, maybe Jupiter, that had been overhead at the Limpopo was now displaced thirty degrees. I wondered if we were going to see Halley's comet. Before I drifted off to sleep again I heard the distant whooping of hyenas and the answering yelps of jackals. I was woken at dawn by the loud explosive screeching of red-crested korhaans that must have been nesting near the camp site. Bob told me over coffee that he had heard the lion several times.

We visited Mzima Springs before breakfast and saw hippo and crocodiles, baboons and vervet monkeys, but there were no elephants that I had watched coming to water twenty years before. It was lucky that we were early, however, because an invasion of packaged tourists arrived in a dozen kombis, having had their breakfasts first at the Lodge. Later we called at the Lodge to have cold Cokes and beers on the deserted verandah and to watch zebras, wildebeest and waterbuck drinking at the waterhole in front of the building against a backcloth of the red earth and acacia scrub of that Heart of Africa. In the distance, Kilimanjaro reared its white-topped massif against the blue sky, and we were enchanted with our luck at being there on a perfect morning. I took a classic picture postcard photograph of a well-marked reticulated giraffe standing out against Kilimanjaro.

Ted was sitting next to me: "There's nothing much you can say, is there?" he almost pleaded, gesturing at it all. I shook my head.

103

A waterhole at Kilaguni Lodge, Kenya.

We passed through Mombasa in the yellow dusk on our way to a camping site on the south coast at Diani Beach. I was tired and we had had a long day and I did not recognise the city even though I had once lived for three months close by. I craned my head this way and that, but I saw nothing familiar. The neon signs beginning to blaze in the twilight and the river of buses, cars and bicycles in the streets told me that I was certainly not in Dar-es-Salaam, but there was an otherwise quickly observed similarity. It was the hordes of people.

"My word," I said to Ted. "I don't believe all these people. It was never like this, the population of Mombasa Island must have doubled, trebled, maybe more."

"You were here before, Denis?" asked Julius.

"Twenty years ago I lived in a small cottage by the sea at Bamburi."

"That's wonderful!" Julius grinned his pleasure. "When my father drove the steam engines on the railway before he took retirement, we used to live in Mombasa. So I understand your surprise. Mombasa is not as it was then, it is terribly crowded with people now. And very dangerous to walk alone at night."

"I'm sorry to hear that," I said. "We used to come to town and go to the cinema and have a meal in the evening sometimes. It was always quiet and peaceful."

Julius laughed. "Not any more, Denis!"

We stayed a few days at Dan Trench's camp-site at Diani Beach and used the facilities of a packaged-tour hotel. The sunburned throng from Europe lounging around the swimming pool seemed to be from a different planet.

The giant nuclear aircraft-carrier, U.S.S. *Kittyhawk*, was anchored offshore and her support fleet was in harbour, so Mombasa had been invaded by several thousand American sailors and marines and many shops in the main streets had signs advertising, 'Special discounts for U.S. Navy'. I laughed at these and pointed them out to Katie.

"Oh, yeah," she smiled. "I hope those guys know that it means a 50% increase. Mind you, I guess they can afford it. Do you see all those new handwritten signs for massage-parlours?" She shook her head. "Maybe you can't get AIDS from a hand-job."

There had been a lot of talk in our group about AIDS in Central and West Africa and the authorities warned that 58% of Nairobi prostitutes had been checked out positively. This figure had climbed to 80% by 1988.

Bob said half-seriously that in Zaïre everybody drank beer out of bottles, not from glasses, these days.

The American servicemen were mainly dressed in blue-jeans and sparkling white T-shirts with their ship's crests on them. I had forgotten how popular baseball caps were with American men. They looked scrubbed clean and so neat but did not seem to be enjoying themselves all that much, walking the streets quietly, staring at the curio 'bargains', sitting in the open air café-bars toying with a beer or Coke. There was a big Negro in one bar with a Walkman plugged into his ears to combat the sound of the blaring boogie music and he contemptuously waved off the approach of a pretty, wriggling prostitute with a negligent flick of his wrist. Very cool, baby! I did not see any with girls on their arms or singing. What has happened to jolly Jack Tar in these dreary days of public relations, national images and frightening venereal diseases?

For a couple of hours we spread around the town centre, Julius guarding the truck. In daylight, it was more like the Mombasa I remembered. There were a couple of new office blocks, but the 1950s colonial style was undimmed. The famous tall steel elephant tusks that bestride the main boulevard still stood, and they were freshly painted. The streets were reasonably clean, the shops bright, cheerful and well-stocked, the crowds orderly and well-dressed. It was certainly not Dar-es-Salaam. I found remembered landmarks and especially the Manor House Hotel where Barbie and I had many coffees, cold drinks and beers twenty years before. Of course, I had to go there for a drink, and sat on the verandah over-looking the street and the Cathedral with absolute *déja-vu.* I remembered sitting there once, so clearly, when Barbie had gone to get her hair dyed after she had tried bleaching it and it had gone green. I could almost feel her anger again as she came back from the hairdresser who had given her a lecture on hair care in the tropics. How could any little African girl lecture a sophisticated Aussie? An elderly British colonial couple, he in baggy shorts and long stockings, she in flowered cotton dress and straw hat, delighted me. They drank from tall frosted glasses of fresh lime juice and chatted with a middle-aged American couple who were evidently house-guests. They completed the nostalgia for me.

Charlie parked the truck in the moat of Fort Jesus so that we could do the Old Town. On my previous visit, Fort Jesus was still being converted from a prison to a museum, but that process had long been completed and I was pleased with the result. A green lawn planted with scarlet hibiscus and a few shady flame trees covered what had been a red dirt inner courtyard and the unobtrusive, newly constructed museum building was simply and tastefully arranged. There had been no unnecessary 'improvements' to the fortress itself. Similar to the fortress of São Sebastião on Mozambique Island, Fort Jesus is located at the north-east corner of Mombasa Island, standing on old hard coral rock that defies easy mining operations. Otherwise, there is not much similarity. São Sebastião is a finer building, classical in style, a great deal larger and constructed to the plans of masters in fortifications which were drawn up in Portugal in the 1540s, whereas Fort Jesus was a more hurried work, planned by the resident engineer in Portuguese India and completed in 1593. Fort Jesus' lack of elegance, however, did not detract from its efficiency, and while Mozambique was never conquered in nearly five hundred years of European colonial history, Mombasa suffered one of the most gruelling sieges of any time, and certainly the fiercest in East-South Africa.

There were several minor engagements, but the great siege lasted from 13th March 1696 till 13th December 1698, two years and exactly eight months. The agony of this siege for both the Portuguese and Swahili defendants and the attacking Omani Arabs is a terrible saga of starvation, plagues, bloody skirmishes, lost opportunities, despair and strange quirks of fate. A relief expedition from Goa, for instance, arrived off Mombasa just five days after the final surrender. Thousands of men, women and children died from battle, famine and sickness. None of the original garrison lasted and at the end there were only fifteen survivors from an intermediate relief expedition and local followers. At one stage, in August 1697, there were no Portuguese in the Fort at all and it was defended by Indians and Swahilis under the command of a local Swahili-Arab aristocrat. With the loss of Mombasa, although it was recovered temporarily, Portuguese power in the Indian Ocean declined and her East African colonies were restricted to Mozambique. The Omani colonial empire in Africa took over and the dynasty of the Sultan of Zanzibar lasted until the Independence of Tanzania in 1960 when thousands of Omani descended Swahilis were slaughtered on Zanzibar in revenge for the years of slavery in one of Black Africa's many shocking post-colonial bloody episodes.

I toured the museum and a tower over the north-west bastion that had been internally arranged as a replica of an Omani apartment. The Museum contained relics from several archaeological digs along the coast illustrating the Indian Ocean trading systems: Arabic style pottery from the 9th to 19th centuries, Chinese Celadon ware [14/15th centuries] (also found at Great Zimbabwe), Chinese Ming porcelain [15/17th centuries], weapons and artifacts. I was specially interested in Indian and Persian glass beads in pale pastel green, pink, yellow and blue, exactly

107

corroborating Julius' remarks about present day Kamba and Masai jewellery. The replica Omani apartment was simple, airy and spartanly comfortable, ideal for the climate. My son was then working at Sohar in Oman and I felt very close to him as I stood on the swept coral cement floor and looked over the decorated wooden furniture and examples of long Arab robes. Sohar was an important Arabian Gulf trading port during the Omani colonial period in East Africa.

On top of the 'Captain's House', on the seaward side, there was a refreshment kiosk built into the old walls with a fine view over the north channel into the old harbour and the ocean beyond. Ted, Val and I had several glasses of delicious fresh-squeezed iced lime-juice and chatted to a friendly man who was on the curator's staff. He had two exquisitely dressed little girls in traditional Swahili costume with him, his nieces, whom he encouraged me to photograph. Beyond the battlements, with their 16th century cannons in place, the top-heavy shape of the U.S.S. *Kittyhawk* lay out to sea with the bombs to obliterate any city in Africa in her belly. It was weird to stand there, leaning on an old coral rampart in the tropic sun, sipping lime-juice, chatting idly with the Swahili man and his prettied-up nieces and looking at 20th century mega-power framed by coconut palms.

I walked alone through the old Arab town at the foot of the brooding fort, past the Mombasa Club with its British colonial style, and into the winding narrow alleyways. Immediately I realised that here was an unchanged part of the city. One of the characteristic 'phallic' minarets of the Swahili Coast stood at the end of a vista. The minarets of the old mosques all the way down to Kilwa were traditionally built in the shape of modern space rockets with openings in the sharp point through which the muezzin made his call. At one time there was solemn speculation that the normal style with some kind of gallery around the top had been perverted by African paganism and corrupted to being giant phalli. But that idea was discredited when it was shown that Africans of the Bantu culture do not worship in that way, therefore there could be no transfer of culture. Probably the simple reason is that a rocket-shaped minaret resembles a stretched grass hut and is aesthetically pleasing to an African eye. It was pleasing to mine too.

In the same street was an old house with a first-floor covered verandah decorated with wooden fretwork. I knew that I had a photograph of it from twenty years before and I took another with a feeling of pleasure. I was rewarded again by the sight of a dhow tied up to the wharf. The wharf master would not let me take a picture from close up because it was government land but he talked to me, explaining that he had not seen a dhow from Arabia for a long time, but that there were a few that were kept in good order in Mombasa. Just beyond the dockyard a giant new mosque, with conventional minaret, was under construction and the askari allowed me to clamber over the building material and take a photograph of the dhow from there. Fleets of dhows were still plying the monsoons in centuries old fashion back and forth to the Yemen and Oman, and onwards to Pakistan and India as late as the 1950s, but they have gone, so I was particularly pleased to see a fine example in Mombasa. It was bigger and better kept than the one I had seen in Dar-es-Salaam.

Wandering back to the truck through narrow alleys, the savoury spicy aromas of the midday meal hung in the air and bright-eyed children ceased their noisy play to stare politely at me. I stood aside for black swathed women who drew a veil over their faces when they saw me. A middle-aged fellow with grizzly hair took my arm and said: "You must hold that camera firm. There's plenty of snappers here!" I grinned at the apt name, but looped the camera strap round my body. I was sorry to get back to the truck, I could have spent another week in Mombasa old town, especially if I could have got a room at the nearby Mombasa Club with a view of the sea from the shadow of the fortress.

At my request, Bob drove to the Nyali Beach Hotel where I remembered taking Barbie to an old-fashioned dinner-dance, but it had a $5,000,000 face-lift in 1982. A huge rectangular swimming pool shimmered where a garden had been and was flanked by geometric rows of loungers all occupied by oiled human seals baking on them like a giant's barbecue. We drove past Bamburi Beach which had become up-market suburbia and my jaundiced eye looked balefully out at pleasant modern villas with two-car garages and swimming-pools and chic town-house complexes. The sight of a 'tropical nature trail', amongst exotic casuarinas and local secondary scrub bush in a depression which I knew had been a coral rock quarry for the nearby cement factory, finally forced an amused laugh out of me. I closed my eyes to doze most of the way to Malindi on the new, fast toll-road, and allowed waves of nostalgic memory to wash over me.

It had been important for me to visit Malindi for its history and I was therefore pleased to find that it was one of our most enjoyable camping places on the whole safari. The site next to the derelict Silver Sands Hotel was a long strip of well kept lawn right on the beach, with a few coconut palms, bougainvillaea and varicoloured crotons. There were some other campers about but plenty of space for us all. The water supply had failed but lack of water was something that had ceased to be of great concern by then; when it was available, it was an unexpected pleasure. I pitched my tent in the lee of a baby coconut palm and slept well there.

The next day we did the usual round: banks, post office, the market. A local bus was parked near the bustling produce stalls and the driver engaged me in conversation, starting with the usual enquiries about who we were and where we were going.

"If you are returning to Nairobi, you should take the back road," he advised. "Your truck is strong enough for that. There is one place which tourists used to love, where there is a high place and you can see a long way along the Galana River. It is very fine and there are animals."

I thanked him for the information and then remarked: "I don't see many tourists."

"No, they don't come any more. I don't know why; some trouble with the hotels." He shrugged. "But you take your hotel with you."

"That's right. And we can see more and we meet people, which I like."

"Good!" He took my hand and laughed. "Maybe some black will rub onto your skin and you will be a little more African."

His companions grinned and one put his arm round me. "What is the best method for this man to get some black onto his skin?" A howl of laughter followed this suggestive question.

"I don't have enough time for that," I protested. "We leave tomorrow."

That was greeted with a leer. "It's because you are *Mzee* [an elder]; you need time to make a good *connection!*" More laughter, and Julius came over.

"What are they doing to you, Denis?" he asked, concerned.

"They think my skin should be helped to go a little black, but I'm saying that I need time for such arrangements."

"Because he is *Mzee*," explained the driver carefully.

Julius bent over in a fit of giggles. "That's wonderful, Denis! . . ." We said good-bye with more joking. The driver sounded his loud musical horn which I told him I admired, so he played it continuously until I had climbed aboard our truck and waved farewell, to the amusement of our group.

"They enjoyed your company," Julius said and I could see that he had been impressed by the casual little episode.

"I enjoyed them too."

"There are not so many White people who can be easy with Africans like that. I can see that you have really travelled a lot in Africa."

The special historical importance of Malindi is that it was there in 1498 that the famous Portuguese explorer, Vasco da Gama, hired an exceptional Arab pilot, Ahmad Ibn Majid, who was able to navigate his fleet directly across the north-west Indian Ocean to Calicut. If da Gama had blundered on further north to the Red Sea and the Arabian coast, he may not have survived. The reason for da Gama's success in getting help at Malindi was because the old Sultan was feuding with the Sultan of Mombasa and he gambled that by befriending the obviously powerful Portuguese, despite the fact they they were not Moslem, he would have their protection in future. His gamble came off, because the Portuguese did not forget this unique friendship on the otherwise universally hostile coast and until the Omani colonisation two hundred years later, there was a firm alliance. Ibn Majid, the pilot, published a definitive guide to navigation in the West Indian Ocean, and da Gama's experts discovered that the sailors of this region had sophisticated instruments and knowledge for oceanic voyaging long before Europeans. Arabs regularly traded with Sofala, the port for Great Zimbabwe, and further south.

Malindi was, therefore, one of those crossroad points in history that I love; a place where one can play the 'what if' game. What if the Sultan had not been feuding with his colleague down the coast, what if Ibn Majid had not been there or had been unwilling to hire himself to the Christians . . .? If da Gama had failed to return, Portugal may have given up the attempt to reach India. European penetration into the Indian Ocean would have been delayed and another series of 'what ifs' are launched.

Bob drove the truck along the sea front where our cooks tried to buy fresh fish. While the bargaining was going on, I stared across the small roadstead sheltered by a tongue of coral from the southerly monsoon. There, before me, was the place where da Gama's alien fleet anchored in April 1498, within hailing distance of four newly-arrived Indian ships. In the sunshine, on the blue sea, local lateen-rigged fishing boats and some pleasure craft bobbed at their anchor lines exactly where a historical vortex had occurred 487 years before. The small number of participators, the peacefulness of the events, the remoteness of the place, and the massiveness of human result, thrilled me.

We drove on to the point and Ted, Nick, Karen and Val walked with me past some luxury residences hidden in the trees out onto the rough coral rocks of the promontory. At its end, a white pillar preserved the exact position of Vasco da Gama's *padrão* that he had erected there before departing for India on 24th April 1498. I told my friends why that place was so important to me and we were all quiet for a while. I was breathless with hidden excitement; I had waited twenty years to be there.

That evening, Bob, Ted and I had dinner together at the Coconut Village Hotel. It was the first meal I had had in a smart restaurant in months, since before leaving England. I felt that I could indulge myself in a celebration and Ted and Bob were in the right mood.

It was the first of four outstanding restaurant meals that we had on the safari. After drinks and hilarity, (Bob had a gargantuan sense of humour and Ted's was sharply dry) we were given a large corner table. I had smoked sailfish, locally produced and as good as any salmon, a superb steak with green pepper sauce, savoury fried rice and a mountain of fresh salad, and three flavours of ice-cream. We drank three bottles of Bardolino which had been sensibly chilled, and finished off with fine Kenyan coffee and different brandies; I chose Fundador. We smoked cigars. We were filled with *bonhomie*.

When it came to paying the bill, the friendly headwaiter admitted that he did not know how to work the American Express machine so the manageress was called and Bob refused to allow any transaction to be completed until she sat and had a drink. Suddenly, outside in the warm night, singing and laughter began and our new friend took us out onto the lawn to watch. The hotel guests were all young Italian package tourists and they had decided to have a gala evening. The men had dressed as women and the women as men, they were dancing folk-dances and singing. The extroverts were miming and parodying to the gales of laughter from the rest of the group. It was marvellous innocent fun, the kind of jolly evening that I could remember from my youth at old-fashioned resort hotels in the Christmas holidays.

Walking back along the beach, my feet were above the sand, the warm sea swished gently, the campsite askari escorted us with his wicked bow and arrows slung over his shoulder.

Before leaving Malindi, there was an important archaeological site to visit. Gedi is a tourist attraction, either tagged onto those package tours that take in the north coast of Kenya, or tourists may go there for a day's outing from their luxury hotels at Nyali. It has never had the attention that Great Zimbabwe has received for it is a Persian and Arab colonial settlement and therefore trendy historians give it low-key treatment whilst exalting Great Zimbabwe as proof of Negro 'civilisation'. Basil Davidson, for example, in *The Story of Africa*, gives Gedi no mention at all in his long description of gently benevolent Swahili city-states, exciting Zimbabwean civilisation and rapacious Portuguese plundering. My conclusion is that Gedi is quietly ignored because it is a reminder that Persians and Arabs were medieval colonists in Africa in a style which may have been more rigorous and absolute than that of the Europeans. A thousand years of cultural mixing between local African tribes, Persians, Indians, Yemeni and Omani Arabs, Portuguese and British have created the Swahili towns of the East African coast. They are exciting examples of centuries of virile influences at work from all sides; of bloody local conflicts, exploitation and revolt, imperial wars beyond the horizons but mostly of long periods of quiet trading and living together in harmony. The Swahili are a cultural and racial mix, and I love the modern towns. But Gedi is different: it is a foreign, colonial town and its ruins that were lost and buried in the coastal jungles for several hundred years prove this.

Gedi was founded at the height of Moslem colonial expansion, probably in the 12th century, and abandoned in the 15th with a temporary and partial reoccupation in the 17th. Its history strangely parallels that of Great Zimbabwe in time. There is speculation about the reason for its abandonment, and one reason is based upon a suggestion that it was known as Kalepwa, 'The wells that dried up'. Another speculation is that the lagoon on which it was situated became silted and its function as a commercial port was therefore gradually lost. As always, there were probably several factors that combined to doom it. In particular, it was overrun by warlike Galla tribesmen. The local people then shunned it in the universal African tradition because it was the home of old, lost spirits. Its modern name probably comes from the Arabic, Gidah, meaning 'Buried'. There is no mention of Gedi in Portuguese records despite the existence of a Portuguese trading station at Malindi for two hundred years, less than fifteen miles away. It was not 'discovered' by Europeans until the 1920s. In the last thirty years it had been cleared of bush, archaeologically explored and tastefully presented as a vast open-air museum.

A modern building stood outside the town walls where there was an extensive collection of Chinese porcelain (Celadon and Ming), Persian ware, beads, Chinese and Middle-Eastern coins and local pottery that had been dug up there. The comparison between the fineness of the imported ceramics and local earthenware was most marked, emphasising the difference in cultures. The landward sides of the town were guarded by high stone walls and gate-houses, further proof of its alien status, and we entered to wander entranced beneath the cathedral dome of magnificent giant coastal forest trees that have been left towering above the geometrically laid out town. The trees dominated the ruins and for the first few minutes my eyes were lifted to them, delighting in the variety of massive trunks and differing feathery canopies. Some were straight limbed with smooth bark and fine pale green leaves, others were gnarled and twisted with heavy dark foliage. "It's a cathedral", I kept muttering to myself.

Under the living roof sixty and more feet above us, light and sound were subdued, shafts of flickering gold and the distant swish of air in the highest branches accentuated the feel of enclosure. The old coral stone buildings seemed to represent high altars, side chapels, choir stalls, pulpits, screens and stunted arches scattered in profusion to some vast and strange unconventional plan. The buildings were not small, it was the size of the centuries-old trees sensibly preserved that made them seem so. With Nick, Ted, Marie and Val, I walked quietly about examining the carved archways, a bathing pool, several wells, the kitchen fireplaces, the water conduits, religious ornaments, the intimate layouts of merchants' or officials' villas and homes. The museum curators had named the buildings romantically after principal objects found within them: 'House of the Chinese Cash' particularly took my fancy. The two largest buildings were the Great Mosque and the Sultan's Palace. The squared network of streets were enclosed by the town walls, but the guide told us that there were other minor stone ruins in the forest and excavation had not been completed. There was no 'native' quarter within the walls.

Gedi simply shows that early Persian and Arab colonists preferred to build Persian and Arab towns in East Africa and aspired to maintain the culture and standards of their countries of origin just as Dutch, French and British did in Southern Africa five centuries and more later. It may be that it was during the disruption of the Portuguese period that the widespread cultural and genetic mixing occurred which blurred the outlines and resulted in a broader Swahili culture as seen in the Old Town of Mombasa or in the seedy remnants of Bagamoyo. The Portuguese depressed the Arab ruling classes to a powerful middle rank of traders without political privilege, creating a new 'indigenous' class between the levels of the new expatriate rulers and the native Africans who were not directly affected. Portuguese dropped out into the growing Swahili group as the years went by and so added to its enrichment.

Back in the truck, I felt that the first half of my safari had now decisively ended. I had touched the edges of the Indian Ocean trading system. Now, we were heading away from the Swahili Coast, at the very beginning of our journey westwards: the most dangerous stage of our route.

CHAPTER NINE: 'THE WONDERFUL BIG LINE'

Sitting on a stool outside his mud hut,
The Mzee scratched his head in a slow motion,
Trying to recall.

MAJI MAJI. Jusuf O. Kassam [Kenyan poet]

We visited Julius' family home on the way to the Kenya Highlands for a grand 'party' that he and Charlie had been planning. It was a matter of prestige for his family, so anxiety began to grow after we turned off into the Machakos Highlands and it became clear we would be late.

The sun set while we negotiated a rough track into the hills, switch-backing over ridges and plunging into dry river beds. We had nothing to contribute to the party so Charlie stopped in the only village we passed through to buy beer. Julius directed us to the bar, lit by a paraffin lantern, but they had only a few bottles in a cool box. Loud discussion eventually produced a tribal authority policeman who took us down a backstreet to a warehouse. The roaring of our engine, the shouting and our swinging lights in the darkened village resulted in dogs barking and running children. The mud-walled warehouse was filled with bales of cotton and an old hand-operated baling press, but in a clearing in the centre next to an antique weighing machine, five or six elderly gentlemen were sitting quietly in a circle of battered armchairs sipping beer from litre bottles round a hissing pressure lamp. They seemed unimpressed by our sudden appearance out of the night and watched us with dull eyes as the policeman negotiated the purchase of two cases of beer from a cache stored in a little room at the side.

The road deteriorated further after the village and Julius became disturbed, reassuring Charlie frequently that we would be all right. But eventually we had to stop where there had been a deep washway in some recent rains. The air was chill and wind moaned through pine and eucalyptus trees. Our torches met deep blackness when we shone them over the side of the track, and there was that particular dead sound that comes from any empty abyss.

"This is it," said Charlie decisively. "I'm not taking any more chances. What do you say, Bob?"

"No way," Bob agreed. "This earth is soft and we can't see what's ahead. We'd better camp up here, I suppose. I'm for a beer, anyway."

Dazed, most of us stood around silently, expecting a miserably cold, hungry night on the mountainside. Julius seemed numbed by the disaster and I could sense his shame and humiliation.

"It must have been a heavy storm just a few days ago, Julius," I said. "How could you know about it?"

"Thanks, Denis." He clasped my shoulder. "But we can still reach my home; we can walk from here."

"Speak to Charlie then, before he starts organising the camp."

"I am nervous," he murmured. I saw the flash of his uneasy grin.

"Go on, Julius. It's going to be all right."

It was all right. A night porterage appealed to Charlie's cavalry spirit and Julius became galvanised into action, running off to call down the mountain for help from his relatives and assembled friends who came racing up to us, breathless and bathed in sweat half an hour later. Each one of us seemed to acquire a guide who helped carry our gear, mine was a teenage boy who went just ahead of me chattering away, asking questions about me and our safari, telling me about his family and how they had worried about our late arrival, carefully shepherding me on the track in the dim starlight with a steadying hand on my arm or leg. Our stumbling descent took forty-five minutes to arrive at the hullubaloo of an African welcome; dogs barking, children screaming and giggling, loud laughter and calls from the women, conflicting instructions and relieved talk in English, Swahili and Kamba. We had arrived. It was ten-thirty at night, but we had arrived!

In 1957 the family had built a substantial four roomed house with corrugated iron roof and it had been cleared for our accommodation. We sat for a while in one room with our gear piled about, sipping beer, waiting for what was to happen. Eventually Julius came to tell us that a goat had been killed and he was frying meat in Blue Band margarine on a fire and we should join the family and drink sugar-cane beer. The children and younger women had been sent to bed and we squatted around the fire while the freshly butchered meat sizzled in pans over the flickering flames. A pot of scummy beer went the rounds. It was quite unlike the sorghum beer of Southern Africa, with a sharp astringent taste and a much higher alcohol content. Julius was the dashing host, introducing a number of male relatives, giving his people a thumbnail sketch of each of us, explaining several times why we were late and apologising for the road.

The meat was inevitably tough and badly cooked and I gagged on a half-raw lump of gristle. I had to wander discreetly to the hedge at the end of the compound to dispose of it. But the effort made to feed and entertain us was deeply heart-warming. Suddenly Julius stood up and summoned several of his menfolk to him.

"The stars have gone," he explained. "It may rain, so we shall go now to safeguard the truck." They took off up the mountain at a fast pace carrying shovels, hoes and a lantern.

Charlie, Bob, Nick and Katie had stayed with the truck to guard it and the rest of us clambered into our sleeping bags scattered through the empty rooms, quite exhausted. As I fell asleep I thought of Julius' kindness and care for us.

I woke at dawn to hear the low murmuring of women's voices and the soft clatter of utensils gently handled. The compound was being cleaned and all made fresh for the new day. One of the older women came in with tea in our red mugs that had somehow been brought down the mountain. She explained shyly that the milk had been boiled so that it was safe to drink.

Outside as the sun peeped over the mountain behind us I was confronted with an extraordinary view. We were halfway down one side of a giant volcanic caldera, perhaps two miles in diameter at the rim and two thousand feet deep. Opposite were hundreds of small kraals, resting on terraces cut out of the steep slope, each with its tiny patch of maize, vegetables, sugar-cane, a few precious coffee bushes and scattered eucalyptus and indigenous trees. Scars of raw earth abounded where erosion had caused landslips. There were roofless, abandoned huts where the top-soil had washed away. In the quiet air, cocks crowed, goats bleated, dogs barked and children's voices bounced about us in the acoustic chamber of the crater. The area was grossly overpopulated and it reminded me instantly of parts of the immediate hinterland of Durban in Natal where Black commuter workers tried to maintain a semblance of their rural life. But we were nowhere near a South African city, this was a tribal reserve in Kenya where people had to survive on their pathetic patches of land without the support of wages from nearby White man's industry. I was appalled, and sat for a long while nursing my mug of tea and staring at the ravaged land.

Later, I talked to Julius about it and he gave me the expected explanation. Populations were growing fast and pieces of land were divided amongst the sons as best they could. Most men tried to get work in Nairobi, and some disappeared into the shantytowns forever, but there was never enough work and the number of kraals on available family plots kept increasing. There was a tribal cooperative that coordinated the gathering and marketing of coffee and cotton, the slim source of community revenue, and sometimes Government officials came to offer advice.

"You can see that life can be a great struggle for us here, Denis," he said sadly, looking out over his neighbours. "Our family is a strong one because our father worked as an engine-driver on the railway. So he was always a man of importance with our elders, and he saw that we were educated. We have five acres of land which is quite a lot. I keep a room in a house in Nairobi and I can bring money sometimes, especially like now, because Charlie pays for this party. But others are not like our family."

"How big is your family?"

"There are five brothers, three working, one here on our shamba, one still at school. I have good sisters too. The boy who helped you in the night was my younger brother; I told him to watch for you."

"You're a good man, Julius," I said.

He giggled, embarrassed, and took my hand. "Come, Denis, enjoy yourself. Drink some of our sugar-cane beer."

Julius and Charlie had come down with the others early, having dug the road level and secured the truck, and the party began about 9.30a.m. Julius' father, the Mzee, emerged and we were joined by his elderly friends from the neighbouring kraals and about twenty respectably married women dressed in bright cotton Western style clothes and strings of beer-bottle tops strung around their shoulders that made a rattling hissing noise as they jiggled their bodies. They had come to dance for us. As the bottled beer that we had brought and the potent sugar-cane beer circulated, plastic buckets were brought out to work as drums.

The bucket-drums began to thump, the visiting women and the girls began singing and the dancing started, our people joining in. My poisoned leg, fast healing now, was an excuse not to be drawn into the dancing so that I could sit lazily in the sun enjoying the fun which went on for several hours. In between the dancing, archery and spear throwing competitions were held, aiming at an effigy of a Masai warrior set up on an earthen bank. One of Julius' brothers pulled off a great feat: he split the first arrow of a group cleanly with the next shot and this set up a great roar of approval that echoed around the caldera. Beer flowed.

I spoke with the Mzee who told me about his years stoking and then driving wood-burning locomotives on the old East African Railways system in colonial days. He described life in Mombasa and Tanga in the 1940s and 50s. He was a quiet, dignified man with a grey beard and a delightfully sly twinkle in his eyes. He reminded me strongly of a less corpulent Jomo Kenyatta, the first President of independant Kenya, and I wondered if he would have been flattered had I said so. At one point he got up and went into the house to come out with an old sword-stick which he demonstrated to the respectful crowd. He strutted elegantly with the

119

stick, aping a European Edwardian gentleman, then suddenly swung about, drawing the sword and flourishing it menacingly. The crowd collapsed in laughter and cheers.

It was an unforgettable day of simple play under the hot sun in that caldera of poverty. After a lunch of corned beef and fruit, our gear was packed up and we trooped slowly up the mountain. All the people joined us; it was a great colourful snake that wound its way, singing and calling out.

"What a wonderful day, what a great sight," I said to Julius, pointing to the people going up the path, the singing flowing on the air.

"We are so happy that you came," he said. "And that is a wonderful big line." He stared at the long file of our party mixed with scampering children, dancing ladies, young men acting as porters, old men trudging, that stretched for quarter of a mile. I thought of Livingstone passing through Africa.

"The 'Big Line'," I echoed. "That's what it is." We always referred to it afterwards by that name.

The younger brother waited for me and insisted on carrying my camp-bed. When we reached the truck we were all very thirsty and as I was gulping, gratefully, from my mug, my eye was caught by a bent old man who was standing at the fringe of the crowd. I had not been conscious of him at the party, but he had walked silently beside me in the Big Line for most of the way, matching my pace and occasionally glancing at me with a shy smile. He was watching me and I noticed froth on his lips. I realised instantly that he must be badly dehydrated but was too shy to ask for water, so I refilled my mug and took it over to him. He held it with both hands in the African way and drank deeply. When he returned the mug he took my hand and would not let go, following me back to the truck. He spoke in Swahili, but I had to shake my head in lack of understanding so I took him to Julius who explained. I was surprised to see tears in his eyes.

"You see this old man, Denis," he said, his voice rough. "He says that he loves you. He knows that you must go, otherwise you would stay with him and his family. He wants to go and kill a chicken for you."

I was horrified. "No, Julius. Don't let him do that! Tell him how grateful I am, how I also felt him close to me as we climbed in the Big Line. Explain it carefully, but please don't let him do that."

Charlie was calling to us to get aboard, and after Julius translated, the old man clasped my hand more firmly, finally giving me the African hand-shake before backing away in the crowd. As we drove off my eyes were held to his until we turned a corner.

"I was so surprised about that old man," Julius said to me later. "He is so poor and he lives in a small house with just a daughter and some grand-daughters. They scratch for life."

"What was it about?" I asked.

"I don't really understand, Denis. He loved you. That's all."

"I think I loved him too," I said quietly. I feel his presence as I write.

The next few days in Nairobi became a bore, waiting for visas. I did some sightseeing, taking in the fine stone Cathedral which had been enlarged years ago by the father of an old friend, and the Nairobi Conference centre with its tawdry revolving restaurant. The comparative glitter of Nairobi after desolate Tanzania had faded by then and my eyes had penetrated beneath the surface glamour. One evening some of us went to Buffalo Bill's, a rip-roaring 'pick-up joint', where a galaxy of prostitutes awaited their prey. They were smart looking girls from a variety of East African tribes; many were refugees from Uganda. There were an equal number of carousing tourists, local 'expats' and Asian and Black business-men and the crowd thinned as the girls went off with their partners of the night. I felt cold thinking of the AIDS virus being distributed.

Our new companions to replace those who had left arrived one evening by the cheapest route from London: Aeroflot to Moscow and, after sleeping in the foreigners' transit hotel there, on down to Nairobi; a thirty-six hour journey. We met them at the Grosvenor Hotel for a welcoming beer while Charlie briefed them. I watched them with sympathy: tired, disoriented, laughing nervously, joining the residue of an established party who had already travelled Overland four thousand miles in two months. But there were enough of them to have their own group strength, and they had their own stories to tell about the flights with Aeroflot and the stop-over in Moscow. Well-travelled Al was the only new American. The others were Cathy and Claire, two bright and cheerful English girls; Sarah and Rob, both university graduates; Aussie Steve from Queensland; Angie from Newcastle, New South Wales, and Graham our youngest, a fine mature lad from the Home Counties, who became my new cooking partner, Val having departed.

CHAPTER TEN: *THE GREAT EASTERN RIFT VALLEY*

"We viewed the Rift Valley, near another Equator sign, and saw Nakuru below – it looks a nice town – and beyond to Lake Nakuru, blue in the sunshine. Quite hot now as we went on to the mountains and to Uganda. Glad we are coming back to the Rift Valley later."

– My diary: 22 August 1965.

"At the Kenya National museum I learned something more about the Great Rift Valley. There were clear displays showing its origin and development between 70 and 50 million years ago. (70 million years ago the dinosaurs died out. The same global catastrophe probably contributed to both phenomena.) Volcanic activity has continued in an around the Eastern Rift Valley until a few thousand years ago and up to the present along the Western branch bordering Zaïre."

– My diary: 20 October 1985.

The view from the escarpment into the Great Eastern Rift Valley was as enormously spectacular as I remembered it. We gazed down 2000 feet at the flat floor stretching away to the misty barrier of the escarpment on the other side, twenty-five miles or more away at that point. On the top, the vegetation was lush and green with small shambas growing vegetables and maize whilst stands of pines and eucalyptus trees merged with patches of bananas and paw-paws. Down below, the grass was sere and dotted with acacia thorn. On the sides of the escarpment the thorn was thick and studded by giant euphorbia candelabra trees. We stopped at Nakuru for a beer and a look-see in the late afternoon. It was drizzling with rain and Ted and I walked down the main street, full of bustle and movement.

I took Ted into a bar for a beer out of the rain. In front there was an eating house advertising roast chicken and the drinking took place in a strange corridor at the back. A narrow alleyway between two houses had been covered by rusting corrugated iron sheets and a motley collection of settees and old arm chairs from European homesteads were set on the muddy earth floor. We were served cold beers by a busy, sweating girl with huge plump breasts and sat in the company of four or five men, drinking companionably in silence. A door into one of the houses burst open and a well-dressed man emerged laughing and joking with two grinning girls who shouted affectionate abuse at him as he left. The girls eyed us and giggled together.

"I would never have come to a place like this on my own," Ted said to me.

"It's just a friendly 'Affie Bar' and local whorehouse. The atmosphere is pleasant," I reassured him. I felt relaxed and happy. "You've got to get into training: from now on there'll be many 'Affie Bars' for beers and cold Cokes. The European style hotels are going to become quite rare."

"If they are as innocent as this one, I won't mind."

"Come on, Ted," I teased him. "What did you expect? Hashish dens and girls performing with donkeys?"

"That's what you could find in Tangier thirty years ago when I was a lad doing National Service in Gibraltar," he said seriously. "But I suppose Black Africa was always different."

We camped that night in the Nakuru National Park where we had a camping site to ourselves with a water standpipe and clean pit latrines. In the morning we were invaded by baboons. They attacked with clever tactics. Having observed us carefully for a while, several males advanced from different sides and before we were alert to what was going on, they had got away with a loaf of bread and a plastic bag of cooking refuse. One of them grabbed a big plastic jar of 'Mrs Balls' Cape fruit chutney from the camp table and Ted pursued him hurling washing up bowls that he had been cleaning. I collapsed with uncontrollable giggles imagining the baboons sitting around with their prizes and carefully spreading hot chutney onto thinly sliced pieces of bread. Ted returned flushed and triumphant carrying the chutney and the bowls. No chutney sandwiches for baboon breakfast after all.

Since I was cook, I stayed with Julius drinking coffee and chatting by the fire while the others went on an early game-drive. In between the two of us shouting at the baboons, Julius told me about the problems his family had over their shamba where we had stayed the night. There had been rival claims on the property and an influencial KANU Party man had inveigled against them. They had gone to court and proved their ownership from documents that his father had providentially registered many years before. Having failed by legal means, their enemies resorted to poisoning one of his uncles and people squatted on the property, threatening the womenfolk. Eventually it all ended up in the High Court in Nairobi with more expenditure in bribes and lawyer's fees. It was a bad time and might not yet be over. He was always glad to take

Overland groups to the shamba for a party for it was a way of 'showing off' and increasing their prestige. It proved to all the peoples in that great caldera that his family were sophisticated and were friendly with foreign White people, which implied an intimacy with the larger world.

"Why did all this start?" I asked, appalled at the waste of money and effort. I had read several reports of civil court actions over land in the Nairobi papers.

"Because we are short of land as you saw for yourself. There is only so much land reserved for our tribe and now our numbers are many times what they were, and we are all short of land. Because my father was educated and had a good job with the railway, he made sure of our property, and others are jealous of us."

"What will happen in the future? Populations are still growing so fast in Kenya."

"I don't know, Denis." He sighed moodily, tossing a stick at a baboon. "We don't know the answer to that."

Food and land shortages are the fuel of political unrest and Kenya had become one of the prominent African nations with political detainees without trial and had also been victim to the African political coup disease. Julius told me about the unsavoury Ujonjo treason trial that was in session, and I had read a couple of reports in the local press. Ujonjo had been Jomo Kenyatta's brilliant right-hand man and held the powerful portfolio of Attorney-General. He had not been nominated as Kenyatta's successor because he was a Kikuyu, the majority tribe, and Kenyatta thought that Arap Moi would be a better head of the Kikuyu dominated ruling party since he was from a minority tribe. Ujonjo had naturally resented this and was now being discredited and destroyed through a long-running criminal case, accused of engineering the 1982 coup attempt and hiring South African mercenaries. Julius laughed as he told me how Ujonjo was reported to have nine passports and investments in South Africa.

"What is particularly funny, Julius?" I asked.

"Well, everybody knows that some of our party rulers have business in South Africa. Ujonjo's lawyers even brought evidence that our President was seen in Pretoria." He laughed again. "Some politicians are corrupt, Denis! They are just going to fix Ujonjo by whatever means they like and South Africa is a good excuse nowadays."

Later, after packing up the camp, we saw the famous Nakuru flamingoes. The great flocks lay like giant pink skeins over the blue of the alkaline water, shifting in the light of the bright, clear sun that followed the rain of the day before.

At Nyahururu, in the heartland of what used to be the White Highlands, we camped in the grounds of what was called Barry's Hotel in colonial days and after walking the well-kept grounds and admiring the view of Thomson's Falls and the richly forested gorge, I went into the bar. The atmosphere of an English settlers' pub was still discernible. The walls were pannelled in smoke-darkened wood, there were heavy beams in the ceiling, the furniture was well-polished wooden settles and beer advertisements decorated the bar. A great fire burned in the brick hearth for at nearly 8,000 feet it was cold outside. I sat by the fire nursing a whisky and heard in my mind the loud echoing voices and laughter of suntanned settler farmers and their womenfolk congregated for a Saturday night party. My aunt and uncle had lived not far away at Ol'Kalou.

The next morning we tidied up the truck in the campsite surrounded by pine trees and did some washing. A middle-aged man was struggling with a motor mower and I went over to chat with him. He was glad to rest from pulling at the starting cord to talk. He told me that he had been a Mau Mau guerilla fighter in the 1950s and had lived for many months in the forests of the Aberdares where it had been a cold and miserable existence. They had often been desperately hungry in the last days when the British army patrols had become more efficient and raiding parties on the farms below had become hazardous. Village girls had brought food and comfort up to them, but that too had become increasingly dangerous. In the end they had given up and he had spent seven years in detention in the Samburu. Those years in detention had been pleasant and indolent, he had quite enjoyed them. But, "Those bad days all finished now, Kenya is a good country." He had wicked, yellowed eyes and a mischievous grin. He told me he had worked in the garden of the hotel since his release in 1960 and he supplied vegetables from his five acre shamba that his children farmed. He was fifty four, almost my contemporary. I asked him if it had been worth it, the loss of ten years of normal life. He said he would never regret the comradeship and the spirit of those days which changed his life, but whether what they did was good or bad for Kenya, he was not sure. "Then, it was important to us; after twenty five years, who can say? I am happy now and that is enough." Indeed it should be.

Some of our group wanted to climb Mount Kenya so we dropped them off at the Nara Moru River Lodge, a converted settler homestead situated in a loop of the river with well-tended gardens and a bar lounge gay with the pennants and printed T-shirts of many expeditions. Mount Kenya is the second highest mountain in Africa, just over 17,000 feet high, lying almost exactly on the Equator with permanent snow and glaciers at its summit. Like Kilimanjaro (19,560 feet) and the Ruwenzori (16,790 feet) it is a volcano and the massif covers many square miles. Africa, like Antarctica, has no really spectacular folded mountain ranges such as the Andes, Himalayas or the Alps: Africa is a stable old giant, except for its isolated great volcanoes along the line of the Rift Valley.

Forty miles from Mount Kenya, we faced one of the awesome views that Africa suddenly thrusts at you. We were travelling north, descending to the great dry plains of Northern Kenya that surge away into the vastnesses of Ethiopia and the Sudan. Somewhere in the hazy distance the Great Rift Valley snakes its way to Lake Turkana, scene of so many discoveries about ancient man. The map told me that the tarred road we were spinning along did not last long and quickly changed to dirt, then to a track and finally to a thin pecked line which was suitable only for cross-country vehicles because of dangerous sections. Beyond that great plain ending in blue horizon were the human horrors that had appeared on television screens throughout the West: the sticklike children of the refugee camps of Ethiopia and the Southern Sudan, victims of civil war enhanced by yet another drought in a land of many droughts. The clearly evident, almost instant change from the richness of the highland vegetation and the quiet prosperity and rural good manners around Mount Kenya, to the harshness of the dry nomadic plains ahead, prompted talk in the truck of the Band-Aid concert and the need to help famine-racked people of Africa. I listened to the old arguments about self-help, the corruption of government officials, the distortions of news-hungry reporters, the selfless efforts of Aid workers. None of my companions seemed to have realised why these horrors had occurred, because the media had been shy of probing the failings of socialism, I supposed. I reflected that I had watched only one documentary, by a Canadian TV reporter, which had boldly shown that the Ethiopian famine had been triggered by the war between the oppressive Marxist regime and nationalist Eritrean rebels. As always, those who suffer are the common people; food stores pillaged, lands ravaged, villages burnt, crops unsown, Aid intercepted and tens of thousands of refugees wandering pitifully to die in the dry season, their lives totally disrupted. Farmers had been forced into semi-desert lands which a thin scattering of nomadic herders had always regarded with great respect.

Elephant family at Samburu, Kenya.

127

Four thousand feet below the escarpment we passed through Isiola and there was more evidence that we were in a new country. A large mosque dominated the town and there was Arabic writing on some of the dukas. The women wore lengths of cloth wrapped around them, bright green and red with boldly printed patterns. Beyond the town there was a serious military checkpoint with heavily armed soldiers and a grid of steel teeth in the road in case a vehicle was tempted to burst through. I had last seen a similar barrier in Israel. We were stopped and carefully examined in contrast to the perfunctory checks that we had come across on the roads to the south. This reminded us that we were briefly entering a different Africa, the Africa of endless war and banditry.

Short of Archer's Post, an evocative colonial name, we turned off into the wilderness of the Samburu Game Reserve and immediately saw game amongst the patchy thorn scrub. There were species that I had never seen before such as gerenuk, an antelope which can stand comfortably on hind legs to browse from the acacia thornbushes, Grevy's zebra with their finely etched stripes and Grant's gazelle, pretty cousin of the delicately marked Springbok of South Africa's dry lands. We saw our first camels. There was the local race of oryx, larger than the beautiful dun-coloured desert antelope of Southern Africa with long straight horns that even lions fear, common in Namibia and Botswana but not seen in the thousands of miles in between. Africa *is* a mirror, I thought for the hundredth time. We saw a distant herd of elephant and the ubiquitous impala which is perhaps the most successful of Africa's antelope. I noticed Claire making notes in her diary and we agreed to compile a list of animals together.

We sited our tents carefully under the giant riverine trees beside the Ewaso Nyiru River because recent rain had formed channels in the earth. A twelve foot crocodile basked on a sandbank in the middle of the stream and a scruffy campsite baboon watched us. Along the sandy shore line there were elephants' footprints and their football sized droppings. There was no sleeping under the stars at Samburu. Later we all went for a game-drive and were rewarded by a close encounter with a herd of elephants. There had been a shower of rain and their wet skins showed shiny black through the scrub. Charlie judged their line of march carefully and parked so that they came past our truck, on both sides, close to, taking little notice of us. One of the females had lost her tusks and one of the males was very old with a shrunken frame and deeply lined face. There were several young, some not more than a few months old, walking beneath their mothers. In order to get close to the same herd, a fleet of kombis carrying tourists from the nearby Safari Lodge left the road to follow it and on the way back we came across the subsequent disaster. One of the kombis was down to its axles in soft earth, another had just escaped a similar fate with mud and grass thrown up over its polished sides from the spinning wheels. The others waited at the road side. The tourists, mostly middle-aged Americans in obligatory immaculate 'safari' outfits and hats trimmed with nylon leopard skin, stood about angrily while the drivers yelled and shouted, two or three heaving at the bogged vehicle while its engine screamed. Charlie stopped our truck and shook his head.

"Those drivers obviously aren't used to the bush. I bet they don't usually go further than the Nairobi National Park." He turned to us. "I suppose we Brits will have to get them out. Out with our sandmats and shovels, chaps. It'll be good training for Zaïre."

"I'm no Brit," grumbled Adie.

"Pretend you are," said Charlie. "Let's show those Yanks what the Empire was made of."

After talking quietly with the tour leader, an elderly black man with his muddied uniform trousers rolled up to his knees, Charlie took charge. He and Dave dug around the wheels of the kombi, we set our steel sandmats across the soaked depression that had caused the trouble, then with a half dozen of us pushing alongside the drivers, the engine roaring and shrouding us with blue exhaust smoke, the kombi tore itself free and went bouncing and crashing back to the road. We had mud splattered all over us and one of the girls broke the straps of her sandals. We stood, panting, as we watched the well-groomed Americans climb aboard. They did not thank us for our efforts to get them back to their hot baths and dry-martinis.

"That was a bloody sour bunch," said Charlie, wiping mud off his face.

"Why didn't we leave them alone?" asked somebody.

When we got back to our camp, Julius, who had stayed behind as our askari, was full of excitement. A crocodile had come ashore and nosed about, forcing him to retire to a sensible distance. After he had thrown tins at the crocodile and banged things about, it had lazily returned to the river. A lone elephant had wandered through our tents and I was sorry to have missed that.

After we had cleaned up, Charlie drove us around to the Lodge to fill the water tanks and watch the regular evening feeding of the crocodiles and leopard. A large hose was being used to wash down the muddied tourist kombis and the drivers, who had been grateful for our help, were ready to fill our tanks. But an askari from the Lodge stopped them and we had to wait half an hour for an assistant manager who told us blandly that the charge for water was twenty shillings a litre. (Petrol at the nearest town was eight shillings a litre.) I looked at the men hosing the kombis before us all and was dumbfounded. I could not believe it, and I saw Charlie going white with rage. We later quietly filled our tanks at the Lodge's staff quarters where a sympathetic worker showed us a defective standpipe where purified water gushed to waste night and day. Unbelievable! The Lodge was operated by a well-known hotel group.

We visited a Samburu village that was set up near the northern gate for tourists to visit. We saw a different herd of elephants on the way and a great collection of vultures, on the ground, perched on trees and circling in the sky. The weather was fine and hot and after the previous day's rain the air was clear with a pale blue sky relieved by whispy clouds. I was struck by the massive scale of the landscape, the endlessness of the wilderness. It was the Great Heart of Africa again, but with a different texture and colouring to Tsavo. The line of the river was distinguished by the dark green of the tall trees that grew on its banks and we saw doum palms for the first time. They are the distinctive multi-branched palms of the Nile valley and the Sahel region, the southern threshold of the Sahara that stretches the width of Africa. We were to get to know them well in the wadis of Chad.

The Samburu village, I was told, housed two hundred people, mostly women, children and older men. Many of the younger men worked away from home in the universal tradition of modern African migrant labour and returned periodically. These people were Nilotic nomadic herders and their huts were almost identical to those of the Hottentot (Khoi) of Southern Africa: withies were bent and fastened to form a hemispherical shell which was then covered by cattle hides or goat skins. Within the simple, temporary huts there was one partition, separating the woman from the man and their children and I was interested that it was the woman who had the private compartment in contrast to the Bantu people who build a separate hut for the male head of the household. In that village it was sad to see the hides and skins replaced by tattered sheets of plastic and flattened tins. An embryo of a rural slum was in being.

Whereas the Hottentots had been Neolithic herders who had been overwhelmed by Iron-age Bantu culture from the north and the Western civilisation of the White man, these Nilotic Samburu were still proud and independent. It was the women who were the most striking. An old man with severe cataracts in his eyes led me about, telling me about the village in quite good English and when I asked him if I could photograph some of his people, he led me to a group of handsome women in their twenties who were emerging from a larger hut, dressed in their finery of beads, forehead decorations and multitude of brass bangles, necklaces and anklets. I noticed that the beadwork on the girls was in bright, primary colours, similar to that of the Zulus and Ndebele of Southern Africa, in contrast to the pastels of the Masai and Kamba, and I guessed that glass beads must be a recent innovation to their culture. There was no coyness or giggling among them, they looked me over boldly and with feminine interest; it was as a man that I was examined rather than as a tourist from another world.

"You older man," one stated without emphasis. "You strong?" She looked me over, and I felt an instantly powerful sexual contact.

"Yes, I'm strong," I replied. "I've travelled a long way."

She held my eyes. "You can show me?"

I shrugged, at a loss. "Maybe," I said, grinning, after a moment, and her finely shaped lips lifted in a faint Mona Lisa smile before she turned to her companions and they talked in their own language, watching me. None of them laughed. There was nothing funny or silly about the incident, and it was several seconds before I raised my camera and shot off a few frames at them before some of our group came up and the mood was broken. I walked away with the old man but turned back after some steps and she was looking after me, still with that subtly provocative smile on her lips.

"You like that woman?" the old man asked me, peering closely at my face.

"They were extraordinary," I said to myself still bemused, then nodded to him. He cackled suddenly and touched my arm: "Samburu woman very strong, like strong man." I thought of the separate compartment for the woman in the small hemispherical huts.

He told me that there were four hundred cattle and five hundred goats belonging to the community which were herded together in the surrounding bush by teen-aged boys with a few mature men to supervise them. They lived on the milk of their animals like their Nilotic cousins, the Masai, and the Bantu Zulus of far away Natal whose pride and bearing they resembled. It is strange how people who live close to animals, who traditionally herd cattle as their principal motive in life, seem nobler than pure agriculturalists. Is it the high protein diet, the wandering life, the need to fearlessly combat natural and human predators? The latter would be the strongest influence, I thought. The old man told me that they used to move about, but stayed in that place the year round now, because of the revenue from the tourists who came from the Lodge in the Game Park. In the lifetime of those bold young women would they become degraded, I wondered, and feared that it might be inevitable.

Samburu women's fine beadwork, Kenya.

Ted and I walked to the Lodge in the late afternoon so that we could watch the crocodiles. Below the rambling main building, sensibly designed so that it was largely hidden in the great riverine trees, a terrace with a low brick wall edged the river, and on one side there was a cleared area where bones and offal from the kitchen were thrown out every evening. This arena was lit by a powerful floodlight. Sitting comfortably with cold beers we watched egrets, ducks and storks flying home along the river to roost. Soon afterwards the crocodiles gathered. Great swirls in the river showed where they kept station in the current. Their heads occasionally broke the surface, but usually there were only the knobs of their eyes and nostrils to be seen. We reckoned that there were up to ten of the monsters there at any one time, but if we had not been searching for them we might not have seen them. It was a frightening thought.

Almost unnoticed, so sudden and quiet were their movements, there were three crocodiles on the bank, their heads poking through the grass at the perimeter of the arena. The heads did not move for several minutes as they observed. Then, the leader advanced in a rush, like a giant radio-controlled toy that had been electronically switched on, and stopped beside the lump of meat and bone awaiting it. Gradually, it subsided onto its belly and began to chew on the meat in a leisurely fashion. Bone cracked sharply and it shook its head to worry at the food. The others did not move a centimetre until the next one somehow decided that it was its turn and it advanced close to the first, which, after an interval, moved aside and returned slowly to the water. Another had meantime taken the vacant place on the bank and waited with that incredible stillness for its turn. From time to time a Lodge servant came down to replenish the supply of raw meat and bone. The display continued for an hour or more until all the meat was consumed by the silent and deadly procession. That night I was aware, absolutely clearly, of the difference between a mammal and those giant reptiles. The awful stillness and contempt for time struck me most forcibly; no warm-blooded animal could be so patient and unmoving, so conserving of energy until it was needed. And when action was indicated, those crocodiles moved instantly, like sprinters at the gun, but they moved with total economy and precision. They were magnificent but terribly alien. So powerful and competent, they proved unquestionably the dominance of their type 70,000,000 years ago. Later, a leopard came for its nightly feed of bait in the dead tree across the river and it was almost lovable with cuddly familiarity in comparison. I was enthralled to watch the lithe cat leap like a golden streak into the bare tree trunk and stand there proudly, his eyes glinting in the light as he watched us.

I walked back with Ted, Dave and Graham. There was a moon and it was spooky. I could see crocodiles' shapes between the silhouettes of the riverside trees and whole families of leopards were padding behind me.

I woke at six again next morning and since the rest of the group had stayed late at the bar in the Lodge, I was alone but for Julius who was scouring for firewood. It was a fine morning, warm and clear and the previous day's sunshine had dried the earth so it had a covering of pale grey dust. I wandered up river, along the road, hoping to see the elephant that had entered our camp the previous morning. I was about to return, after watching some impala and a shy dik-dik when I heard crashing in the undergrowth towards the river. Adrenalin flooded my body and I prepared to run, thinking it was the elephant.

A grey shape swung high in a tree, and I relaxed and was about to light a cigarette when it struck me that I might get a close look at the troop of baboons who were moving away from the river. So I trotted along the road to where I judged they would cross and squatted down on to my heels, like a proper naked ape, and waited to see what would happen. The first to appear was a large male, a clan elder, who came out onto the road and looked carefully up and down. He saw me, of course, and I could sense him hesitating and weighing my presence. We stared quietly at one another for at least half a minute and I was glad that I had decided to be an ape squatting in the dust. Satisfied, he walked with dignity across to an open area in the scrub and took up station on a dead tree. The rest of them soon followed and they settled in this open space where I observed them closely for an hour or more. At first, they glanced at me frequently until I became accepted. I was afraid to move, but when my legs started to ache I had to shift my weight and apart from a quick glance from the leader, this did not disturb them. It was an amazing experience, for this was a wild troop, not campsite scavengers, and I was openly amongst them, not safely encased in the metal bubble of a vehicle.

They exhibited every kind of activity. Some broke up an old dead branch and delicately picked at the termites they found, popping them into their mouths and swallowing contentedly. Others groomed each other, some just sat together, two females actually holding hands for a few minutes. There were three large male leaders that I could distinguish, the first who remained on his dead tree and two others who placed themselves on the periphery of the open space. There were children everywhere, scampering about, wrestling with each other, running up the dead tree, swinging on the low branches of another, clinging momentarily to a mother or other female. One even climbed on the back of the old male who looked round with majesty at the youngster until it slid down and ran off. Indulgently, a female would admonish a child if it became too boisterous and one received a sharp slap which rolled it over in the dust when it took no notice. There were two very young babies, still covered in black fur, who clung to their mothers. One youngster ran towards me and for a split second I thought it was going to play with me, but it was called back by a sharp bark from a female. I had not brought my camera, it was locked in the truck, but I was so absorbed that I did not think of that until later.

Perhaps the most interesting was a female that was in oestrus, 'on heat'. Two or three males watched her and their penis's were erect. She presented her behind to one and he mounted her in conventional baboon fashion, standing on the backs of her bent knees. The coupling was over in a few seconds of rapid thrusting. She went over to another male who had pale grey fur and he mounted her too, but his activity seemed more leisurely and sensual. She approached one of the leaders, sitting on his tree. His penis was firmly erect but apart from a glance at her hind-quarters, presented to him, he did not move. He clearly was able to override sexual instinct. She waited a while, then walked off, wandering in a circle. A teenager, then came to her and climbed on her back, his legs were too short to make connection in the normal way, and she let him thrust in her for a while before shrugging him off and going to the pale-furred one who mounted a second time. While this was going on, the rest of the troop took no notice, the children played and squabbled, the females watched them and groomed one another, others sat in the sun. Ten minutes or so later, the three male leaders, at some signal that I missed, got up and, continually glancing about, wandered away. The one closest to me gave me a careful look, as if in farewell. In moments, they were all out of sight.

I walked back to our camp, dazed by the extraordinary feeling of intimacy that I felt I had shared with the baboons. My naked ape companions were packing up the truck. I had missed breakfast and had to rush to strike my tent and get my gear together.

We stopped at Isiola to shop in the market and as I was wandering about, admiring the market people and their produce, a twelve year old boy attached himself to me. He began by asking me many geographical questions and I was reminded of the older boy way back in Malawi who wanted to study in South Africa. He told me that he was from Somalia and his father, "who is a rich merchant", sent him to the boarding school attached to the mosque in order to learn good English. The local boys were rough and he missed his own people, but he thought he was learning well. He followed me to the truck, holding my hand, and when I got onto the step he suddenly asked for a pencil, which I gave him. As we drove away, his large solemn eyes followed mine, the pencil in his fist clutched firmly to his chest. He looked lonely and sad.

We camped that night at the Naro Moru Lodge at the foot of Kenya again and our climbers returned. They had had a tremendous experience. Their socks had frozen and they had been miserably cold at the highest camp. Rob had been ill with altitude sickness, vomiting and prostrate. But the views at dawn had been mind-blowing. For some hours there had been no cloud anywhere for the hundreds of miles visible from the summit, and Mount Kilimanjaro had been sharp and beautiful away to the south, a rare experience. So they were exhilarated. All were stiff and sore but talked in floods. The high altitude bogs had been the hardest going and the snow ridges at the top the most frightening. Listening to the excited chatter, I felt the loneliness and fearful emptiness of high mountains.

That night, something brought me to full consciousness and I was drawn to climb out of my warm tent. The moon was approaching full and there was not a breath of air. There were no clouds. I stood watching the black forest in the foreground, the medium grey dome of the lower massif and the reflecting brightness of the great snow-covered peaks. The sky was pale grey. I stood in awe, trying to think of all the things I should be thinking.

From Mount Kenya we returned to the Youth Hostel in Nairobi for final preparations. Then we were off. I felt nostalgic at the conclusion of the first part of our grand safari. It was the soft part, the most 'touristy' part, the most 'civilised' part, Charlie kept reminding us. I knew that he was right, of course, and I wondered if my companions had an idea of the hardships which I knew were ahead. It did not matter, it would happen, willy-nilly.

We stopped two days in the Masai Mara game reserve. I did not like it, because I was eager to get to grips with the reality of Central Africa and

Zaïre and was surfeited by 'tourism'. But there were our newly joined friends to consider; they had to have their share of game viewing. I suppose that my dislike was enhanced by the filthy campsite. Plastic was blowing from the rubbish tip where a dirty old baboon scuffled for rotten food. There was no water at the junior staff ablutions which we shared, and our girls particularly suffered. Going out to squat and expose naked white bums on open grasslands was normal later, but not yet.

But there was magic, of course. There was a good moon and in the night hyenas 'whooped' and I heard the grunt of a lion. We also said goodbye to Julius. That was difficult, and I vowed that I would maintain my friendship with him; and I have.

We headed from the Mara, through the Reserve, to Suna on the main tarred road from Nairobi to Mwanza in Tanzania. We were all tired and thinking of the new world that faced us when we had pitched tents in a field outside the town. The newcomers were especially subdued.

CHAPTER ELEVEN: *THE GREAT EXPLORERS*

Who left heart
And guts to find new life
In Africa. The corpse they

Tramped back
To Westminster and a cramped lot.
It's a hundred years since he died.

But he's still here
Within the exhibition stands. A piece
Of cloth, a sweat-rimmed helmet:

The awed hush
Of bent tourists straining to hear
A dim heart-beat.

LIVINGSTONE. Mike Nicol [South African poet]

We went shopping next morning in Suna, our last chance in Kenya, and Charlie met a berobed old Arab in a duka who told him that his grandfather was a slave-trader in that area, and I admired three Arab ladies in the market dressed in long gowns with veiled faces. The youngest was very tall and slim wearing a delicately embroidered, filmy white gown. Her dark eyes in her pale face were heavily made up with kohl. I was reminded again how strongly people hang on to traditional culture in an alien community as generations pass by. The massiveness of ethnic momentum and inertia is immeasurable.

I had not thought much about Livingstone since leaving Bagamoyo. Waiting to go through the formalities at the Kenya-Tanzania border, sitting on the springy grass under some sweet scented pine trees, I focused on Livingstone, and the other great Victorian explorers into whose territory we were now entering. Livingstone had not travelled into the immediate vicinity of Lake Victoria, but if anybody is to be considered the founder of European exporation in Central Africa, it has to be him. In his earlier years he concentrated on the Zambesi and Lake Malawi and was propelled by his zeal in combating the East African Arab slave-trade. He believed the introduction of British Civilisation and the commercial upliftment of Central Africa would give the native peoples protection from the slavers, because they would no longer need to sell their brothers and sisters to obtain the cloth, glass beads, guns and ironmongery that the Arab traders brought up from Zanzibar. His writings stirred the interest of geographers and ethnologists, as well as the general public, in African exploration in a period when the concept of colonial Empire was popular and growing. Britain had many energetic young men with training and experience in far places, especially India, who had ambition and time on their hands to follow him.

In Central Africa, prominent amongst this new breed which followed were Burton, Speke, Grant, Stanley, Baker and Gordon. Burton, Speke and Grant were soldiers. Stanley was a journalist despatched by his newspaper proprietor literally to follow in Livingstone's footsteps, he was an adventurous foreign correspondent experienced in exotic travelling in Turkey, Persia, India and Egypt. Baker was a wealthy man, a 'sportsman', who travelled and explored for complicated motives. Gordon, at the end of this chain of names, was a bridge between two eras: the period of European exploration and the period of colonial activity.

Livingstone became influenced by the men whom he had directly or indirectly inspired. Burton and Spekes' obsession with the unexplored great lakes and the source of the Nile with the vicious controversy between them over the respective merits of Lakes Victoria and Tanganyika, caught Livingstone too, and his last years were spent in the same cause. Sadly, Livingstone, perhaps too strongly oriented to Southern Africa, exhausted himself following a false trail. He was convinced that the Mountains of the Moon, the legendary 'fountains' described by Ptolemy, were the source of all three great rivers of Central Africa; the Nile, the Congo and the Zambesi; a truly grand design. Therefore he sought them south-west of Lake Tanganyika, where he died.

All of these men had to be mystics to a degree. All were complex and complicated men. There must have been times when they were unbalanced, badly depressed, perhaps quite manic. They all suffered from long periods of tropical diseases, typically malaria and dysentery. Months were spent languishing in villages and towns in the interior held up by sickness, waiting for stores, the whim of local African chiefs or general ennui and depression. They spent years on their journeys. Livingstone's terminal period in Central Africa lasted seven years, from 1866 to 1873. The efficiently ruthless and well-funded Stanley, following others' paths for much of his great trans-continental journey, took 999 days to complete the explorations of Lakes Victoria and Tanganyika and traverse the Congo River. I have most sympathy and affection for Livingstone and most respect for Stanley. Livingstone undoubtedly had a true understanding and feeling for the Black people among whom he travelled; they certainly had a love for him that no other European explorer of the time remotely inspired.

Apart from these men and the many minor characters on the same stage, there were the unsung Arab and Indian explorers who have not been sympathetically chronicled, for they were unashamed traders and trade in Central Africa at that time meant the slave-trade, in addition to ivory, rhinoceros horn, exotic skins and other plunder of the environment. Wherever Livingstone travelled in his later years, there were Arabs before him. His earlier great feat, the traverse of Southern Africa, was carried out in the wake of Arab and Swahili trading forerunners. Our chauvinism dismissed all of these people, almost casually, as if the only exploration of any worth had to be carried out by Europeans educated in appropriate European schools.

Alan Moorehead in *The White Nile*, describes the European explorers and first colonial giants in Central Africa between 1856 and 1900, and he wrote this of them:

'A curious combination of hatred and love drew the explorers back to Africa. They were like men who make a life at sea; having once committed themselves to its hazards they feel impelled to go back again and again even if Africa kills them. At one time or another most of them rail against the country and its inhabitants, declaring them to be ugly, brutal, scheming, debauched and finally hopeless . . .'

Maybe they could not understand the great continuity and depth of African culture because they could neither respect nor begin to explain it. Victorian Europe was so stuffily conscious of its civilisation. Livingstone loved the African people but he was a missionary and one of a kind, so he could get away with his eccentric sympathy. But I like to think that those other Victorian heroes could not spend so many years, and could not be drawn back again and again, without some form of love for the people too. Moorehead quotes Schweinfurth, a 19th century explorer of the upper Nile:

'The first sight of a throng of savages, suddenly presenting themselves in their naked nudity, is one from which no amount of familiarity can remove the strange impression; it takes abiding hold upon the memory, and makes the traveller recall anew the civilisation he has left behind.'

While we were travelling in Tanzania, three young Britons were walking in Stanley's footsteps from Bagamoyo to Ujiji, where Stanley met Livingstone ["Dr Livingstone, I presume!"]. George and Christine Tardios and Andrew Graham took four years to complete the modern journey . . . At the end, Tardios wrote in the *Sunday Telegraph*, on 30 March 1986:

'The trip has hardened us. Ideals we once held have been turned on

their heads. Weary of lies, greed, corruption, the despoiling of nature and wild life, gross misuse of foreign aid, we now appreciate what we left behind. We were too naive. We have become wiser, but not necessarily nicer.'

I read this with sadness. The remarks were an extraordinary echo of those made by their illustrious exploring forbears a century before.

Because of the seemingly endless civil war in Uganda, all the freight traffic for Rwanda, Burundi and Eastern Zaïre was being funnelled along the road that we were travelling. At the border post, into Tanzania, trucks were parked nose to tail in a snake about three miles long. On the Kenya side, a village had sprung into being as if the immigration and customs offices had become a bonanza. There were bars, doss-houses, provision shops and many open market stalls. There were hundreds of shacks, thrown together with bright, crudely lettered signs, and a busy crowd swarmed.

We got through quickly because we carried no cargo, but evening was approaching as we crossed two low ranges of rocky hills, separated by a small plain.

"Where are we going to camp, Charlie?" I asked.

"By Lake Victoria, I hope. It's where the Serengeti corridor comes through."

"Speke Gulf?" I asked, suddenly excited. I had not known Charlie's plan.

He grinned at me. "You'd like that, wouldn't you?"

Passing over the last ridge, we came in sight of the fifteen mile wide tongue of the great Serengeti Plain that reaches out to lick at the shores of Speke Gulf on Lake Victoria. Here, the millions strong herds of wildebeest and zebra used to come to water at the height of seasonal droughts. In the golden light of late afternoon, it was a view that filled me with mixed wonder. As a geographical spectacle it was fascinating, flat and green it swept away eastwards to a far horizon, beyond which lay the Eastern Rift Valley and the volcanic giants of Ngorongoro, Meru and Kilimanjaro. Scenically, it was different country, grassland with dark clumps of tropical bush and fairy fronds of palms, dotted with black specks of easily grazing wildebeest and, at the edges, multicoloured specks of native cattle in an untroubled merging at the unfenced frontiers of game reserve and tribal territory. Historically, here was where John Hanning Speke on 3rd August 1858 first set eyes on the great Nyanza, the

141

inland sea, that Arab traders had told him about and which he decided, intuitively, was the source of the Nile. We drove along beside the new road which international Aid was constructing on a causeway raised above potential floodwaters and I wished, as always, that we could have stopped so that I had time to catch up with the impressions crowding my mind.

The pale blue waters of the great lake to the westward were bounded by the low hills of the two arms of Speke Gulf, washed pink by the evening sun. Distant white triangles of fishing boats were returning to their ports. Vegetable gardens bordered the water and there were small kraals of round, pointy-roofed grass thatched huts. We parked on a hardened area where cattle came to drink, a few yards from the gently breaking waves, and I watched the sun set in a red-gold ball across the waters. We pitched our tents in the afterglow as the hills turned to sharp black silhouettes and the nearly full moon rose as we ate our dinner. As I drifted off to sleep, my imagination heard the little waves washing in a sibilant chorus: "Speke Gulf, Speke Gulf, Speke Gulf . . ." What exulting thoughts did Speke think as he slept for the first time on that shore 128 years before?

When I woke at six, immediate excitement was in my belly and I pulled on my shorts and crawled out of my tent quickly. The sun was nearly up and the scene in front of our camp showed blue and pink water enclosed by the earthy arms of Speke Gulf, still there. A small tropical storm, part of Lake Victoria's private weather system, had threatened the night before with flashes of purple lightning in the distance, but the morning was cloudless and serene with clean sharp air. I climbed onto the roof of the truck with my camera and watched the world come alive. The triangular white sails I had watched the night before were setting out from a fishing village across the bay. Women and children were coming down to wash themselves and collect water in battered tins and plastic buckets, laughing and talking loudly. The older children stopped to watch us getting up and preparing breakfast, standing in a quiet semi-circle. Later they collected cans and bottles from our refuse when I offered them. These people were physically well proportioned and cheerful with very black skins and broad fleshy faces.

To my intense delight, one of the fishing craft came in to beach itself close to us. It was constructed of planks with raised, pointed bow and stern and was quite beamy. It had a short mast and a low-cut lateen sail with a long yard: an Arab rig!

"You see, Ted," I said excitedly. "The Arab influence is absolutely clear here, right in the middle of Africa –"

142

He grinned at my enthusiasm.

The crew, mostly young men, came ashore and splashed about, washing themselves, while a boy shinned up the mast under the direction of the white-robed master to clear the jammed main-halyard. Stanley was the first European to circumnavigate the lake and prove its size and he must have hired boats just like this one.

We entered Mwanza after an hour's drive and it was a town that I enjoyed, lying on a wide estuary about half way across the southern shore. It had been a German provincial capital at the turn of the century and a German colonial residence with gables and mock timber frames stood on a rocky hill in the centre, surrounded by flamboyant and jacaranda trees. It was almost identical to a similar building in Windhoek, Namibia. The town itself was alive. It was by far the pleasantest Tanzanian town we visited. The two main streets were faced with shops and small apartment buildings in reasonable repair, painted white with concrete trellises around the top of their facades. The majority had obviously been built by Arab and Indian entrepreneurs with dates on the buildings from the 1930s and 1950s, as in Arusha. But, whereas Arusha seemed to have declined beyond the stage of genteel poverty, into a dismal era of total defence against social cancer, Mwanza was still fighting back. We parked beside a modern hotel, the New Mwanza, and walked about. Near the waterfront there was a healthy tamarind, defeating the tropical sun, with a plaque saying that it was 'The Coronation Tree', planted by the British Provincial Commissioner in 1953, and I had an instant vision of white uniforms, ladies in wide-skirted frocks and wide hats, and the Police Band with at least one trombone out of tune playing the national anthem.

We went shopping and everything manufactured was very expensive, many goods from Kenya or Rwanda smuggled in fishing boats. A bar of Imperial Leather toilet soap cost £4.00 at the official exchange rate! I asked a quiet, dignified elderly Indian shopkeeper if he thought I could photograph the old German colonial building on the hill and he gave me a sad little smile: "You must know what these people are like. If you photograph it, you disappear . . ." It now housed a military radio station, the only sure communication with the outside world.

I asked how the local people could possibly pay such high prices for the manufactured goods we saw in his and other dukas. He explained that there was a parallel economy in Tanzania. Farm produce was supposed to be sold to cooperatives at controlled prices and in many parts of the country that happened. In some areas, where there was laxness or the officials turned a blind eye, produce was smuggled to Dar-es-Salaam or over the borders and higher prices were obtained. In turn, goods were smuggled in either directly or by falsifying documents. These were procedures that astute men had established in the twenty years of doctrinaire socialism and steady decline. "People will always find a way, out of necessity. Our official policy is not natural to us . . ."

Ted and I walked around the market and he was especially fascinated by the cottage industry going on in lean-to sheds built against the old cement block walls of the fresh produce section. I loved a workshop that was producing a range of oil lamps from tin cans, the brass bottoms of old light bulbs and plaited string for wicks. Here is the African genius for improvisation, I thought, as we had also seen it in Malawi.

The Showground at Mwanza must have been one of our more bizarre campsites on the whole safari. It was a large area of about five acres, surrounded by a high wall and controlled by two families who lived in huts at the gate which was always kept closed. Faded and dilapidated permanent exhibition buildings were dotted about an arena in the centre. On one side there was a building with modern flush toilets without any piped water connections and in one corner there was a well with a pump that was operated like a pogo stick. It pumped with a great gush as you leapt on and off it, but the water had a greeny tinge and a bad organic aroma because of the town's sewage settling ponds nearby.

Angie had discovered a compatriot in the New Mwanza Hotel, not only a compatriot, but one who hailed from her neighbourhood in the Hunter Valley of New South Wales, ("Wow! it's a small world!"), and he joined us for dinner that evening. He was the General Manager of a Ugandan road freight company owned by a multi-millionaire German and a Ugandan in Kampala. He was a pleasant, confident Aussie in his early forties who had been in the trucking business here and there around the world and was settled in East Africa, for the moment. He told us many stories about Uganda, a country for which he had a high regard. He thought the Ugandan people were the most sophisticated and intelligent in Central Africa and had made several very close and lasting friendships. The world had thought that Julius Nyerere of Tanzania had been such a fine man because he had sent in his army to dislodge the monster, Idi Amin, and instal his friend Milton Obote who had been in exile in Dar-es-Salaam. Whereas Amin had been unpredictable and his secret police had been murderous, the country had still worked after a fashion. But Obote and the Tanzanian army had reduced the country to a

144

standstill and the slaughter had been worse than in Amin's days because it was systematic. Our group listened wide-eyed to some of his anecdotes.

Barbie's Diary: Monday, 23 August 1965.

". . . *gravel road until crossed into Uganda, then v. good tar from there on. Stopped in Tororo for groceries – modern clean town, good choice in shops. Lots of neat tea and coffee plantations – tea has avenues of trees. Den says they are windbreaks. Stopped at Jinja, the source of the Nile! All around are grounds like a huge park, grass mown and flowering trees, bougainvillaea. Rippon Falls pub, like back home in Aussie. Women washing clothes on rocks below the big dam wall where the Nile starts ...*

Went straight to Entebbe, friendly black people directed us to campsite on edge of Lake Victoria next to the Entebbe Sailing Club. Big trees and nice smooth lawn down to the sandy shore. The yacht club lets us use their hot showers and loos. There is also a German party camping; 2 men and 1 dolly-bird in one tent. African watchman popped over to see if we were OK. We had good dinner with fresh vegies and I slept well; a few mossies."

In the evening, Rob, Sarah, Ted and I went for a walk down to the lake shore, about five hundred yards away through maize fields and past two kraals. The people there were friendly and welcoming, naked children ran out waving. Along the shore there were neat vegetable patches like those at Speke Gulf, and further on a small forest of masts showed where a fishing fleet was beached. There was a storm hovering with some angry clouds, but the sun was setting under them with a rich golden light, so I hurried to the fishing fleet to take a photograph if I could. There were people bailing the boats and tidying their sails and we warily watched each other for a while until some young boys came up and cheekily greeted us. I showed one my camera and he screamed with delight, insisting that I take a picture. The adults signed that we could do so, but quietly moved out of the way. At the waterfront there were a number of birds, incredibly tame, picking at fish offal and the fresh water snails that teemed there. There were sacred ibis, yellow-billed and marabou storks, sea gulls, a hammerkop (exceptionally tame), wagtails, egrets and a large black bird with a divided bill that I could not identify. The mass of snails warned of bilharzia, for they are the host of this dangerous tropical parasite and I warned my friends about it.

The last night in East Africa, we camped in a deserted shamba where fields had not been ploughed for several seasons. It rained heavily at 1.30 in the morning and a thunderstorm centred itself over us at dawn. The lightning and instant cannon blasts of thunder were almost continuous and there seemed to be no movement of the black mass above, so we packed up in the teeming rain. The inside of the truck was full of steaming, wet bodies and soaked bedding when we set off.

Biharamulo was the last town in Tanzania that we would pass of any size, so Charlie stopped so that we could food shop. It was clearly a British colonial town for it stood magisterially on a hill and the storm-washed track that led to it off the main road had an ancient pine tree avenue. In the centre, bouganvillaea ran wild over a ruined building. It was an abandoned town though, except for a military post. The main street and market square were lined with dukas, many bearing their proud founders' names and dates: 'S. Moola and Son – 1936'. All were shuttered and closed but for two manned by sleepy Black women, selling the tail-end of old stocks. In the market, inhabited by about a dozen people, a couple of stalls sold tomatoes, onions, bananas and maize kernels. Towards the top of the hill, where colonial officialdom had comfortably roosted, there was a rickety metal tower with a microwave dish and next to it an air-conditioned, high-tech telephone exchange was being constructed. That is what the prim, official contractor's board proclaimed. I wondered what horrendous bureaucratic mess had produced that wasteful incongruity; maybe it had been scheduled fifteen years ago and some Commonwealth Aid finance had finally come through, so it was being built anyway to service a town that had now died. A smart army Landrover with regimental badges stood near the new building and an immaculate officer gestured with his swagger-stick. He was talking to an engineer in well-pressed slacks and long-sleeved shirt, wearing a bright yellow hard-hat. A hard-hat in Biharamulo!

In the afternoon, after entering increasingly mountainous country with volcanic looking rocky outcrops, we swept around a corner to see a large, steep-walled valley with a flat floor. Papyrus swamps bordered a swollen, muddy river that plunged over a foaming waterfall. The Tanzanian and Rwandan border posts stood on either side of a modern concrete bridge. This was the Kagera, considered by many to be the true source of the Nile. Apart from the shorter Mara River, which we had passed over twice, there are several major rivers and dozens of smaller streams pouring into Lake Victoria. But the Kagera with its two main tributaries is the greatest of these, a handsome river on its own, five hundred miles long, and it is claimed that its volume is great enough to produce a noticeable movement of water from its mouth in Lake Victoria to the main Nile exit at Jinja.

In the *National Geographic* Magazine of May 1985, Robert Caputo wrote, in *JOURNEY UP THE NILE*:

"From there [where the Kagera forms the boundary between Tanzania and Rwanda] I followed roads through Rwanda and Burundi that wound their way in and out of supremely beautiful agricultural valleys, the land of the Tutsi and Hutu people. Finally on a windswept hill in southern Burundi, I came to the end of my journey and the beginning of the Nile. A tiny trickle of water issued from the earth. Caput Nili, read a weathered metal plaque on a little stone pyramid – 'Source of the Nile'."

While Charlie had our passports processed together by the officials, we were able to stand on the border bridge and watch the thundering brown stream pour over the Rusumu Falls that lie only yards upstream from the bridge. That was an important moment for me. In December 1955, I had landed at Khartoum and observed the great joining of the White and Blue Niles. On 1st August 1965, I had seen the Nile at Cairo and several months later had watched it spout from the outlets of the Owen Stanley Dam at Jinja, on the site of the Rippon Falls. Lately, I had camped on the shore where Speke had first sighted the great Nyanza of which the Arabs had told him and which he had named Lake Victoria. That day, I stood clutching the concrete guardrail that trembled to the thunder of the waterfall beneath me, conscious that I was watching molecules of water that would flow into the Mediterranean Sea. I somehow felt linked, through it, to the mystery of more than four thousand years of civilisation which it had stimulated and supported.

147

PART FOUR:

ZAÏRE

CHAPTER TWELVE : *THE CULTURE VORTEX I*

VORTEX . . . 5. *fig.* A state or condition of human affairs or interests comparable to a whirl or eddy by reason of rush or excitement, a rapid change, or absorbing effect: 1761 . . . Shorter Oxford English Dictionary. Third edition 1944.

The farmer ploughs into the ground
More than the wheat-seed strewn on the ground
The farmer ploughs into the ground
The plough and the oxen and his body
He ploughs into the ground the farmstead and the cattle
And the pigs and the poultry and the kitchen utensils
And the afternoon sunlight shining into the window panes of the
voorhuis
And the light entangled in the eyes of the children
He ploughs into the ground his wife's brown body
And the windmill above the borehole
And the borehole and the wind driving the windmill,
The farmer ploughs the blue clouds into the ground;
And as a tribute to the holocaust of the ploughshare –
To the sowing that was the parting of the Juggernaut –
The earth rendered the farmer in due season
Corn.

SEED. Herman Charles Bosman [South African poet]

We drove through to Kigale, the capital of Rwanda, along a fine tarred highway. The road gave the country a strange feel, accentuated by the abrupt change in scenery and the appearance of the people. We travelled on a plateau which was riven by valleys; not very deep and not precipitous. The plateau was in a state of gentle erosion by high monsoon rainfall. Looking into the distance there were no outstanding mountains, just an endless landscape of interlocking valleys carrying the water away into the great lakes that surrounded this elevated island in the centre of Africa.

The population had a high density. In that part of Rwanda, the land was thoroughly cultivated and small villages and family kraals were distributed evenly as far as we could see into the hazy scene of hills and valleys. An early impression of the people we saw by the road side was the neatness and uniformity of their dress. Many of the women wore skirts and blouses of plain cloth, some had dark blue skirts and white blouses. The men were also neat in slacks and shirts. It gave the population a tidy and disciplined look, an air of purposefulness. This was reflected in their cultivation. What was outstanding about the landscape was the endless plantations of bananas. For mile after mile, bananas dominated. Along the course of the streams in the valley bottoms there were tidy emerald terraces of rice paddies, maize fields, carefully demarcated plots of coffee, mangoe orchards, paw-paws, sugar-cane, yams and cassava. Sheltering beneath the bananas, beans and ground-nuts were cultivated together with green vegetables, similar to what had impressed me around Arusha and in the well-watered country north of Lake Malawi. Wherever the hillsides were too steep for terraced agriculture there were clearly defined paddocks of pasture where cattle and goats grazed. The cattle were in great health, solid beasts with heavy uniformly shaped horns, local but selectively bred. Rocky hilltops were not abandoned to the bush, there were coppices of exotic eucalyptus for firewood or timber. This was peasant agriculture of an extremely high standard. I had never seen anything like it elsewhere in Africa and I watched with amazement. Looking into the hazy distance it all seemed the same, it was not a ribbon along the route of the highway.

We reached Kigale, the capital, in mid-morning, and it too was something different. A futuristic city was being carved out of a vast saucer where several shallow valleys joined, at a cost of tens of millions of dollars. The nuclei of residential suburbs, industrial parks, commercial and administrative centres were growing far apart with new roads under construction to link them. In the vacant spaces, the banana plantations and smallholdings were still there but being steadily cleared. The ugly rash of shantytowns, the universal African curse, was beginning.

"Do you know anything about all this?" I asked Charlie.

"No, I don't," he said. "It's quite amazing, isn't it? The last time I came through this way, we drove through Burundi where the countryside was similar, but there was nothing like this."

We stopped two days at the St Leon Mission in Gitarama. Charlie had often told us about the great Belgian Roman Catholic missions in Rwanda, Burundi and Zaïre, and St Leon was the most magnificent, in traditional style, that we visited. Apart from several chapels attached to the school, the convent and the seminary, there was a vast cathedral. Several hundred acres of farm were administered by the mission for their own needs and to teach improved methods to the peasants. One morning, Ted

151

and I walked up to the cathedral, a great yellow brick pile in a much simplified but traditional European Rennaisance style and to get there we passed through several quadrangles surrounded by residences, offices and meeting rooms. I spoke to a genial old Belgian priest in a mixture of English and Dutch: he had been there for many years.

A young Rwandan priest escorted us through the maze of buildings to the cathedral. He had been educated in Kampala, Uganda. I asked him if there was any trade in the huge quantities of bananas that were grown in the country, but he said there was none. They were all consumed locally. Bananas were the staple diet of the country, some were dried to make a sort of flour, others were processed into alcohol. In the villages, they were eaten raw, cooked with other vegetables to make a stewed dish and fermented to make a strong beer. He explained that the boys in the boarding school came from the élite Tutsi tribe and they were taught in English because although French was the official language, Rwanda was commercially oriented to Kenya and Uganda and English would be the important language of the future. He had heard that we had been mobbed by the boys the night before, and thanked us for our indulgence. It was good for their education, but they had been told to leave us alone that evening.

The cathedral was finished in fine style within. The floor was quarry-tiled in an attractive pale colour, the pantiled roof was supported by rough-cut but well-seasoned and selected beams of prime forest timber. The regular, fixed lines of hundreds of benches were of clean cut and polished pale hardwood. I sat at the back thinking of the incongruity of this great, lavishly crafted cathedral in the heart of one of the poorer countries of Africa, when all the children from the primary school filed in for their daily Mass. They wore uniforms of dark blue skirts or shorts and white shirts, echoing the clothing of the women I had seen along the road. The children peeled off to sit in their rows in complete silence, shepherded by young, attractive school-teachers. The whites of their eyes flashed in their dark faces as they peered sideways to see me. A priest entered at the far end and singing began. Four or five hundred young voices, singing familiar hymns with an African lilt, without accompaniment, resonating in that great building, was an exceptional sound. There were goose-pimples on my arms and there was water in my eyes.

The vast and complex question of cultural conflict was triggered in my mind that day at the St Leon mission. The quite extraordinarily vast banana plantations sharpened previous ideas about the evolution of the

Bantu cultural and tribal group, so important to half of Africa. Years of thought and reading seemed to explode in my mind as clear themes.

Rwanda is a small country with periods of distasteful history since Independence. Together with its neighbour Burundi, it was a German colony in 1914 and after World War I, Belgium took up these two territories and ruled them as League of Nations' Mandates. When Belgium precipitately abandoned the Congo in 1960, Rwanda and Burundi followed into immediate Independence without regard for the tribal structures in these two, apparently insignificant, little countries. For the previous fifty years the tribal political structures had been held in limbo. But there are two dissimilar tribes who inhabit this region, the minority but select Tutsi, who are Nilotic and related to peoples who live in the north of Uganda, and the Hutu, who are of the great Bantu cultural group. In the post-Independence period there had been frightful massacres and anarchy as tribal ascendancy and political stability was sought after the long period of colonial control. However, new stability in Rwanda gripped by the MRND party machine and its President, Juvenal Habyarimana, had been achieved in 1973 through a military coup. Lately, democratic structures were appearing.

Rwanda had achieved home-grown political stability, but its economy and development was largely in the hands of expatriate advisers, the neo-colonists. The astounding revelation of a 'new-improved', pre-packaged city in the style of a mini-Brasilia under construction at Kigale seemed the ultimate example of this. The universal panacea for Third World countries was being applied in little Rwanda: if in doubt, build a modern, hi-tech city as an industrial focus, a 'growth point', and all will be well. That it may draw wide-eyed, hopeful peasants from producing food on the land to build lawless, chaotic shanty towns inhibiting industrial investment in the future is a problem for local politicians and the advisers who will follow after. Presently, they concern themselves with the more exciting projects of managing the finances, training the security forces (defence budget 1982: US $30 M), devising commercial strategies and spending Western capital on possibly inappropriate infra-structures. (External public debt in 1982: US $189 M). Therefore, who was engaged with the perceived orderly milieu of the peasants who are still 95% of the people? The answer seemed to be the basic Bantu tribal culture supported by the discipline of the Catholic Missions and the Government party machine. According to U.N. figures, Rwanda has a per capita GNP of about US $250,00 per annum, (remarkably similar to Malawi), but observation showed that the people were poor but still not impoverished, any more than in Malawi.

Therefore the apparently catastrophic GNP indicates that most of the economy is still outside the monetary system. The people are largely self-sufficient peasant farmers. Presently, it seemed to me that this was highly satisfactory. But for how long? Could the inertia of established peasant culture compete with the influence of expatriate aides and advisers working hard to convert them to a model of their own devising? Development was no doubt being pursued as the only perceived panacea for exploding populations, which the Roman Catholic Church had fostered and was actively continuing to do. (46% of the population below the age of 15 years; 3.5% growth per annum, a doubling every twenty years). Rwanda seemed to me to illustrate the dilemma of Africa in microcosm, especially since it seemed to be an ideal country to 'engineer': small and fertile with high rainfall, industrious people, commercially virginal, and the rural social environment kept in order by the morally irreproachable missionaries and national Party machine.

African spiritual belief had been held to be primitive and savage, principally because Christian Europeans and Moslem Arabs could not find a dogmatic religion to grapple with. Missionaries found that they seemed to be working in a godless, illiterate vacuum crying out to be filled. To their astonishment, early Christian missionaries discovered that it was almost impossible to convert the heathen and this confirmed their heathenness and stupidity, they were incapable of visualising the glory of civilised religion. But, apparent success miraculously followed the imposition of formal colonial administration and the significance of this was misinterpreted. It is only recently that many missionaries have come to accept that their dogma may not be suited to Africa, and the response has usually been to 'Africanise' their services, allow drums and marimbas into churches, portray Christ as a Black man and add other interpretive changes. Privately, priests will acknowledge that Christianity is losing its following since Independence. Others insist that a new, African-style Christianity is emerging. In the long term, the latter view may be correct in practice, but what is emerging is not an Afro-Christianity, but a reasserting of African beliefs with the acquired clothing of some of the forms of Christianity.

Lyall Watson wrote in *Lifetide* (1979):

"It seems appropriate too that in these new endeavours it is the most

154

heavily funded programmes, those sponsored by purely practical and military concerns and involving the most complex machinery in elaborate experiments of great scientific precision, that are turning out the most simple poetic truths. . . . We are beginning to feel involved. To experience the universe and our participation in it as one dynamic, inseparable whole; an organism, ever-moving and alive; spiritual and material all at the same time."

In Africa, the physical is not the total of life. The base of all African cultural tradition is the real acceptance of the fourth dimension of time, so that the line of one's ancestors with the complete matrix of the past is woven into one's present existence. Taken to its logical limit, all people, all Life in fact, are clearly linked to the Creator in a simple unshakeable faith. Like all things in Africa, I have found that traditional philosophy has a symmetry of perfection that has been lost in the complexities of Civilisation. Especially, this becomes a revelation, when the spiritual aspect of a problem is related to the physical world. One simple example may be that practical good sense recommends that after unusual death or epidemics to people or livestock, it is wise to move to a new site away from pollution or other sources of disease. Consideration for the peace of soul for those who have passed on is the supporting spiritual imperative for a physical upheaval which otherwise would be unpopular.

In the grander concept of ultimate connection with the Creator in infinite time, it is interesting that our modern science is now speculating on the universality of life and its relation to its incredibly far distant origins, probably beyond our own Earth, through the descent and evolution of genes. Genes are the living link, and we can isolate and study them within their DNA chains. Lyall Watson has pointed to the growing speculation that members of species such as humankind, which have a demonstrably finite existence from birth to death, are merely the pathways taken by the ever-living genes in their eternal march through the fourth dimension of time. Substituting spirits for genes, this is the reality of universal life that is accepted by African peoples, whereas the grand Civilisations have manufactured complex religious dogmas that seem to have little relation to the Universe as we now observe it. It is only through the clarity of micro-biology that we are wearily circling back to the traditional beliefs of Africa.

The importance of the belief in the spiritual links backwards to the foundation of all Life, the Creator, is that the total practical wisdom of the tribe in survival technique and in maintaining social stability is reinforced by the power or force of the combined spirits of the ancestors.

155

Spiritually reinforced practical wisdom relates to the conservation of the environment, hunting and gathering, herding and breeding of livestock, ploughing and sowing of seeds, harvesting and storage, medicines and curing, birth-control and child-rearing, education and marriage, property and land, death and inheritance. Thus, practical lore and social laws are inseparable from the spiritual matrix of past generations who developed the love and the laws. What is horrific is that the pool of human wisdom in Africa has been diluted, if not polluted, by the missionary zeal of classical Civilisations and their religions.

In South Africa at the beginning of the safari, I had been reminded of the powerful African churches. South African Blacks have been subject to the most vigorous European cultural influence of all Africans. Therefore it is not surprising that in South Africa the strongest para-Christian or neo-Christian movements have arisen in reaction to the sterility of European dogma in its attempts to tackle the grander problems of life in an African context.

An article appeared in the South African *The Daily News*, of 1 August, 1986, written by Garry Brennan, and an extract is relevant:

"The independent churches and mainline, orthodox churches seem to be poles apart, with misunderstandings on both sides.

"The rift in religious movements is a worry to church leaders and academics who are aware of the tremendous growth of the independent churches and their influence on Black perceptions.

"In 1930 the [South African] Zion Christian Church, for example, had 926 members; today it claims a membership of more than four million.

"In 1948 there were 800 independent denominations. Today there are 3270, with six million members. Membership has increased from nine percent of the Black population to almost 40 percent today . . .

". . . In some of the churches there is an over-emphasis on the Holy Spirit, Umoya. This must be seen against an African cultural background in which power, the vital force, is seen in everything: the body — sometimes leading to muti (magic objects) rites — and plants and of course the sea. . .

". . . the independent churches [of South Africa] are the fastest-growing religious movement in Africa. Mainline church leaders — especially Anglican Archbishop Desmond Tutu, who has been critical of the Zion church in particular — will need to study the extent of their differences with the independents and come to terms, or risk losing control of more of their flocks."

156

The observation of the extent that bananas are the staple food of Rwanda and the uniformity of Bantu language and culture over half of Africa may seem to be unrelated, but the bananas were confirmation by direct observation of the likely reason for this vast uniformity.

When Speke and Stanley separately first visited the lands which make up modern Uganda in the 1870s and 80s, they also found that the staple food was the banana. I was aware of the importance of the banana in Central and West Africa when we entered Rwanda. Nevertheless, I was astounded by the enormous acreages of land that were planted with this rich food producer. Those bananas were planted and tended by peasants for local consumption long before Europeans arrived. The greater significance of this is that the banana is not indigenous to Africa. It was introduced by Indonesian, Indian and Arab traders of the Indian Ocean system probably about two thousand years ago. The banana plantations of Rwanda are spectacular evidence of the importance of exotic plants in Africa, but there are many others introduced long before European contact such as: yams, sugar-cane, citrus, rice, cotton and coconut palms. Sophisticated agricultural methods, plantations and extensive terracing were being employed by Africans from Uganda to Zimbabwe, when Europeans first entered their lands. Maize was introduced later by the Portuguese.

Most authorities seem agreed that the origins of the Bantu cultural-tribal group were in the deciduous forests, north of the rain forest, of Eastern Nigeria and the Cameroon more than two thousand years ago. These related tribes must have been numerically small, but fate had placed them in an extraordinarily strategic position, located on the edge of the Sahara and immediately to the north and west of the Congo Basin. They were pastoralists, herding cattle and goats. A stimulus started a population explosion that led them to expand, not migrate, in two directions, probably synchronously. One expansion route was around the top of the impenetrable Congo Basin to today's Uganda, Kenya, Rwanda-Burundi, eastern Zaïre and western Tanzania. They were prevented from northward movement by long-established Nilotic and Cushitic peoples. The other expansion route, necessarily more difficult and slower because of areas of rainforest, was down the west coast and thereafter into the savannahs of southern Zaïre, northern Angola and Zambia. In this zone, the two movements met, but there was plenty of land to the south occupied only by Neolithic Khoisan hunter-gatherers and herders. The fact that this extraordinary colonisation of half a Continent took place through expansion and not migration, suggests that the stimulus was not flight from territorial conquerors, but a population explosion resulting from the introduction of new food and technology cultures.

The sources of these are clear. Firstly, across the Sahara came iron smelting and agricultural technology based on Sahelian grains. Iron and agricultural know-how triggered the Bantu into moving east and south. They could not expand westward, because the neighbouring Black people also received the same technology which stimulated their own growth. These West Africans could not expand therefore they developed a series of sophisticated kingdoms and empires with large towns, Ghana, Mali, Yoruba, Benin, over the following millenium and more. Secondly, high-value, exotic foods were being introduced to East and then Central Africa from the Indian Ocean and were filtering through to West Africa. The Bantu, already expanding eastwards with newly acquired Iron-age agricultural know-how, were able to exploit the yams, bananas and others that they encountered and this stimulus added impetus to the population growth and furthered expansion into the whole of the southern part of the Continent. Quite rapidly the whole of East-Central-South Africa was thinly occupied by Bantu people between about 100 and 300 AD. Linguistic and cultural differences suggest that the vanguard of this movement was broken into three main parts, the Nguni tribal group along the eastern coast, a central group from Zaïre southwards, and a western group in Angola and Namibia.

Much later, there were other events that disturbed the Bantu peoples before the middle of the 19th century, when the sustained European colonial period began in earnest. The first was in the 9th century when Moslem Arab trading expansion to Sofala and further south triggered the Katangan and Zimbabwean empires. The second was the introduction of maize and expanded Portuguese trade into southern Mozambique and Natal in the late 18th century which triggered the Nguni invasions of Central and East Africa and the rise of the Zulu kingdom. The influence of Moslem Arab and Portuguese colonies on the East African coast caused disruption in the interior too and warrior tribes thrashed about. European slaving in Angola and intensified Arab slaving in Central Africa in the 18th and 19th centuries caused shock and disruption.

My thinking expanded and crystallised further, later on in Zaïre.

We stopped for lunch by a lovely, clean mountain stream rushing down from the high forest. Views were superb towards the Western Rift Valley with grey-purple-blue monsoon cloud cover and mist trailing from the trees.

Suddenly there was sight of silver Lake Kivu and mountains rising into cloud on the other side, in Zaïre. There was a lump in my thoat and my belly twisted with excitement – we were truly entering another Africa. To the north, three volcanoes – one perfect steep cone, and two others with jagged peaks stood, all over 14,000 feet. They had a strange, ominous look. The whole atmosphere of that approach to Lake Kivu had a weirdness to it, an unreality. I kept reminding myself that it was me there in real time, in that truck, with these people, in that place.

Our descent into the Western Great Rift Valley became an emotional watershed for me and I was conscious of its power. Retrospection has not reduced it. Our entry into the rainforest, the monsoon weather that was prevalent, the intense changes in the social environment that we had begun to experience were strong geographical effects. Intellectually, I had been looking forward to visiting this part of Africa, because of its great historical importance. All my expectations were exceeded. Comparisons between this and that part of the safari are pointless, but the next six weeks were to have an almost traumatic impact.

Leaving Rwanda was easy, but the Zaïre border post on the other side of a bridge was the curtain-raiser to the different bureaucracy of Central and West Africa. It took hours and a US $40 bribe to save us from stripping the truck for customs inspection. The bribe also exempted us from filling in currency declaration forms and having all our money (about US $10,000 in cheques and bills at that stage) counted out by sticky fingered officials. Charlie had half-heartedly suggested to the Chef that we would need stamped forms when we left the country, but he was smilingly assured that there was a new law, we would be all right. This proved to be a mistake, but Charlie was understandably keen to get away from that post while the Chef was still amiable. He had commenced his midday drinking routine and Charlie had also given him a bottle of whisky.

We drove around Bukavu for a while before parking in the long main street that descends a gentle hill to the lakeside. It was the largest town that we were to pass through between Nairobi and Bangui, the capital of the Central African Republic. The centre occupied a promontory that stuck out into the lake. On the mainland shoulders and on two smaller promontaries there was a substantial 'European' suburbia, neat brick and pantiled bungalows stood in ordered rows. Verandahed houses and Mediterranean villas of substantial size in large grounds with mature eucalyptus, palms, mangoes and monkey-puzzle trees lorded it on the heights above the town and along the waterfront. Bougainvillaea and flowering oleanders provided colour. Several steamships were at the small port furnished with warehouses and cranes and there was a yacht basin. The main street was lined for a distance of about a mile with shops and boutiques in the recognisable style of the 1930s with bland curves and high façades. There were two hotels, one was the commercial, town-centre establishment, and the Riviera Hotel overlooked Lake Kivu from a fine position at the end of the promontory where tourists could languish at ease. The streets were lined with palms and flame trees. The feathery outlines of jacarandas, that powerful exotic symbol of European settlement broke the skyline.

All the evidence of a thriving, bustling town was there. But it was almost deserted. Most of the brick bungalows were closed and heavily shuttered. The gardens were overgrown. One of the suburban promontories was shut off by a security barrier manned by an armed askari; there were still some of the local élite hiding there. The steamships in the port were sunk or beached, the cranes rusted and the warehouses empty. The shops in the main street were in disrepair with mould-stained paintwork and cracked or broken windows, several were long abandoned. Most of those that were open had few goods, spread optimistically on dusty shelves. One small 'supermarket' owned by a Belgian had imported stocks and European delicatessen and we mobbed it with relief, but outside the concrete slabbed roadway had cracks and broken patches. The Riviera Hotel was shabby and run down, its 1930s colonial charm lost forever.

That evening we camped by the lake, about five miles out of town. A scenic road had been built along the shore and an old rickety sign proclaimed that the area was a public garden and resort. We pitched our tents on a flat-topped mound between the road and the steep banks and we had a good evening. The mouth of my tent opened onto the panorama of lake and distant mountains. Several of us swam in the clear water, we washed clothes and built a crackling fire. Aussie Steve played some of his non-rock tapes and we all had a few drinks around the fire, talking and joking easily. Socially, our group was now blended, and we were used to each other and there was cohesion. Marie had recovered from a bout of malaria and we were all fit. The rain held off and there were no mosquitoes.

The next morning Charlie went into town to see if he could buy tyres to replace two that we had to abandon since leaving Nairobi and to find out how we could visit the gorillas in the nearby *Parc National du Kahuzi-Biega*, on the road to Kabunga, in the hills of the Rift Valley escarpment above us to the west. The more famous gorilla sanctuary is in northern Rwanda, in the forests clothing the volcanoes which we had seen and which had so impressed me. The research station where the American, Dian Fossey, lived and worked for many years with several groups of gorillas was placed between Mounts Karisimbi and Visoke which stand on the Rwanda-Zaïre border. She was to gorillas as Jane Goodall is to chimpanzees in the Gombe sanctuary on the shore of Lake Tanganyika. Dian Fossey devoted eighteen years to her gorillas with little publicity and it was at her camp that Nicholas Humphrey (*THE INNER EYE*) had begun to achieve his insights into the mind of apes and men. Some of her story about her beloved gorillas and their steady depredation by poachers seeking saleable souvenir hands and skulls was told in *National Geographic* Magazine of April 1981, *THE IMPERILED MOUNTAIN GORILLA*. Dian Fossey was killed, probably by poachers, in December 1985, just a month after we drove past the rugged peak of Mount Karisimbi. We would have visited her sanctuary but for the fact that the rainy season had made the roads in that area suspect and so we had come to Bukavu.

Charlie returned with the news that tyres were unobtainable, but we had to get a move on as he had made arrangements for guides in the Kahuzi-Biega Park. We drove up a valley through the busy village of Tshibinda, where children called and waved to us, until we breasted the crown of the escarpment and parked by the side of the road near the guide post. A smart young man who spoke good English awaited us with three rugged older men in worn blue overalls. High up, the clouds were gathered and the forest dripped with moisture, but the rain held off. I did not know what to expect, but was determined to get pictures so I dug out my 200 mm lens and fixed it to a camera. We set off in single file down a footpath into the valley to the west, clambering over tree roots, ducking through heavy growth, squelching across marshy patches of the stream we followed, the soft earthy smell of the rainforest in our nostrils. It needed all my concentration to negotiate the steep path and look after my camera and its heavy lens. Occasionally the guides cut at a hanging creeper or intruding branch with what I thought of as a 'token hack at the jungle'. Inconsequentially, in my nervousness, I saw us tracking romantically through the impenetrable jungles of the Congo, Tarzan and Jane were close to us.

Suddenly, the young *Chef des Guides* held up his hand and warned in a low voice that we must not panic or move abruptly. There was the noise of bodies moving in the thick growth on the hillside above us to the left. We all turned in that direction. I cocked my camera, time was moving in slow motion.

There was the sound of heavy hands being clapped. "He's beating his chest," I breathed, "like King Kong!" Dave, standing in front of me, turned to give me a nervous smile. Then he was there! Five feet away! Dave involuntarily stepped back into me and I steadied him without thinking. The great silver-backed male crouched there, quietly, unmoving, watching us. He was directly in front of Dave and I, and I looked straight into his eyes for moments that seemed to last hours. I *knew* that we communicated. It was like a psychic electric shock, and I kept saying inside my head, over and over: "I love you, brother. I love you, I love you, I love you." Time really stood still. But my complicated human mind was working; I had to take photographs and raised my camera. Of course, it was the wrong lens. He was so close that I struggled to focus on the whites of his eyes and the shine of his nostrils. I changed the speed to 1/60th but it was still insufficient exposure in the darkness of the forest, but I dared not reduce the speed further, so I shot off a couple of hopeless frames. I became aware of the clicking of cameras all around me, and the tension was broken. Suddenly he was gone and there were crashing sounds all about as the troop moved away.

I stood as the others scrambled past me until I was alone. Without warning, sobs of emotion wracked me. I had met our closest relative in the Universe and we had stared at each other, peacefully, with curiosity and with tremendous emotion on my part. I knew that we had met each other's psyches. Tears ran down my face. Katie came back to me and hugged me. I was grateful for her understanding, and I stumbled down the path after our group.

We stopped in a clearing and the *Chef des Guides* explained that he knew where another family troop might be, and he would take us there. He was explaining the composition of the troop and describing the habits of gorillas. I could not tolerate the atmosphere of a guided tour that inevitably was growing, so I called out that I wished to return to the truck. He was nonplussed, I think, but Charlie had also grasped how I felt, and asked if one of the other guides could be spared. So, a kind, ugly-faced older man was detailed to take me back. I explained to him in my awful French that it had been an *"experience encroyable"* and that *"j'ai fait tout, c'est finis."* He smiled at me and gripped my shoulder.

The giant silver-backed gorilla at Kahuzi–Biega, Zaïre.
(Photo: Katie Hale)

Back on the lakeshore we drove north along a narrow dirt road that was well maintained to begin with but gradually deteriorated. Heavy cloud came over and it began to drizzle. We passed several abandoned colonial homesteads, barns and sheds, most still in good external order, none of them occupied, yet alongside there were wattle-and-daub, palm thatched huts with chickens scuttling and children waving tentatively. Small patches of bananas, manioc, coffee, beans and maize were cultivated in the forest. It was a pattern that we became used to. Through gaps in the dark trees we caught sight of the shining silver lake with the black shapes of islands floating irregularly in it. It was sombrely beautiful.

Next day after an uncomfortable, damp night, the three volcanoes were suddenly quite close, each with its head buried in a menacingly dark purple cloud. Charlie told me that successive lava flows from the volcanoes of this area had devastated the landscape during this century. At the northern end of Lake Kivu, we drove over a lava causeway and onto a tarred road that ran in a straight line for seventeen miles across a rolling sea of dark-grey, clinkered lava, fuzzed with light vegetation.

"When did this happen?" I asked Charlie.

"I'm not sure. I think somebody told me the 1940s, but there would have been many earlier eruptions."

The sun was shining from a torn sky when we entered Goma, a town built in a modern rectangular grid on flat land fronting the lake. Like Bukavu, the colonial centre was practically deserted, but its flat spread showed no hint of the charm that Bukavu must have had. We parked outside the Masque Hotel which was a sudden oasis of Europe. There was the faint aroma of garlic and wine hovering in the bar-restaurant furnished in dark, polished wood. The water ran falteringly from the taps in the loo. Outside, there were chairs and tables set on tiled paving beneath pergolas with flowering vines. I drank an ice-cold Coke and watched an immaculately uniformed Belgian para colonel chatting up two slim, designer-clothed, dishy blonde girls. His gold-striped black kepi stood on the table with leather gloves folded carelessly on the top; his greying hair matched his eyes which crinkled in charming smiles as he talked to the girls, who lounged, touching their coiffed, sun-streaked hair and adjusting their giant, graduated sunglasses. I found him alien with his smooth paunch stretching his crisply pressed, pale khaki, finely woven shirt with its gold badges and insignia. My bush-sensitive nostrils could smell the mingle of his after-shave and the girls' perfume. They gave us one amused glance.

At some time I had read an article by an old Congo hand who had returned after twenty-five years to the Hotel du Lac on one of the Western

Rift Valley lakes and had written wittily on its appearance of having stood still since he had been there before the catastrophic chaos at Independence. The barman at the Masque Hotel told me that there was such an hotel closer to the waterfront, so I persuaded Ted to accompany me there. It was indeed the Grande Hotel du Lac, but it bore no resemblance to the description in the article which told of views from a hillside, an elegant dining room in Swiss 1920s style, with the original leather-bound wine-list still in use, but with no wine in the cellar. The Goma version was probably from the 1950s and had little style. Its present state was similar to that of the Riviera Hotel in Bukavu. I asked the clerk in reception about my problem and he grinned.

"Ah. Je comprends. L'hôtel est à Kasenyi près du Lac Albert. Pas du Kivu. C'est très bien."

"Sorry, Ted," I apologised. "Wild goose chase."

"Well, let's see if the beer is cold," he suggested.

The visit was not wasted, because we came across an interesting scene. It was a Sunday and the shabby dining room was filled with smartly dressed Whites, some of the women quite elegant as if they were lunching in Cannes. It explained the senior Belgian army officer in full regimentals and his chic girls. But what were they all doing in Goma? The clerk tried to explain when I asked him on the way out, but I could not follow his French. I understood vaguely that they were from nearby.

We eventually pitched camp in spitting drizzle, in the dark, on a raft of lava by the lake shore in the compound of a battery-chicken farm. There was not a breath of air and the black night seemed to lean on me. The tent pegs either disappeared into cracks in the sharp clinker, or bent as we hammered them into unseen solid rock. I lost one and it took ages to get my tent up. I was exhausted and seemed to pull my clothes off and climb into my sleeping-bag in some slow-motion movie observed from a height. I felt drunk, but had only consumed about half a litre of Primus beer hours before at the Hotel du Lac.

In the morning, I awoke with the sun shining on my tent. It was 7.30 a.m. and I could not understand it. I lay for what transpired to be about another half-hour, half-conscious, telling myself to get up. My naked body felt strange to my hands. I thought that I had to be ill, but knew I had no fever. Eventually, I crawled out and found the rest of the camp still pitched, to my relief. Rough mounds of grey-black clinker reared around us, patchily covered with a tough green ground-creeper. A rugged, lava mountain loomed above us close to. Most of my companions were sitting moodily about, some were washing clothes. Charlie and Katie, who were sharing a tent by then, were looking pale and wan.

"Charlie's not well," Katie told me. "We had a terrible night. You don't look good, either."

"I feel drugged," I said. "I can hardly move a limb."

"Charlie says it's the gas from the lake."

I couldn't think. "What do you mean?"

"There's gas in this lake, but Charlie thought it would be all right here by the chickens. An Overland-type girl died further along last year. She was swimming and suddenly gave up; just went under. Apparently a dog was found dead by the water last week and an African who was boozing didn't wake up after falling asleep in a hollow in the lava."

"Jesus H. Christ, Katie," I said, my brain straining to work. "We could have died last night."

"You're absolutely right!" she nodded. "We nearly did. Charlie was hallucinating in the night. We moved our tent up there and it took about two hours, falling around on this lava. He's cut his legs. It was awful."

Bob came around. "O.K. Let's get the show on the road. We're getting out of here. Let's go!"

It seemed a great effort to pack the camp until a cool breeze blew up and we all received an infusion of energy. By the time we had reached Goma I felt fine. We regained our spirits, teasing Al about being 'over the hill' because he was forty-one that day. He was happy because he had caught Radio South Africa on his short-wave set that morning and was full of world news that we had not heard since leaving Nairobi. Al liked to keep up with events.

North of Goma there was a tarmac airfield with an aircraft museum parked around it: several battered Dakotas, a D.C.4 with faded 'Liberian Airways' logo, old-fashioned turbo-prop planes, which Al said were Russian, and something that looked like a 1950s-style British piston-engined airliner. The airfield explained the Belgian para colonel and although I did not see military aircraft, they had to be there somewhere. The airfield bordered the extensive lava field which filled the whole width of the Rift Valley north of the lake, It was like a glacier composed of coke and power-station ash. Parts, which were demonstrably older, were tempered by a light covering of green, whilst tongues and giant puddles with dark surfaces proved fresh flows. In the middle of the clinker glacier there were cones and lumps like giant, frozen bubbles and bursts where minor eruptions had occured. The road crossed the lower slopes of Mount Karisimbi (14,790 feet), with its great cone all jagged at the top, clouds trailing wispily across it. I watched it pass by, trying to imagine the sight and thunder of a major eruption. I had no thought for Dian Fossey amongst her gorillas, my mind was full of the awful power of molten rocks in the heart of our world, and the sly killer breath that can sneak out on a still night, frighteningly touch you and so easily snuff fragile warm-blooded life away. We had been very close to death.

The clouds bore down on us again in Rutshuru, a long straggly new town, definitely African in style with an old colonial administrative building in the centre, plastered with M.P.R. [Movement Populaire de Revolution] party slogans. In contrast to Bukavu and Goma, the streets were busy with relaxed people. This was the Zaïre I had been looking for and I felt a close rapport with the atmosphere. In my diary, I described the style as a sort of 'controlled social anarchy': a remarkable air of ease and lack of all pretensions. I knew I could squat at the side of the road and chat with a friend and no one would give me a second glance; a trivial thought perhaps, but it was the feeling I had. Charlie asked us if we wanted to stop at a hotel or carry on into the bush. With a grin, he suggested that we had not properly celebrated Al's birthday. There was no doubt about Charlie's preference and we loudly agreed. We pitched our tents in the tidy compound of the Katara Hotel, which was no more than a row of rooms, a simple shower and toilet combined, but without a bar or restaurant. There were several open-sided thatched rondavels with seats under their shelter.

"Where's the bar, then, Charlie?" asked Steve, anxiously.

"There's a super bar-restaurant across the road, but this place is much cheaper for camping."

We had a great evening in what one of us described as a five-star Affie hotel. Within a rectangle of rooms there was a courtyard with numerous small palms, red-flowering hibiscus bushes, variegated crotons and patterned beds of ice-plants. In the centre of the court was a cement dance floor and a smart, intimate lounge area with four large booths around a central circular bar. Coloured lights were strung around and the bar was softly illuminated with yellow and orange bulbs. Zaïre boogie played through speakers scattered about; the volume was reasonable and the sound system was hi-fi. I was delighted with the place and joined Charlie, Katie, Al, Bob, Ted, Cathie and Claire in one of the booths. We were presented with an elaborate hand-lettered menu and wine list by a gentle barman in a crisp white uniform. The prices were the most reasonable I had seen since Malawi. On the walls of the bar were several polite notices addressed to 'Chère Visiteur'. One of those great, spontaneous parties built naturally. Charlie decided that I was the most sophisticated of our group, therefore, for some obscure reason, I should have a bottle of Ricard and a bucket of ice placed before me. The girls sampled liqueurs, Charlie found some single-malt whisky, whilst iced Primus beer flowed down Bob's throat like a waterfall. A few locals happily joined us, well-dressed professionals or officials, and Charlie outdid himself in the role of an English gentleman-explorer. The rest of our group occupied other booths. Angie decided that she "just loved" Zaïre music and Zaïre men. (We had been told quite a few times that she had a 'big' West Indian boy-friend back in the U.K.). From time to time we all went onto the dance floor to boogie, dancing without partners, like Kunduchi Beach in Tanzania. It was marvellous. With some surprise in her voice, one of our girls said I was the best boogie dancer in our group. I decided that Zaïre was definitely a very fine country.

In the morning, I asked the hotel clerk where to chuck our garbage and he kindly took it away for me. Garbage was an emotive subject. I could have prepared a catalogue over the whole safari of the particular shortages in different areas, dependent on what children and other spectators selected. In some places it was always tins and bottles and in others it was any kind of paper or plastic bags or wrappers or old reading material. Only once, in Niger, did I see children meticulously scraping together all our vegetable peelings, so it was not food they were after. Somebody once asked me if I did not find it disturbing to let our garbage be picked over, but I was not embarassed because the children or people who did it were not. We were not introducing luxurious and exotic garbage; we bought goods and food in the local markets and town shops, we were frugal and did not waste. Our garbage was no different to that of any local urban family.

We proceeded northwards along the floor of the Rift Valley. It was narrow with steep sides, filled with rain forest again for a while. After the town, cultivation and people disappeared for we had entered the Virunga National Park which included the Valley and all of Lake Edward ahead of us. Quite abruptly, the great escarpment wall faded away to our right hand and simultaneously the vegetation changed to savannah: grass and scattered thornbushes. It had to be the opening up of the Rift to a distance of many miles that caused a drop of rainfall and thus a decline in the high trees, I thought. We also came across a strong river flanked by rich riverine vegetation running northwards and drove alongside. It was the Rutshuru River which rose in mountains in Uganda whose border lay just about eight miles east of Rutshuru town. The river flows into Lake Edward, which empties via the Semliki River into Lake

Albert which also receives the Victoria Nile, and these combined waters then flow away north to the Mediterranean. Once again, as at the Kagera, there were molecules of water which were starting off beside us on that gargantuan journey. Truly, there were many fountains of that great African artery, just as Ptolemy had foretold. Beside the river, where we stopped to brew tea and met a British Overland truck going south, we walked in baking sunshine on washed sand with many plate-sized prints of elephants and the spoor of antelope. There were hippos grunting in the water, and crocodiles on the opposite bank. How many have heard of the Virunga Park? Later that day, driving across a grassy stretch we stopped to watch a whole pride of lions with gambolling cubs. In addition, we saw Cape buffaloes, warthogs, waterbuck, crested cranes, baboons, vervet monkeys, and Uganda kob (similar to the lechwe of the Okavango in Botswana). In the distance, Lake Edward came into sight, a thin silver-blue line on the horizon beyond the pale green of the savannah. Purple thunderclouds roved the far eastern escarpment, well into Uganda.

From the western escarpment wall, up which we slowly laboured, the panorama was breathtaking. We stopped for a while to take photographs and absorb the view. Whereas the Rift Valley north of Nairobi had been dry and sere, here it was green and humid. In Kenya the enormity of nature's majesty was tempered by the knowledge that there were many people about: vehicles constantly rushed along the tarred highways, there were the bustling towns of Naivasha and Nakuru. Above all, the Kenyan Rift Valley was so public; so many books had been written, so many tourists had raved. Saying farewell to the green emptiness of the Western Rift there and looking into the soft milky haze of Lake Edward across to the dim mysteries of the mountains in Uganda, I was acutely aware of the absence of people, the remoteness of contaminating civilisation. Only the thin red line of the rutted dirt track connected us with the rest of the world. The only humans we had seen the whole day were fifteen Overlanders, like us, adventuring in this Eden.

> The beasts that roam over the plain
> My form with indifference see;
> They are so unacquainted with man,
> Their tameness is shocking to me.
>
> THE SOLITUDE OF ALEXANDER SELKIRK – W. Cowper

CHAPTER FOURTEEN : *RENDEZVOUS WITH A MERCENARY*

I cannot blind myself
to putrefying carcasses in the market place
pulling giant vultures
from the sky.
HOW CAN I SING? Odia Ofeimun [African poet].

From the crest of the grand *Escarpement de Kabasha* our route led us north along the jumbled landscape of highlands west of the Rift Valley, then westwards through the green jungle-lands of the famed Ituri Rain-Forest.

Shortly after leaving the spectacular panorama of the Rift Valley and Lake Edward, we approached a large, sprawling town surrounded by extensive terraced agriculture and pockets of fruit trees. It was an African town, entirely composed of mud-brick buildings with thatched roofs spreading over a hillside and along a shallow valley. Its layout was decidedly African: the huts lay in a pattern, but the pattern was shaped by the contours of the land. From a distance, it seemed a formless mass; at close range, the natural curves that the lines of huts formed, converging and separating, crystallised into pleasing lines. We halted by the small, busy market and walked around. Some of the stalls stocked manufactured goods with the same extraordinary origins that we saw all over Zaïre: Imperial Leather soap as always, 'cold-water' Omo from South Africa, Johnny Walker whisky; other goods from Thailand, Kenya, Belgium, France . . .

The carefully swept, tiny yards around the huts in this town were bounded by neatly clipped hedges that would have graced Home Counties suburbia. Hibiscus bushes bloomed; I saw carefully tended crotons, Christ-thorn and red-hot-pokers with their luminous columns of blossom. Each hut had an enamelled metal number-plate, odd numbers along one line, even along the next. It was the first time that this particular phenomenon, exclusive to Zaïre, was so forcibly impressed on me. Here were typical indigenous homes with the atmosphere and style of undisturbed Africa, yet integrated into the milieu there were selected bits and pieces of Europe; cultivated decorative plants and an unselfconscious orderliness. In this town, and in hundreds of villages and kraals that we passed through in the next weeks, across tribal boundaries and hundreds of miles of bush roads, this amazing integration of culture persisted. This town showed no evidence of old colonial presence, the only official building was a large mud house near the market with a hand-lettered sign, M.P.R., proclaiming it as the local Party H.Q. Elsewhere in Africa, as we had seen,

African villages co-exist with European culture, with simple copies of shops and churches, the more elaborate houses of the wealthier residents constructed as mirrors of colonial bungalows. Zaïre was different. I had been puzzled by the large, empty colonial towns of Bukavu and Goma. I had not yet solved the problem of abandoned Belgian villas and farmsteads. Now, I was wondering at the first large town we had encountered which had obviously never had White residents. There was a magic to this country that was growing in my mind.

A strange incident occurred as I returned to the market which shocked me and sharpened my thoughts as powerfully as a lightning strike. The scene was normal: people wandering about the stalls, bargaining, gossiping, laughing or lazing. Suddenly there was a rush down one of the alleys between the curving rows of huts and a blood-curdling ululation that was to become familiar in other places: the sound of hundreds of children calling together, a strange hyena-like call, a rising "wh-o-o-o-o-o-p!" issuing simultaneously from dozens or hundreds of throats. My arms goose-pimpled and my throat was dry. A neatly dressed, pretty young woman came into the market, panting and stumbling, pursued by the whooping mob. Sweat ran down her face and stained the armpits of her white blouse. There was a trickle of blood on her temple. She paused on the roadside near me and screamed an appeal to the people about, who stood silently, watching without comment or interference. Hurled rocks began to clatter on the hard clay of the road around where I was standing. One struck the young woman heavily on the shoulder and she shambled away, wincing with pain. The whooping went into a crescendo and more rocks flew, one passing close to my head. Taking my cue from the other people in the market, I remained stock-still as the mob coursed by, following their quarry down the hill. The noise suddenly faded and the youths and children began filtering back. The market place came to life again with excited chatter and loud laughter. The people nearest to me gave me friendly smiles and a middle-aged man came over to touch my arm in reassurance.

"What was that about? I thought you were in real trouble then." Graham's English voice at my shoulder was like a cold douche over my body. I started and shook my head. "I don't know . . . She must have broken some village law."

"Not much law here," said Graham. "Not a copper in sight."

"That was the law at work," I replied, deep in thought. We walked back to the truck together.

Abandoned colonial farmstead, near Lubero, Zaïre.

Late that afternoon we reached an abandoned colonial farmstead where we were to camp. We had passed several, but Charlie remembered this particular one from his last safari. It stood on a hilltop with an avenue of eucalyptus and pine trees leading to it, surrounded by close-cropped exotic pasture grass. On a twin hilltop was a smaller dwelling and a collection of barns and sheds. The main homestead was elaborate with a wide verandah and Flemish gables. Inside were what would have been three comfortable bedrooms, two reception rooms with fireplaces, two ravaged bathrooms, one still containing a massive cast-iron bath with brass taps, and store rooms. A covered walkway led to a separate kitchen, scullery and servants' quarters.

"As far as I know, this belonged to a wealthy farmer who had several small properties around about," Charlie told us. "He must have had managers at each one, you can see a cottage over there next to the farm buildings."

"Why are all these places abandoned?" Marie asked. "These are all nice homesteads. This one's much better than many you'd come across on a station in Western Australia."

"I've never had a proper answer to that question," Charlie replied. "Here, the farm land is not actually abandoned. You can see that the pasture is looked after and there are cattle and sheep here. There is a local who looks after it for some fellow in Kisangani: an African, politician maybe."

"So why doesn't the foreman live here?"

Charlie shrugged. "I don't know really."

It was a puzzle that had no solution at that time, but fell into place later when I had understood more of extraordinary Zaïre.

The road was not too bad until we had stopped at an Equator sign for photographs. "We're leaving the Southern Hemisphere for the last time, aren't we?" said Ted mournfully. "I don't suppose I'll ever see it again in my lifetime." He was upset and moody for a while.

Thereafter, in troughs between hills, flood water accumulated and successive trucks created ever-worsening soft patches. Without attention and until the water could drain away, more traffic made it worse. All that afternoon we slithered and splashed northwards along the deserted road. We did not get stuck, but we were introduced to the gut-twisting noise of our turbocharged engine bellowing at high revs and the stink of volumes of blue exhaust hovering alongside us, mixed with the hot oil smell of hardworking gear-boxes. Our truck had eight forward gears and that day was the first time that we had to go into low range on the flat since leaving Johannesburg. It was to become commonplace from then on. In the evening we came to the first really big mudhole. A truck was buried axle deep in it and there was a queue of vehicles. Exhausted, muddy men were sitting about smoking and talking quietly, they had been working at it all day.

So we went back to a conveniently placed mission on a rise close by. This was the first Zaïre mission we stayed in and it was a small station; Catholic, with a substantial brick church and a straggle of simple buildings behind, supported by a banana plantation and a field of maize and manioc. We were given the mission's primary school classrooms to use, for which we were grateful as it began to rain again. There were four small classrooms in a long rectangular building of wattle-and-daub with rusty corrugated iron roof and Aussie Steve, Angie, Karen, Adie and I slept in one. There were no desks, only battered stools, a rough table and chair for the teacher and scratched and worn blackboards on easels. A shelf on the wall carried slates and closely scribbled, torn notebooks. I looked at some of them, staring with smarting eyes at the precious and pathetic accoutrements of learning in this unmarked place in the middle of the forest. There was nothing especially emotive about that bare little bush school, it was one of hundreds of thousands in Africa, and they did have a rough building at least. It was its revealed intimacy that suddenly affected me at the end of an anxious day.

The sun shone hard and hot in the morning and a grader arrived to pull trucks through the mudhole. Also on the scene was a grizzled and frenetic Belgian, the counterpart of the Aussie in Mwanza for he managed a trucking enterprise for a local tycoon in Kisangani with whom he was a partner. He was trying to get south to shepherd a twenty-four ton articulated vehicle through this bad stretch and was travelling in his four-wheel drive eight-ton Mercedes breakdown truck. We were to meet him again later but he was a great help to us at that first big mudhole we encountered. There was no way that we could have got through this particular one for days without help, it was a six-foot deep cauldron of sloppy red mud and we drove around it, willing bystanders joining our people in clearing a path.

174

The main trunk road near Beni, Zaïre.

Our new Belgian friend tethered his four-wheel drive truck to ours, together with a freight vehicle that was waiting. The driver of the Belgian's truck had a mad gleam in his red eyes and would tackle anything. Blue exhaust smoke rose and there was shouting and bellowing from Bob, the Belgian and various helpers. We got clear after four and a half hours of effort.

That afternoon we stopped on the edge of an escarpment, about 500 feet up, and gazed into the gigantic Congo Basin, a thousand miles across, that we were descending towards. The air felt thicker: was warmer and more humid, the sun not so sharply burning. I stared across the flat, olive-green roof of the rainforest extending to a misty, undetermined horizon. Streaks of gently drifting smoke exuding from the forest showed where kraals were hidden. I looked to the west, where my map showed no roads, no towns, just jungle. There were no streaks of smoke there. Did people live in that immensity? What was there? Did anybody know? We met a man who told us that as a refugee during the Civil War he had been lost for weeks and had met pygmies who had not recognised iron or cloth.

At the bottom of the escarpment lay the pleasant town of Beni, dominated by a large mission station and seat of local administration. Giant oil-palms which must have been fifty or sixty years old lined the main street. We bought fresh provisions and I found old-fashioned sulpha antibiotic powder which I prefer to the modern varieties in a pharmacy. We waited on the verandah of an old colonial hotel while Charlie changed money and Katie chatted to a tall, bearded White man in his thirties. She brought him over.

"Denis, this is Paul. He speaks beautiful English and you have to talk to him. I told him all about you." She leaned over, whispering loudly, "He knows Mozambique!" Katie knew of my love for that country.

I greeted him, shaking hands, "You don't mean Mozambique Island?"

He laughed, replying in scholarly English with a strong French accent, "Yes, I was there on several occasions." He held up his hands. "Don't trouble to ask. It is all right, everything is in good condition. The FRELIMO is safeguarding all the treasures in the Palace and the army is using the Fortress. Everything is in order, even though there is no commerce and the people are suffering poverty."

"When were you there?"

"I was based on Nampula from 1977 to 1983, looking for coal. I am a geologist."

"Marvellous," I said. "This means we have to have a beer."

We talked animatedly of Mozambique Island which he also loved, and the coral fringed coast. He told me how the few towns were surviving after

Independence in that vast northern territory of the country. He had to leave eventually because the opposition RENAMO rebels had finally cut communications to his prospecting areas and the project had to be abandoned. He was presently working as the field geologist on an American university's archaeological dig near Lake Albert. They believed that they had found proto-human and human remains earlier than the Leakey family's in the Eastern Rift Valley but it would be years before the public would hear. He could not discuss details of course. We shared my enthusiasm for the remote beauties of the Western Rift Valley. "You should fly up and down in a helicopter. What an experience! There is a special sensation to the earth there." It was tremendous luck to have met him.

Charlie later asked him about gas at Lake Kivu and described what had happened to us.

"Was there any odour, like sulphur?" Paul asked.

"None at all. I thought it was methane."

"Methane is organic, so it was probably carbon monoxide. You were indeed lucky, and could have been killed. That end of Kivu is very volcanic, as I'm sure you know. Gases will escape through fissures from time to time, maybe leaking constantly. When there is no breeze, they accumulate . . . and, pouff. It is all over." He grinned. "Anyway, you are here!"

In the afternoon, passing through a village with frangipani and crotons and neat hedges as usual, I saw a flash of white in the cloud mass off to the east. I called out to Bob and he stopped. It was the Ruwenzori, the true Mountains of the Moon, the centre of the many fountains that source the Nile. We took photographs of the 16,760 foot, snow-capped and glacier-clad summit peeping coyly through the clouds. I sank back in my seat, so grateful that I had been allowed that fleeting glimpse.

The next morning, I was up early, as usual, and wandered about. The rising sun was fighting its way through the night mist which trailed from the tops of the trees and in our clearing there was a damp quiet, the air deadened by the high trees, yet also touched by a feeling of vibration. I had sensed this before and found it hard to describe to myself. In my head, it seems that the enormous mass of living vegetation in these tropical forests has a tangible presence, a kind of benign pressure. The normal sense of hearing is constricted and at the same time confused by soft echoes. This extra feeling seems psychic. In the mopani bushveld of Southern Africa it is different but also tangible. The 'taste' of it there is astringent, like a delicate sweet-and-sour sauce; in tropical rainforests it is more robust, like an unsweetened chocolate pudding. Often, I find that I can best describe atmosphere or ambience to myself in terms of imagined tastes.

There were loud whooping noises in the forest in the early mornings. Of necessity, animals of the high forest have to have penetrating calls, delicate songs are no good. The whoops would echo and tumble through the air and it was difficult to locate the source. That morning I watched two magnificent black hornbills with sharp white markings, similar to the trumpeter hornbills of the southern savannahs. Bulbuls came into the camp and pecked at some scraps. Safari ants were busy, but they did not attack us. Butterflies were waking up and fluttering in the undergrowth. Colobus monkeys swung around the trees on the periphery. During the night we had heard our first tree hyraxes: small nocturnal mammals who have an extremely powerful screaming call, like a human baby amplified several times. When they are first heard, the calls are bloodcurdling and disturbing; just as you are drifting off to sleep the call comes, then just as you are drifting off again, the call shakes your nerves. It naturally struck me that the eerie and spontaneous whooping alarm call of the children in that part of Zaïre was an association with the monkey and bird whoopings of their jungle.

We waited three hours for a log bridge to be repaired that morning and I lay across the front seats in the cab, reading, and from time to time gazing upwards at the trees silhouetted against the segment of blue sky broken by tufty fair-weather cumulus clouds. The infinite variety of leaf patterns, colours and skeletal shapes of the great trees, many of them hundreds of years old, was a constant delight, almost an ecstacy. The thought of razing these trees to plant patterned rows of food crops was as repugnant and disgusting to my mind as slaughtering whole herds of antelope or the 'scientific' culling of thousands of elephants in Zimbabwe. As the food mountains of Europe and North America grow monstrously and there is fear of farmers being bankrupted by official quotas, we humans are destroying forests and wild herds in Africa and South America in order to put more land to the plough. I am sick with shame for us! What will our great-great-grandchildren think of us?

We diverted to buy tyres, now clearly essential because of the bad roads. On the way east, towards Bunia, we abruptly left the forest but there were no visible people. No kraals dotted an amazing savannah plain, there were no cattle grazing on the green immensity. The yellow road wound across the rolling land until it breasted the farthest ridge in the blue distance. Nick was jumping about in excitement: "What a place for ranching. What's the matter with the locals, where are they?" he kept asking. I was puzzled too, of course, but in the back of my mind an unpleasant thought hovered: the Congo Civil War was fought fiercely in this province, the Chinese and Tanzanian-backed suicidal 'Simbas' had plundered it and finally been defeated by South African mercenaries hereabouts. I rooted about and found Colonel Mike Hoare's *Mercenary* in our library box and put it away in my bag to read when we stopped.

In the late evening, we reached the large Protestant mission complex at Nyamkunde, spread about in a great shallow bowl nestling on the northern side of a group of old, eroded volcanic cones. It had an instantly perceived comfortable feeling of tranquillity. There was a large hospital, school, administration, accommodation for workers and schoolchildren and on the higher slopes of one of the hills were the expatriate staff houses. We were able to camp on a cropped, green lawn, pitching our tents under pine trees on the verges. It was an oasis of Western culture. White children speaking English with American and Scandinavian accents came to watch us as well as Black children from the boarding establishment close by. Electric lights on poles illuminated the grounds of the residential area and the roadways. We had ample, safe water. We carefully dug a pit for our cooking fire and most of us were early to bed in the cool, dry air of this savannah plateau. The clean smell of pine needles surrounded my tent and there were many fireflies about.

A number of us had medical problems: flu, diarrhoea, strange rashes, and infections, so we used the facilities of the hospital which, besides being the major medical base of this extended mission activity over the Orientale Province of Zaïre, was also a teaching hospital for nurses and paramedics. The cap on one of my teeth had come loose and it was stuck back in by a gentle dentist from Hull in the north-east of England, using the opportunity to show some of his assistants what an artificial cap was like. When I asked about the fee for the service, I was told it was Z75.00 (about sixty-five pence).

"That's not enough," I protested.

"That's the way we do it here," the dentist said. I gave him a £5 note and felt guilty at the smallness of my donation.

We had to idle for three days at the mission because Bunia, where we had to get tyres, was closed down as there was no currency available. The mission's chief accountant came to explain. In Kinshasa, the World Bank was counting the total currency in circulation in the country while reviewing the National Debt, and eleven tons of notes and coins had been flown from Bunia to the Central Bank by the army.

"Counting the currency?" I asked, wondering.

"Yes," he laughed. "It does sound improbable, but they have been printing money without controls, so the World Bank has insisted on a physical count. It's being done region by region."

"I would never have believed it were I not here."

He shrugged, smiling. "Zaïre is different."

Cicadas singing and bulbuls chattering in the pine tree by my tent woke me at 05.20 one morning. For a while I sat on the parapet in the garden of a vacant house then decided to climb the nearest hill and watch the sun begin to flood the plain to the north with light. It was an easy climb through fields of manioc, cabbages and tomato plants to where a watertank stood on the crest. The pearly fingers of the rising sun touched a veil of high cirro-stratus clouds and gradually the colours on the rolling grassland before me changed as horizontal golden shafts hardened. Immediately around the hills and the mission there were several kraals, the smoke from their cooking fires rising in grey smudges and the calls of women and children carrying clearly together with the crowing of cocks and the occasional bark of a dog. Beyond, there were no kraals until in the far distance I could see smoke rising near another clump of hills about ten or fifteen miles away. It was evident that in this lightly populated country, people settled near hills where there would be springs and streams of water. The emptiness and lack of cattle herds on this prime grassland still surprised me. There were few trees, just occasional thorn bushes, and right to the horizon, beyond the near hills, maybe thirty or forty miles away, there was no sign of change in the topography. I sat for perhaps an hour, thinking of the Civil War that had raged across that very landscape in 1964, before making my way down again. Jeremy and Timothy, shy four and six year old sons of an English doctor and Canadian mission worker, greeted me as I approached the camp. They had genteel manners and spoke very precisely and seemed totally out of place there.

The drive into Bunia to get the tyres, when money became available again, was an hour's journey along a rough, red-dust road, winding through the tall green grass. I thought of the Chinese supported Gbenye who had ruled this part of the infant Congo Republic for months in 1964, terrorising the populace with his 'Simba' army supplied with arms from over the sea through Nyerere's Tanzania and by air from Russia through the Sudan and Obote's Uganda. The Americans were supporting the national government of Tshombe and Mobuto and there had very nearly been an African Vietnam War here. Universally condemned and viciously vilified by the Western media, Colonel Mike Hoare's mercenary brigade of South Africans, Rhodesians, Belgians, Germans and British had saved these people from the horrors of all-out modern warfare by defeating the 'Simba' army in a brilliant infantry campaign that re-captured the entire Orientale Province in a few months.

In 1960, in a state of confusion and political turmoil, the Belgian Government had overruled the advice of their colonial administrators who produced a master-plan for the orderly hand over of the Congo to a democratically elected, indigenous government. A plan which was proposed to take two to five years to implement was thrown aside in favour of hurried legislation in Brussels that produced a constitution and enacted it in six months. This vast colony, the largest in the world at that time, was a geographical but not ethnic entity. Political parties, hurriedly formed and poorly organised, represented tribal interests and there was no possibility of a truly representative national government taking over from the Belgians under the new constitution and in the time available. Patrice Lumumba was assisted and advised by Russians in setting up the structure of a party machine and the hasty Belgians handed over power to him, since he had the only base that seemed to have national roots. This did not suit the leaders of the ethnic parties who had claims to be more representative but whose power was regional. The argument between federalism and centralism was raised and centralism was the form openly pursued by the Belgians, since it was quicker to put into effect, and covertly by the Russians, because it was easier for a central puppet to maintain control with an undemocratic party machine. The argument goes on in South Africa today with both the Afrikaner Nationalists and the Marxist ANC favouring centralism and the democratic moderates who seek peace and progress favouring the more difficult and time-consuming solution of federalism.

A mutiny in the armed forces resulted soon after Congolese Independence following rash and inflammatory speeches by Lumumba, asserting his authority, and several local leaders unilaterally opted for some form of federalist structure. The most important of these was Tshombe in mineral rich Katanga which had a history of strong tribal government over a period of at least five hundred years, contemporary with the Zimbabwean Empire. Moise Tshombe was a pragmatic capitalist and strongly opposed to the Russian-backed Lumumba. Civil War broke out in various parts and Katanga seceded from the new republic. Lumumba was unable to control the situation and called in the United Nations to put down the rebellions. The conduct of the U.N. forces was suspect and bad administrators made matters worse by attempting to take over the management of the country.

After months of bush war, the superiority of the U.N. army which included well-trained Indians, prevailed and Tshombe was sent into exile. Lumumba's regime was supported by the newly emerged African ideologues who were the darlings of Western leftists, such as Nkrumah of Ghana and Nyerere of Tanzania, and Lumumba was given the full support of Russia's diplomatic and propaganda power. However, Tshombe was brought back by the Congolese army under the command of the young General Mobuto who detested the increasing foreign control and ousted Lumumba. Lumumba was killed by his Baluba guards, whose tribe he had savagely repressed, in January 1961.

Federalism then became espoused by Communist-backed politicians seeking regional power after it was clear that central government was lost to them, and the Chinese moved to fill the vacuum created by the failure of Russia's activities. Secession was pursued by Chinese supported regimes, particularly that of Gbenye, based on Stanleyville. Massacres and terrorism of local people became normal behaviour in the country for a long time, in the fashion that has since become tragically standardised in Africa, such as in Mozambique today.

This dreadful Civil War persisted until Tshombe and Mobutu, fearing that they could not win, invited Colonel Mike Hoare to raise an army of mercenaries and solve the problem with White technical efficiency. Hoare turned to South Africans and Rhodesians, because they were familiar with African conditions, but he recruited many from Europe. Hoare's mercenaries, increasingly supported by the Armeé National Congolaise as its training progressed, finally routed the Chinese, Russian and Tanzanian supported rebel forces. Mobutu is still in power, twenty years later, now one of Africa's elder statesmen. Without exception, every civil war in Black Africa, since 1960, has had ethnic origins, or has been fuelled by ethnic animosities. Ideology has been the smokescreen put up by politicians for expediency or to promote their cause. The West's weak acceptance of widespread death and misery in ethnic conflicts because of these ideological smokescreens is extraordinary. Reconciliation and bold reformation is a desperate necessity, not 'rivers of blood' and a succession of oppressive, brand-new demagogues.

Bunia town centre was no more crowded than Bukavu and Goma but it had the relaxed casualness that I had detected at Beni and Rutshuru. There was also an ambience of gaiety. The long main street was divided down the centre by dusty traffic islands with a few tired palms growing in them.

Two pick-up trucks were casually driving the wrong way along one carriageway and we edged past them. A round, jolly-faced Indian girl sold me warm French bread and other groceries. She spoke English with a 'colonial' accent. I could have been in Durban or Nairobi and I spent some time talking because she attracted me. She was from Uganda, inevitably, and loved working in Bunia. "It is such an easy town."

"Why?" I asked. "I can feel something in the air, a sort of lightness." I raised my hands, demonstrating.

She laughed and rubbed her hands together. "It is money. That is what you can feel. They are gold mines near here and people have work to do." While we talked and joked, an old man had been covering a piece of paper with scribbles. I watched his tortuous efforts then took his pencil and smilingly made the sum for him. He studied it with his head on one side, then grinned and shook my hand. The Indian girl had been watching and she explained, "He is nearly blind and is so proud of his literacy, so we have to let him make up the bills." She rested her hand on a calculator. "It is already worked out here."

"Why do you continue to employ him?" I asked, curious.

"Oh! we love him. He is such a nice old man, and he lost all his family in those old troubles, you know?"

After a cold Primus in the hotel five of us went to a restaurant for lunch. There were three middle-aged Belgian miners and a roly-poly wife with tanned leather faces and gnarled hands also eating there. They were drinking plenty of red wine and joking and laughing a lot. The atmosphere was a tonic to our little group and Charlie had got new mud-rib tyres so was in high spirits. We ordered soup, omelettes, chips and tomato salad. Charlie insisted that I have Ricard because my spider bites were better and my tooth was stuck back in. A bottle materialised with a beer tumbler.

"Hold it," I said. "Lots of water is essential with that. I don't suppose there is any hope of ice."

The waiter went away and after some time returned with a Johnny Walker ice-bucket. *"Je m'excuse, mais il n'y a pas de l'eau. Nous avons seulement du glace."*

"Pas de l'eau! Seulement du glace!" I repeated in astonishment: no water! only ice! We all collapsed in laughter: Bunia was unique. It set the seal on a gloriously liquid lunch. Somehow the bottle of Ricard disappeared along with the food and Primus, and Martell Cognac, which did not need water, accompanied delicious local coffee.

On the truck next day I was reading Colonel Mike Hoare's book, *Mercenary* and became excited at what I found:

"*On Boxing Day [1964] I began to hand over to Ian Gordon, . . . Jack Maiden was brought in from Bunia and was to be Ian's second-in-command. I was pleased to see Jack after his long spell of action in the east of the country . . .*"

And again, further on:

"*My sector now stretched over six hundred miles from Aru to Niangara . . . We were woefully thin on the ground, but the fact that the civilian population was with us tipped the scales . . .*
"*Aru was controlled by Lieutenant Gerry Joubert, Aba by Lucky Griffin . . . Dungu by Jack Maiden. My corps of 'District Commissioners' warmed to their task . . .*"

Back in July 1969 I had received a call on a faint, scratchy telephone line from a friend who was the municipal treasurer of Inhambane, an old Portuguese trading town on the Mozambique coast. He was phoning to tell me that Jack Maiden, who was employed by business associates of mine on a tourism project there, had been let down and was out of money and in debt. Jack's employers were not responding to calls for assistance and my friend felt he must alert me to the bad public relations that would result if Jack was sued for debt and incarcerated as a penniless foreign vagrant. My work would be involved since I was acting as a consultant to the tourism project.

Knowing how right my friend was, I dropped everything, grabbed some cash (the amount involved was not enormous), and caught the next plane. Zacca drove me in his jeep out to the Praia da Barra where Jack Maiden had his camp. Beneath the coconut palms and casuarinas bordering the fine sand beach, two miles long, Jack's tents were pitched neatly; clothes blowing on a line, tools and equipment carefully stored beneath slung tarpaulins. The camp was deserted and we walked about somewhat anxiously, but all was in order. I climbed onto a small dune and looked along the beach and saw a large portly figure watching something on the shoreline through binoculars. I recognised Jack and called to Zacca.

"I was watching those birds," Jack said when I reached him. "They're migrants, just arrived." He looked at me closely, his face unable to conceal his worry. "It's good to see you, Denis, I was feeling very lonely here these last couple of weeks. I've had some problems with my own people, do you think you can lend me some money?"

"I know all about it, Jack," I said. "Zacca phoned me. I've brought money and we'll go back tomorrow."

His face creased in a smile.

I had often thought of that lonely figure on the beach. I knew he had been a Congo mercenary, but he never spoke about those days, even though we became friends. He was a slow, quiet man. He died a few years later.

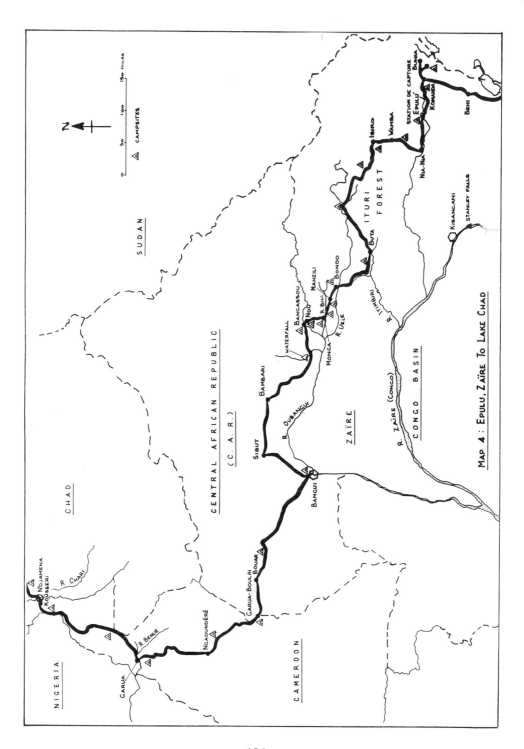

MAP 4 : EPULU, ZAÏRE TO LAKE CHAD

186

CHAPTER FIFTEEN : 'OFFICE DES ROUTES –
OFFICE DES TROUX!'
'Roads Department – Holes Department!' – Zaïrois truckers' joke.

It is the vital deprivation
Of the underdeveloped countries
That they do not have factories
For the manufacture of chewing gum
Nor grandstands for Coca-Cola dispensation.
HEART OF THE MATTER. Ifeanyi Menkiti [Nigerian poet]

After leaving the grand Protestant mission at Nyamkunde, we stopped at Komanda junction where we entered the Ituri Forest again and returned to our planned route. While the cooks shopped in the bright little market I looked into a couple of shops installed in mud huts. An old man asked for a cigarette and after accepting it with the double hand gesture of the Bantu peoples gave me a formal bow. I found a little bar/restaurant whose dirt floor was swept immaculately clean and emptied tin ashtrays sat on rough-hewn tables, shiny with years of polishing. A middle-aged woman came to serve me a cold drink and I sat for a while in the quiet of the morning watching chickens pecking at minute crumbs and a child playing with a home-made toy, singing to itself. On the wall was a stylised colour-wash mural of a man lolling at ease being served by a voluptous maiden, and underneath there was an exhortation which I copied onto my cigarette packet: 'RESPECTEZ BIEN VOTRE COMPETENCE S.V.P.!' I felt so happy to be in Zaïre.

Now began our real traverse of the Congo Basin. The strange towns of the healthy and previously prosperous eastern highlands which had been heavily populated by Belgian farmers in colonial days were behind. In the low altitude rain forest ahead there were none of the isolated brick farmsteads that we had seen in quantity since Bukavu. Apart from three, Isiro, Buta and Bondo, the colonial towns we were to pass through were ghosts. We were to travel nine hundred and twenty five miles through the forest on appalling roads from 20th November to 4th December, a period of fifteen days: an average of sixty one miles per day. Not too bad, considering. Except where traffic was piled up behind the gigantic mudholes, we went for hours without seeing another vehicle. Some days we saw none at all though we were travelling the only trunk road. Even local markets faded away and there were days when we had to subsist on dehydrated food and occasional fine paw-paws, pineapples and oranges bought from Pygmy villages. The only meat that was available was that offered by hunters: monkeys and small antelopes. We bought antelopes, but could not bring ourselves to eat monkey. Mostly our purchasing was done by barter for the people have little use for money, maybe travelling to a market town once in months to buy luxuries like second-hand clothing. In many places money was refused outright and if nothing that we had to offer was needed, then commerce did not occur. They usually wanted clothing, Bic pens and pencils, dry-cell batteries, cigarettes and matches, glass bottles and plastic containers, metal implements, and we rapidly ran out of spares of these things. In any case most of us ran out of cash too, for there were no banks.

We usually camped wherever we could find space beside the track amongst the trees and thick undergrowth. Twice we stayed in a village and twice in towns, and those were notable occasions. It rained frequently and we existed in perpetual damp. Bob had saved all the old engine oil from the Nairobi truck maintenance which he mixed with diesel to get our cooking fires going. We became filthy and our clothes, which were rinsed in streams or roadside ditches, were red from the mud that was every-where. It was always hot and humid and we had some really spectacular tropical storms at night. Nobody escaped infected cuts and insect bites because wounds could not be kept clean. The girls and some of the men were badly affected by sandflies which brought up itchy weals which they scratched in their sleep or thoughtlessly during the day. Three of the girls, in particular, became seriously ill from fevers resulting from severe infections. Of the men, Ted suffered most and his unhealed sores became worse, crippling him for a while. I had yet another spider-bite which immediately became infected but was kept at bay by my sulpha powder from Beni. Of all the group, I was the only one who did not react to sandflies and I attributed that to my many years in Africa which had conditioned my immune system. My particular disaster happened later at Isiro when I twisted my left knee badly, boogying, which had nothing to do with nature, and it did not recover until months after the end of the safari. (It was always my left leg that was poisoned, bitten by spiders or damaged.) I was fascinated by the continued rarity of mosquitoes. Several times I slept in the forest without tent or net and did not suffer bites or infection. Apart from Marie, who had contracted malaria in Tanzania, none of us was stricken with that particular disease. We all had diarrhoea from time to time which became a nuisance rather than a disaster. All in all, we were lucky.

Visible wild life is rare in rain-forests. We sometimes saw monkeys in the trees and the only regular birds seen were coucals, green parrots and the great black hornbills gliding across the road or small clearings. The dawn chorus was deep liquid whoops and gentle twitterings from invisible small birds in the undergrowth. I became used to the nocturnal screams of tree hyraxes and the evening whistles of frogs. Several types of ants and termites were always about and I loved to watch the safari-ants with their efficient and untiring organisation. Always there was the background shrill of cicadas and winged insects. I continued to be thrilled by fire-flies and bored my companions by telling them how rare they were now in the cultivated parts of Africa. For hours at a time our truck played host to stick insects and mantises which moved about the interior; one was six inches long. At first, the girls were horrified, later they took no notice. One was called Safari Joe because it stayed with us for so long.

We never saw a snake.

I rode on the roof from time to time. In Zaïre, apart from inside the few town limits, some of us were always riding on the roof whenever the overhanging trees and bamboos allowed it. From there, your head twenty feet above ground, warm air blowing, it was like riding a yacht across strange seas and there was an intimacy with the naked land that was missing inside the truck. You could also look down into the kraals that we passed and the children would go wild with excitement when they saw you. After we entered the Ituri Forest the people were mainly Pigmy, and the children no longer 'whooped'; their calls became more of a natural sounding, single-pitched scream. Older children often called out, "Tourie, tourie, tourie!" I was continually impressed by the neatness of the kraals and the carefully cultivated little plots of exotic 'colonial' flowers. I saw roses in one kraal!

Halted at the first big hole of this leg of the journey, we pitched camp in a thunderstorm. As we were cooking and sheltering inside our big communal cook-tent, our Belgian friend, Joseph, turned up, his spare grey hair plastered down his face but effusive and happy to see us. While we were at the Nyamkunde mission, he had got his great articulated vehicle through the hole near Beni and was shepherding it with his four-wheel drive rescue truck. He shared our dinner and talked at length with Charlie and Bob who were grateful for his experienced company. He warned that the road to Kisangani was very bad, some trucks were taking

189

three or four weeks to get through.

He told us that his company had a contract to deliver construction equipment to a German civil engineering firm that was building a tarred highway from Bukavu to Kisangani. It was a three year contract which could never be achieved. Giant bulldozers and earthmovers sank above their engines in the mud, trucks were abandoned, people got sick and had to be flown out. Everything stopped for a week when a bulldozer driver working in a stream found a gravel bed with sizeable gold nuggets. He laughed at this and shrugged exaggeratedly, *"C'est Zaïre!"* He said that his twenty-four ton truck was dragging the contents of two ocean containers of 'Portacabin' mobile chemical toilets three thousand kilometres through the forest for the use of local workers who preferred the bush anyway. [I would too]. He would probably wreck his precious truck doing it, it was costing tens of thousands of Zaïres, the toilets would never be used, but proper German consultants had made the specifications and the contract had to be fulfilled.

"Les Allemagnes – ils sont fou!", he yelled repeatedly, screwing his finger into the side of his head. "I am carrying these beautiful English shithouses. OK?" He paused dramatically. "But from where comes the chemicals?" His roar of laughter echoed from the trees in the middle of the forest.

It was grey in the morning with mist drawn from the trees by the heat of the invisible sun. In the big hole a truck's roof was below the level of the road, sunk deep during the storm in the night. Three trucks tethered together like a span of oxen pulled it through and then the work of felling trees and partially filling the hole began. It took several hours.

I was introduced to the camaraderie of the Kisangani road that morning which became indelible in my memory to an extent that when I think of that time in my life, I instantly recall the smell of wet earth, vegetation, food frying in palm-oil over glowing charcoal, and diesel exhaust; I can hear the echoing calls of many African voices, bursts of occasional laughter and that gut-wrenching noise of big engines howling at high revs. I have a vision of a great green canyon covered by grey skies, floored with shining red mud on which a static fleet of burdened trucks stand, heeling this way and that. The trucks are mostly Mercedes, but there are Toyotas and Nissans and an occasional Ford or International. Beneath the trucks there are camps; bedrolls, cooking gear around charcoal stoves, woven grass bags of vegetable stores, chickens clucking in baskets, young women asleep, drivers smoking marijuana and conversing gravely, children sucking at the breast. Mud-coloured washing hangs from the external mirrors of the trucks, sometimes a goat grazes on the end of a string tied to a door handle. From time to time, a deep chorus of musical yells comes from the head of the column and the camps are hastily got together. It is time to haul another leviathan through the mud and chopped logs before repairing the damage ready for the next in line. Always, the truck that has just gone through waits for the next behind in order to tow it through the hole on the end of the long wire hawser that they all carry. Sometimes they wait for an hour or more. There is never discussion about it, it is automatic. Five or six trucks go through one way, then the order is changed and a similar number go through the other way. Ah! those Zaïrois truckers were magnificent!

Near the Epulu River, there was a great frenzy of digging and effort. Joseph, worried about his great articulated truck, ran up and down exhorting, with his crazy red-eyed rescue truck driver. Darkness became complete. Our truck got through with chains. While repairs were going on to the hole again, a Fiat 4-wheel drive jeep broke ranks and got stuck. Tempers were lost, and with shouting from the truckers, the jeep was pushed off the road on its side. Graham and I cooked rice and dehydrated chicken while the others helped at the hole.

Joseph's huge vehicle and its two towing trucks stuck. I watched headlights waving in sky, blue tyre smoke and exhaust rising, engines howling, steel bodies groaning, people yelling; all echoing eerily in the forest. I saw metal Titans fighting for life with hundreds of near-naked men trying confusedly to help. In my fatigue and exultation and filled with my vision, I did not notice hours slip away.

At 10.30 we drove off down the lit tunnel in the forest. At last, we were at the Epulu River and crossed a Bailey bridge to pitch camp in an old Game Reserve base-camp. It was the 'Station de Capture' for rare species for the world's zoos. Steve found a tarantula bigger than his hand and I climbed into bed at 2.00 am.

The next day we discovered that we were in company with a Guerba Overland truck that we were to acompany off-and-on for weeks. It was a converted Bedford British army lorry and we could travel faster on good roads whereas they had four-wheel drive and were better off in sand. So we kept passing each other. But we made friends and at the main stops we rendezvoused and camped up together. There were nineteen of them, mostly Antipodians and North Americans, with only a couple of British. They were not as harmonious a group as we were and there were schisms amongst them. Particularly, they were about evenly divided between a 'serious' group and the others who liked to relax and have a party at the rest stops. We, in contrast, never divided that way. They thought we were a bit wild.

The Station de Capture de Epulu had been established as a veterinary and conservation centre for the Ituri Forest by the Belgians and still functioned to some extent. The ruins of an hotel from colonial days was there, blasted and pock-marked by gunfire from the Civil War. The rare and beautiful okapi forest antelope, a cross between a zebra and a dwarf giraffe, were brought in from the forest and paddocked there for a period until they were familiar with people and could stand the shock of being transported to the zoos of the world. There were two okapi being held and I was thrilled to see them. I remembered the famous Neolithic rock painting of an okapi that I had seen and photographed in the barren Erongo Mountains in the Namib Desert of Namibia, proving that high forest had been spread far down the west side of Africa at the end of the last Ice-age, probably 15,000 years ago, when rock-painting man was busy in Southern Africa. I had always considered that particular rock-painting to be so significant, the link between primitive man, the extended Congo forests and the era of time that brought them together. At the Epulu, I stood watching the beautiful and unusual okapi and my mind drifted to the red rocks and dust of the Namib. Extraordinarily, I did not have my camera. But I did photograph a chimpanzee orphan that Katie cuddled at the veterinary office. A truck driver had brought the young fellow in, presumably its mother had been killed by a hunter, and the attendants were looking after it. It had a baboon orphan for company and I watched the two together with fascination. The chimpanzee was obviously disturbed and missing its family, it would sit quietly staring into the distance, occasionally scratching or shifting its position. The young baboon was active, bouncing about, playing with seed pods or sticks, trying to get the chimpanzee's attention, rushing up to hug or touch it. The chimp would tolerate the baboon for a brief while, then shrug it off or move out of its way. The chimpanzee was being fed on Food-Aid dried milk powder and bananas. I have often wondered if it survived and if it was happy.

The Epulu River was in flood and we cleaned up and washed some clothes. My tent was pitched ten feet from the rushing water. It was a pleasant break and the sun shone that day. Bob, Charlie, Ted and I had lunch in the village in a rough little Affie bar sitting on wooden benches in the shade of a palm thatch roof. I had *Nyama ka Wali* – stewed meat with rice and a palm oil sauce – it was delicious. The menu was in Swahili, which reminded me that this far into Zaïre, Swahili of the East African coast is still the lingua franca. Along the Congo River, Lingala is the common patois, apart from pidgin-French. There are too many local languages for any one of them to be used nationally.

Charlie made his decision to miss Kisangani and told everyone over dinner. Talking to Joseph and several drivers at the big hole who had come that way, it was confirmed that we could lose up to a month following the conventional route, which would make the rest of the safari hard going to catch up. There was danger of damage to the truck in fighting our way through a series of bad holes. Before reaching the junction where we were to divert from the main route, we spent most of another day fighting another big hole which had formed in the last couple of days and this lent weight to Charlie's decision. Once again, the discipline and camaraderie appeared, the working together to repair the hole, the trucks pulling each other through like a giant metal caterpillar. We caught up the Guerba truck on the other side and their leader had also decided to miss Kisangani. Observing our combined group of nearly forty together, I could see signs of wear and exhaustion. Many legs had festering sores.

There was a small village at Nia-Nia, from where we struck north to Isiro, Bondo and the Central African Republic at Bangassou. We stopped in the village to buy fresh vegetables and to have a beer or two at one of the bars. There were woven palm frond seats on three legs on which we sat by the side of the road and we waved and shouted to the Guerba truck grinding by, unable to pause because of their slow speed. The bar owner started up his cassette player and spontaneously we began to boogie in the street, surrounded by clapping and giggling children. It was a special experience. Some of the truckers that we had struggled along with in the last few days also drew up for a beer and danced with us. When we eventually parted there were emotional farewells. A big fellow embraced me, holding me tight. A really rough-looking man ran alongside as we moved off, tears unashamedly running down his face. Africa! Africa!

The road north from Nia-Nia was little used and seldom maintained. For hundreds of miles it was merely two wheel tracks with grass growing between and the undergrowth impinging from both sides. Yet this was the only road connecting the eastern end of the Bunia-Kisangani trunk route and the vast northern territories of the country. Mike Hoare's commandos had roared through there with their military convoys making lightning strikes against the Communist rebels twenty years before, but it had become a track which would have disgraced a private farm in South or East Africa. The old stories about the African jungle taking back its own came to life in front of our eyes. Quite sizeable trees had taken root on the verges and we constantly brushed against vegetation on both sides. The paintwork of our truck took on a sandpapered appearance and three windows were broken by heavy branches swinging back with a crash. Bamboo thickets became commonplace, forming narrow arches like cathedral naves and these were often difficult; each time we approached a particularly dense patch, two or three of our acrobatic younger men went on the roof with machetes to hack ourselves free.

The log bridges were particularly dangerous. Charlie or Bob would stop and we would all get out and then the truck was shepherded across with much hand waving to get the wheels lined up on the strongest looking logs and then the crossing was made with a burst of speed. A couple of times we had to work at repairing the logs. Mud holes were no longer a problem, there was insufficient traffic to have made any, but there were several long stretches in gentle troughs in the slowly undulating floor of the forest when we were glad of the new mud-rib tyres and our chains.

The people were predominantly Pygmies and it was here that money became valueless. We would go on for hours without any evidence of humanity, then suddenly, there would be a little group of small huts almost buried by the forest and a quiet little family waving solemnly as we passed. Sometimes they offered us fruit for barter: excellent pine-apples, paw-paws and sweet oranges. In the silence of the forest, the noise of our laboured approach could be heard for maybe a quarter of an hour. Always, to my endless astonishment, there were the little beds of flowers by the roadside or in patches about the huts with the ground swept clean and tidy between. Apart from the decorative canna lilies, crotons, hibiscus, frangipani or poinsettia, there were occasionally coffee and cocoa bushes and bananas. Aged oil-palms, some of them fifty feet high, were seen in clusters in overgrown villages, long abandoned, with creepers completely covering the ruined walls.

The cultivation of coffee, cocoa, oil-palms and fruit had been encouraged by the Belgian colonial authorities many years ago in order that these tiny remote communities could generate some cash. I assumed that the flowers were a spin-off of this activity, evidence of transfer of the gentler aspect of culture that I had guessed at when I first encountered it from Goma onwards. A White trader would service these roads regularly with his trucks, bringing out simple manufactures and picking up the coffee and cocoa beans, the palm-oil and palm-kernels, the native rubber and surplus fruits, all in their season. Each local community cleared and serviced the roads for an agreed distance on either side of their villages. The introduction of plots of cash-producing trees and bushes to each family group, well separated, seemed an admirable compromise between total lack of development and the creation of Western-managed plantations. Nowadays there were few traders and many communities had been abandoned long ago. But the crotons and frangipani still flourished and the pineapples were some of the largest and sweetest I've ever eaten.

I kept reminding myself that we were seeing the people who lived beside the only road that traversed thousands of square miles of territory. Beyond the fringes of this fragile dirt road, the forest extended into misty blue-green distance, untouched by White-man's expertise. If greater wealth is needed to be generated in the Congo Basin, surely it must be better to penetrate that jungle with simple tracks and extend the limited, peasant cash-crop system that the colonial regime seemed to have been working at, rather than to create a ghastly ribbon of degeneration along tarred highways, costing millions to maintain, felling the forest for poorly managed plantations, and starting up migratory worker systems and rural slums whose evils are seen so clearly in Eastern and Southern Africa? Would the imported Aid consultants and academic 'experts' see that? One morning Al heard on the BBC World Service that another $750,000,000 had been granted to Zaïre for road improvements and water works (after the result of the money count by the World Bank?). Future historians may look back on the old European colonial era with better understanding. There is to-day a sad lack of the restraint and career-long commitment of the old imperial administrators, trained for decades in underdeveloped countries and held to strict budgetting by metropolitan governments.

One night we camped up with the Guerba truck in a large clearing and their 'serious' section invited us over to compete in a game of charades. I did not go, of course, and their tour-leader came over to sit and chat with those of us who declined the quaint socialising. John was a quiet, competent Australian who had been on a number of trans-African safaris. He did not say much, but I could see that he loved Africa. He was not enjoying his group whom he said were bickering a lot and their schisms were growing as times got harder. Marguerite, a forty year old Canadian, came over to talk with Ted and I. She found the earnestness of some of their younger people oppressive, they were far more concerned with organising their camping than the fact that they were having a once-in-a-lifetime safari in Africa (hence the charades). We enjoyed Marguerite's company and thereafter she joined us whenever we met up with our Guerba fellow-travellers for any length of time. I reflected on these two safari trucks in a rough clearing, surrounded by the high trees of the Ituri Forest, with bursts of laughter and girls' shrieks echoing as young Australians and Britons played a Victorian drawing-room game. There was no stirring of the warm, heavy air and purple flashes from a distant tropical storm lit the northern sky, creating instant, jagged silhouettes of feathery branches. There were faint vibrations of thunder.

As we approached Isiro there was evidence of large areas of abandoned agriculture. The forest in these places was gone and the grass stood as high as an elephant's eye. Many old oil-palms, too old for fruit bearing, stood about in the grass. Aged coffee plantations with secondary growth beginning to tower amongst them told the same story. It had not rained for some time in that district and there was red dust on the leaves of flowering spathodea trees and the coffee bushes. We were edging ourselves steadily northwards away from the perpetual rain of the central Congo Basin. I saw a dark-blue red-headed lizard, the common West African type, for the first time. It was very hot and the sun was powerful.

Isiro was the renamed colonial provincial capital, Paulis, one of the earliest colonial towns in this part of the country. A large, disused 'Provincial Assembly' building stood in the centre and there was an abandoned colonial administrative complex. We drove through a suburb of decaying villas and bungalows along roads lined with spathodeas, flame trees and oil-palms. There was a resemblance to Bunia, but it was a larger town and lacking Bunia's gay ambience and comparative prosperity. The Guerba party was also there and Charlie and John decided that we should all camp in the backyard of a still-functioning hotel so that we could change money, do some shopping and have 'a bit of a blow'.

We trailed round three banks who were not interested in my sterling traveller's cheques and I was wondering what to do when Marguerite called me from down the street: an Indian trading store was changing as much as we wanted. A young, English-speaking Indian woman attended to me. As expected, she was from Uganda and her family had been in Isiro for five years. While I was talking to her, her husband joined us. He told me that they could double their capital investment in Zaïre every two years, whereas it took ten to twelve years in the U.K. He told me that everybody preferred to buy South African household goods; they were cheaper, deliveries were good and, most important, the quality and packaging was better suited to tropical African conditions. South African product expertise could sweep the whole Central African market if there were no boycotts and sanctions. He wished that South Africans could help to set up industries in Zaïre, they would know better how to go about it.

After our camp was organised behind twelve foot, glass-topped walls in the back of the hotel, most of our two Overland groups gathered in the restaurant area, roofed with rusting corrugated iron, surrounding an open-air dance floor. There were plantings of blooming frangipani and hibiscus relieving the rough and severe white-washed walls. At five o'clock, music started up, locals began trooping in for the evening and young waiters began rushing about with trays of iced Primus. A smartly dressed gentleman in a three-piece suit and Homburg hat asked in elaborate, flowery French if he might join Marguerite, Ted and I. He was drinking cognac with beer chasers and was quite drunk in an amusing way. After we had satisfied his questions about us, he disclosed that he was the *Chef des Routes* of the area from Wamba to Bondo. We had a lively discussion about our problems travelling the roads and his difficulties maintaining them. He had a jeep, six trucks, a bulldozer and two graders on his establishment. He was in town to have his jeep repaired, five trucks were awaiting spares from Kisangani (he could wait two months for them), his bulldozer had been sent to help fill the holes on the Kisangani road (he did not know when it would return) and his graders were being held in reserve in case there was a major blockage on his section.

"So, if I cannot work; I have to play!" he explained, ordering another cognac and beer charged to his account. An attractive young woman joined him for a while, but when she saw that he was getting drunk, she left him with sharp words which he shrugged off with a charming smile.

I ate an excellent half-pound beef hamburger, (the first since Zimbabwe), with fried eggs, chips and salad, served with a bottle of South African Cabernet-Sauvignon and afterwards joined in the boogying. That was my undoing. Dancing energetically with Karen and then Angie, I slipped on the polished cement floor and twisted my left knee. I thought it was a minor sprain as I sprawled, laughing, but when I got up my leg would not support me. I sat with Ted for a while, waiting for the numbing shock to wear off, but it did not and Nick had to come to my rescue, supporting me to the truck and getting me to bed. Next morning, my knee continued to refuse to function. Nick helped me with my gear and Marie strapped my knee up, ordering absolute rest. I was sunk in gloom. If there was something seriously wrong with the joint, I feared that I could not continue with the safari. A one-legged person is just a bloody nuisance in those circumstances and the inconvenience and pain removed all pleasure from the experience. Everybody was being kind and helpful, but for how long could they tolerate a partial cripple?

We crossed several large rivers since we were now progressing across land that gently sloped to the south and west bearing streams to the Congo itself and to the Oubangui, one of its major tributaries. Bigger rivers were crossed on Bailey bridges, put up by the Belgians in the decade after World War II, and when the rivers became too wide we had to use ferries. The Bailey bridges were admirable. There was not a bolt or rivet holding the great steel trusses together, they were designed to be thrown up and taken down in the heat of warfare in Europe, so they were fastened by a system of levers and clamps. After thirty to forty years these bridges still served in the heart of Africa although they were doubtless intended to be temporary. One day, no doubt, great concrete spans would cross these rivers for the occasional truck to use and the faithful steel girders would be thrown down to rust in the pure green waters.

Bondo was an interesting town. It was dominated by a vast mission church, bigger than some English cathedrals. It stood in the town centre, a long brick pile with tiled roof, surrounded by a cleared area of clean sand and gravel without a trace of litter. Zaïre is the cleanest country I have ever travelled in. An old man with grotesquely swollen testicles wanted to guide Ted and I through the church, but he would have to get the keys from the sacristan who lived at a distance, so we declined his offer. He was grateful for a cigarette. In the market, I limped along with Tony and Dave advising them about purchases, for I was going to direct them in cooking a palm-oil stew. There was an amazing variety of meat, all brought in from the jungle, some raw and covered with flies, some smoked. There were antelopes and several sizes of monkey. I was dreadfully afraid that there were some young chimpanzees. Ugly looking river fish lay alongside each other in different shapes, the largest were a type of mud-fish with long whiskers. Wild birds, hornbills and parrots, hung on a line. To my horror, one stall specialised in wild cats and domestic dogs. My Western-style stomach heaved as I started at the furry carcases, stinking and fly-blown. At a premium, I was able to buy goat meat that was moist and red in colour, slaughtered that day. The vegetables and fruits were more conventional: aubergines, tomatoes, onions, manioc roots, yams, bananas and plantains, oranges, pineapples, leafy stuff which could have been manioc leaves or wild cabbage, maize cobs, garlic, chili-peppers, green peppers, susus, sweet potatoes, groundnuts, sugar-cane, freshly squeezed palm-oil. Other stalls were selling antiobiotics and other drugs in ampules and mountains of multi-coloured capsules, cheap jewellery and knick-knacks, South African consumables as usual, Japanese digital watches and batteries. I asked some of the stall holders if I could take their photographs and after lively discussion it was agreed, so they postured and posed for me. There was one old man who had been following me, dressed in striped trousers, collarless shirt and a dark blue waistcoat with shiny brass buttons. He got in front of the others and came to smart, military attention. I snapped him quickly, but there was a sudden uproar. He was pushed and shoved and there was shouted abuse, so I left the scene. Did they object to him because he was known and disliked, or because he was smartly dressed and aped the old, despised ways?

Also in Bondo market there were gold dealers, a row of them apart from the general hurly-burly. Each sat behind a table on which stood a small scale and a bundle of high denomination notes openly displayed. I was especially intrigued that the weights that were used and trusted by all to measure gold dust were Belgian coins from colonial days. One dealer showed me a sizeable nugget that he had bought the previous day and explained his prices, (approximately US$ 255,00 an ounce, which was pretty fair, I thought). None of them seemed to have bodyguards and there were no guns in sight.

African markets are generally very safe places wherever you are.

CHAPTER SIXTEEN : *CULTURE VORTEX II*

> In Papenoo we had a geniune introduction to the
> Polynesian way of life. There was no idleness, no boredom,
> no rush and no waste. The soil, sea and river provided
> what the little community needed, and no effort was made
> to exhaust the resources in exchange for wealth. Wealth in
> Papenoo was not measured, as among us, by counting what
> we have; what counted there was how one felt. [Tahiti
> before World War II].
>
> FATU-HIVA. *Thor Heyerdal*

A thumping, grating noise from the rear suspension was serious and we crawled slowly for about five miles until we came to an extended village with about a dozen family kraaals established about a large open space, a small church and a thatch-covered open assembly or public lounge. It was perfect for a few days sojourn to carry out repairs to the back axle. Charlie went off to interview the headman while children gathered shyly, watching us with solemn eyes.

We had left Pygmy country at about Isiro where the weather and the landscape had also changed. The forest was now patchy, several square miles of rain-forest were interspersed with areas of less dense growth with huge stands of bamboo, smaller trees and tall coarse grass on higher ridges. The people were taller, their faces were more angular and their skins were coffee coloured, like the Bantu of Southern Africa. Their huts were constructed by erecting the roof on vertical poles and then building the mud walls within this frame; which is a common method in Southern Africa from Botswana through Zimbabwe and Zambia northwards; we had seen identical huts in the Zambesi valley and I have often seen them in Tswana-speaking territory on the edge of the Kalahari Desert. This village, named Manzili, was in one of the areas of dense forest so I felt that we were still encompassed by the Congo Basin, but the touch of the Sahel savannas was beginning to trail itself across our path. Africa's mirror reflecting north against south was beginning to show and soon we would pass on to the fringes of the Sahara with increasing Arab influence.

Charlie came back with two old men and a brisk young fellow dressed in slacks and safari jacket. "Everything's all right, chaps. Here are two of the village elders and the son of the *Chef de Commune*. We can stay as long as we need and camp here." So we settled into Manzili, setting up our tents at one side of the village 'square', as we called the naturally irregular open space, in the shelter of a stand of tall bamboos that creaked and groaned in any breeze. I decided that I did not need a tent. The truck was positioned on flat ground and Bob and Charlie, assisted off and on by Steve, Dave, Aussie Steve and Nick began their uncomfortable task. Before jacking up and wedging the rear of the vehicle so that the four wheels and the springs could come off, we had to empty the truck of our gear, so it was a good opportunity for a thorough clean-out. All the time we were in Manzili, personal possessions, clothing, boxes of tinned and dried provisions, cooking gear, jerry cans and tools were strewn around and we never lost as much as a plastic teaspoon. At night we tidied up, but we did not have anxiety or fear for our security. In the mornings, children came to watch us getting up and preparing food. From time to time women and men would walk by, pause interestedly for a while then move on about their business. If we talked to them, they responded and they were ready to laugh and joke. The people of Manzili were one of the gentlest and best mannered communities I have ever had the pleasure of living amongst.

In the three days we were there, a mission truck and one Landrover passed along that road. We heard them coming for miles.

I read a lot, and thought a lot. Mostly I lay on my camp-bed in the shade, resting my leg. The first evening, I helped Tory and Dave with the cooking of the great palm-oil stew from the ingredients bought in Bondo in the morning. Charlie had been teasing me about it, telling everyone that I was busy with some diabolical Nigerian dish, the cause of the White man's burden and the curse of the 'White Man's Grave', so everyone was aware of something different. We had plenty of time, Bob found some beer and Ted brought out a bottle of whisky that he had been hoarding for the right moment, so we had a lot of fun. All the ingredients were prepared by Dave and Tory and gently stewed for a couple of hours on a slow log fire. I made a separate vegetarian dish with paw-paw, bananas, sugar, salt, cummin seeds, manioc leaves, garlic, ginger roots and more of the rich, red palm-oil. I persuaded Adie (who was the caretaker of our reserve supplies) to issue me with precious South African long-grain rice. Graham and I made a performance of cooking and draining the rice, Graham supporting me as we hobbled together into the undergrowth to get rid of the starchy water. Al came up with some cassettes of ballad pop-music from the sixties that he had recorded at home and we played them quietly. It was another memorable evening together, one of the best.

Ted and I were sitting in the strong moonlight, having a nightcap and chatting quietly at about ten-thirty when we heard male voices singing in the distance, softened by the trees and lilting in the stillness. The sound came closer and suddenly sharpened as about a dozen middle-aged gentlemen swung into view, walking briskly and solemnly in strict single file. We remained on our stools by the fire and watched, entranced. As the column passed us, they carefully gave us a raised hand salute and the moon glinted on their grinning teeth. We gravely raised our hands in reply.

"How about that, Ted?" I asked as they disappeared into the trees beyond the assembly.

"Beautiful. Just beautiful," Ted replied slowly.

There was a burst of laughter and a cheer from the jungle and the singing began again. The single-file column reappeared and marched across the square, saluted us again, acknowledged our response and disappeared down the road.

"I'll never forget that," said Ted. "Never."

I dragged my bed over by the fire in the middle of the 'square' and slept peacefully. There were no mosquitoes.

The next day was Sunday and the village drum sounded twice. Once to wake everyone at six, as it did daily, then again at nine to summon all to the service in the church. The village drum lived near the church under its own thatched roof. These drums are particular to this part of Africa. They are not made of hollowed logs with hide or skin drawn over the end, they are sections of great trees, six to ten feet long, lovingly shaped and hollowed until the correct appearance and resonance is obtained. They are valued and cared for, and I would guess that they lasted for decades, if not centuries. There is no doubt that they were given supernatural authority and were objects of importance akin to that of church bells in medieval Europe. A rhythmic code can be simply beaten out and when struck, they made a deep 'bonging' sound that carried far through the forest. They were instruments of communication as well as accompanists to dancing or singing. In another village where we slept further on, when the drum was beaten in the morning, it was echoed by five other drums, diminishing in volume with distance, within half a minute. There is no doubt at all that a message can be passed by these drums very efficiently.

I asked an old man if I could rest in the thatched assembly because it seemed clear that when it was not used for appointed gatherings, it was a public lounge, but available in descending order of privilege. The old man took my arm with a gap-toothed grin and ushered me along, sweeping his arm to indicate that it was free to me, so I set up my camp-bed in a lower corner, away from the shiny surfaced log seats, and listened to the church service. It consisted of five hymns interrupted by prayers or addresses. The language used throughout was the local one, but I recognised all the hymn tunes, altered as they were to suit the people's rhythm and style. It seemed conventional enough, but I had no doubt that if I had been able to understand the preacher, I would have found great differences in dogma and emphasis in what he was saying to his people. One hymn was particularly evocative: it was sung frequently during Sunday evensong when I was a schoolboy, and we used to sing it in the same slow mournful cadence, lagging behind the organ and choir, which infuriated the choirmaster. I listened, lying on my camp-bed in the jungle clearing, tears mingling with sweat, and pondered on fate that I should be reminded so strongly of boyhood memories in that place.

Karen talked to me about the health of the people in that part of Zaïre. In Manzili, her observations suggested there was evidence of inbreeding resulting in retarded children, stunted growth, strange body shapes. I did not think inbreeding had anything to do with it. Local lore and custom that had evolved over a thousand years together with natural selection would have taken care of that problem. I was satisfied that we were observing the effect of endemic tropical parasitical diseases, such as filaria, amoebic dysentery, bilharzia and various intestinal worms. Added to that horrific catalogue there was malaria, yellow fever, syphilis, sleeping sickness, polio, hepatitis and a battery of other viral infections such as dengue and, nowadays, possibly AIDS. The twisted bodies were probably the result of polio, the stunted growth would come from an accumulation of factors, the symptoms of mental retardation followed from sleeping sickness and general debility. I had noticed people watching us with eyes closing and faces becoming vacant, then being aroused temporarily by some sharp sound, and was sure I was observing the effects of sleeping sickness. The more unpleasant visible features of widespread tropical disease were the hugely swollen testicles of many older men and the goitres distending the necks of older women. The people of the jungle who survived into adulthood would be fairly immune to bacterial and viral infections, but would continue to be steadily damaged by parasites. Other facial or bodily features, strange to our eyes, could have been genetic mixing between Pygmies and Bantu types in this border area between two geographic and ethnic zones.

This train of thought reminded me of the paramount danger to modern

Africa: population explosion. Easy thinking relates this phenomenon to two major factors, reduction of disease and better nutrition, both being the result of 'civilised' practices. In considering massive population changes in ancient Bantu Africa, I had long accepted that new foods were the principal factor and I still believed that there was no argument with that general proposition, especially since the facts exist. Given that improved food and medical care has to have a massive effect, but assuming that a new natural balance should be achieved once a new population plateau is acquired, the African disaster has to be taken further, because there seems to be no sign that a natural balance is starting. Kenya, one of the more developed states in Africa, has one of the highest growth rates in the world (4.3% per annum, a doubling every fifteen years!). There have to be cultural reasons, therefore cultural solutions.

In Europe, North America and Japan, balance has occurred through universal education and the raising of living standards to the point where most of the population has economic-cultural uniformity. Does this mean that in Africa populations will continue to double every fifteen or twenty years until all the people are like Europeans today? If so, there seems to be no hope whatsoever because economic standards are dropping, per capita food production is declining, old colonial infrastructures are failing and the land is deteriorating. Africa could be facing the most extraordinary famines, political anarchy and the destitution of hundreds of millions of people. That scenario would suck Western civilisation into the turmoil. Food production and land degradation are the biggest problems caused by population explosion. An index of per capita food production, using 1961/65 as the base, shows that Latin America achieved a 25% increase to 1981, declining to 15% in 1983; Asia, allowing for weather cycles, achieved a similar growth of 15%. But Black Africa has *declined* to a level of 80% of the base by 1983, and the trend continues.

Demographic research in South Africa supports the idea that Africa has to be industrialised and modernised in total before population growth ceases. It has been shown that rural South African Black women were still rearing an average of between six and eight surviving children, whereas urban Black women produce four and Indian, Coloured and Whites between two and three. Applying other demographic factors but assuming an unchanging proportion of rural/urban Blacks this would result in 12.8 million non-Blacks and 160 million Blacks in 2050. This is an impossibility, of course, since famine would have had a devastating effect long before then. However, if Blacks were increasingly introduced to industrial society, as is already occuring there, their numbers would only reach 67 million in 2050, which is theoretically acceptable, and would shortly stabilise, peaking at about 73 million in 2100 before declining. Other calculations show that the 'maximum sustainable population' in South Africa is about 80 million, so South Africa seems to have a bright long-term future provided commercial development is not stopped by political revolution. But, it should also be remembered that whereas South Africa has an existing, developed industrialised social base of more than 10 millions (of all races), the equivalent segments in most other sub-Saharan countries can be measured in hundreds of thousands. South Africa is the forerunner and the pioneer in sub-Saharan Africa, which is why economic and cultural boycotts are short-sighted stupidity in a Continent facing ruin. Since, for the moment, South Africa is a political pariah, opportunities for co-operation, mutual aid and the vital pooling of advanced thinking are being lost forever. Water under the bridge is water gone away.

So, what of Black Africa? Lying on my camp-bed in Manzili I thought of the tentative conclusions that I had reached over the years and the various coalescences of thought that had occurred on the safari. Most African countries had declined economically in per capita real terms whilst doubling their populations in the twenty-year post-colonial era. On average, per capita food production was declining, and those trends were continuing inexorably. With outstanding exceptions, Aid was still being provided in schemes that seemed to me to be frequently wasteful and amazingly inappropriate, serving little purpose except to provide outlets for First and Second World industrial technology, satisfy selfish political objectives or assuage misled public consciences. Worst of all is the deluge of Russian military hardware tied to distorting Marxist propaganda prompting a lesser but no less significant flow of Western military equipment, enhancing the national debt of already bankrupt countries wracked by civil war or unrest. (Recent figures published on Angola show that that miserable country, which was proclaiming itself a future African powerhouse fifteen years ago, had an external debt of US$ 3.2 billion, *an incredible 65% of which was owed to Russia for war material*).

There had to be another way.

Mangosuthu Gatsha Buthelezi, a descendant of Shaka, the military genius who founded the modern Zulu nation, and Chief Minister of the autonomous KwaZulu state within South Africa, said recently: "Culture has not yet been drawn into conflict [in South Africa] as a major issue facing our land, which makes me feel there is still hope for us to redeem our country from the forces that seek to destroy it." That is a most significant and revealing statement. Buthelezi, during the same address, concluded that the transformation of South African society would come from the efforts of those who served deep moral principles – another important, and seemingly obvious statement which is seldom considered in relation to Black Africa. The extraordinary explosion of parallel 'African' churches in South Africa, the growth of 'Born-again' movements among South African Whites, the wide involvement of Church leaders in politics and the emphasis of moral values by political leaders points the way to the rest of Africa. Maybe the future of Africa hangs on cultural and moral criteria and not on material progress. Maybe that is where Western concern and the Aid that follows has taken a drastically wrong road.

Supported by the cultural Rennaissance and its Enlightenment, the Industrial Revolution was able to transform Europe and the United States, eventually producing population stability, vastly increased individual wealth and cultural uniformity, apparently flowing from industri- alisation. But industrialisation would have been ultimately degrading were it not for the Enlightenment and the non-conformist Christian revival that burgeoned with it. We assume too easily that material imp- rovement of the masses is the only panacea. But Africa seems to be incapable of following this materialistic path to Utopia. Indeed, Marxism has failed most spectacularly in Africa principally because people have universally rejected it, either passively as in Tanzania, or in endless civil war as in Angola. The capitalist brand of materialism, as in Kenya, has created new wealth, but has also created massive population growth and land degradation. I recalled my admiration for Malawi, despite its faults, which is ruled by a capitalist autocrat who also has high moral principles.

Returning to the cancer of population growth which is the virus afflicting the Continent, laying the body open to attacks from all kinds of economic and political killer diseases, I had come to believe that the debate should be moral and cultural. Zaïre was the catalyst of my thinking.

Two years before, I read *Reproductive Rituals*, a social study of the family and fertility in Western society before and during the Industrial Revolution, by the historian, Angus McLaren. I was reading it for general interest, when I became aware that his theses had most important messages for present day Africa. Although principally concerned with population stability in medieval Europe and its explosion during the Industrial Revolution, reference is made to birth control customs in primitive societies in the recent past and today. It is clear from McLaren's specialist research that population stability does not occur in simple or primitive societies because of high death rates and poor food, but is maintained by a conscious and sustained positive effort involving rituals, marriage laws and cultural lore combined with physical methods to prevent conception and to limit birth after conception. Nature tries to space children anyway through hormonic reduction of fertility during the suckling of children, and children were often weaned at the age of three years. Tribal rituals and lore governed abstinence, especially after the birth of a child and at times of epidemic, group hardship or drought. Contraceptive methods, most commonly male withdrawal before ejaculation, were widely used and abortion procedures, either mechanical or by infusions of herbs and animal concoctions, tried over centuries, were employed. Infanticide by exposure or simple cessation of feeding of infants was another method of population control, where children appeared abnormal or the birth infringed the law. Every African tribe has the tradition of 'initiating' youth into adult society. During this period of initiation all tribal laws and customs were taught and of great importance was the passing on of wisdom relating to marriage, sexual activity, procreation and the raising of a family. Many tribes accepted, or encouraged, sexual activity amongst young unmarried couples as well as married people, but they were taught not only how to do it for mutual pleasure and the reduction of sexual tension within tight-knit communities, but how to ensure that conception did not follow.

Examination of the population explosion in Europe, and comparing this event to modern Africa, McLaren sees this as a consequence of the breakdown of customs on top of an increased survival rate of children. As more children grew to adulthood following better nutrition and improved knowledge of infant and childhood disease, a brake was not put on conception. In addition, with the dissolution of older traditions and derision of so-called superstitious customs in a new, 'scientific' age, old methods were abandoned. Another factor was at work in Africa: misplaced respect for the integrity of new customs from a new and powerful overlord, (which may still be seen in misplaced respect for First and Second World political and economic theory).

Another major factor in Africa, often missed, that I see very clearly is family and community insecurity because of greater mobility, itinerant industrial and plantation labouring, and the general and sustained assault on traditional morals and customs from every direction which tends to encourage parents to have more children than they need. It has the same effect as an increase in premature death, (which is also massively occurring in civil war and famine), for the departure or expected departure of children from the kraal and tribal group for an unknown outside world is not so different from disappearance from natural causes or warfare. 'Baby booms' in wartime are normal in the most sophisticated civilised societies.

A multi-pronged cultural and moral assault came about early on in Africa largely through the positive efforts of missionaries supported by official administrations and strengthened by cultural transfer from Europe. Missionaries and colonial administrations actively attacked the 'loose' morals of the African 'savages', outlawed abortion and infanticidal practices, preached and sometimes even legislated against tribal marriage laws and eroded the fabric of tribal custom at the same time as they introduced improved health conditions resulting in increased survival rates. In more recent times, when missions are less dogmatic and have lesser influence, formal literate education has expanded and American, Western and Eastern European culture has flooded in. Culture shock on a massive scale has occurred and the old order of morality and tradition with its accumulated centuries of wisdom has been displaced.

Thinking at Manzili, the problem that had been dogging me in Zaïre – the almost universal practice of ignoring abandoned colonial homesteads, stores, workers' housing estates and formal agriculture – seemed to be resolved. In Zaïre, after the bitterness of the immediate post-colonial chaos and the following vicious Civil War, European influence evaporated. Elsewhere in Africa, after colonial administrations left, they had often been replaced by Russian and Chinese Marxism or the technical, commercial and aid organisations of Western countries: the foreign pressure was increased, often insidiously. But outside the capital, Kinshasa, or the mining and technical oasis of Katanga, the Western presence in Zaïre almost disappeared and the successful campaign of Hoare's mercenary commandoes prevented Russian and Chinese infiltration. For twenty years there was a hiatus and the ordinary people had a generation in which to revert to a semblance of their old ways, strengthened by the promotion of an African nationalism by the ruling political party. *The colonial homes and farms lie abandoned because the ordinary countryfolk find them aesthetically and culturally unappealing and unnecessary.* They are alien.

Zaïre may provide a key. My observation suggested that the inhabitants were in greater harmony with their world than the people of several East/South African countries under their different political regimes aiming for modernisation and technical development. A spectacular omission from the places we travelled through in Zaïre was signs of urban or recent rural degradation. The reverse usually applied: people had left the towns rather than create shantytowns around old colonial nuclei.

Perhaps there was a simple solution, which when I thought of it in Manzili village seemed so obvious that it would be naïve to write it down seriously. The simple solution is to follow a similar path as that taken in Zaïre; to deliberately institute a 'hands-off' policy approximating the experience of Zaïre which occurred in that country by particular historical events. Instead of promoting or acquiescing in the super-highways, electronic hospitals, mechanised irrigation schemes, MIG jet fighters, complex power-consuming factories and vast mechanised agriculture, we should curb all Aid programmes planned and negotiated at central government level. We should insist that moral and cultural principles of the societies concerned are safeguarded and that alien ideologies that suit current leaders' political ambitions are not being imposed. The common people should have time to meditate, discuss, and argue (agonise if necessary) over the development that they need and can successfully carry out. They should be encouraged to review their traditional culture and lore, to openly and combatively question solutions suggested by outsiders that do not appear to be intuitively correct or run counter to half-forgotten accumulated wisdom. There should be a moral and cultural revival of African ways of dealing with the African environment, assisted and helped by technology only when necessary, requested and exhaustively examined.

We should not listen to charismatic political leaders at the top of pyramids, many of whom have obtained their power through vicious civil war or armed coups, promoted and helped by foreign parties seeking selfish advantage or global influence. Particularly we should not listen to them because they so often cause the problems and we should bluntly tell them so. Nor should we listen to embittered academics and intellectuals who seem incapable of positive thinking and trudge aridly along a dreary path of fashionable criticism. We should listen to the 'real' people in the kraals, districts and townships who are actually at risk and are trapped in downhill spirals. National complexities do not exist. The problems are at community level: how to stabilise population and feed the people. Complexity follows after that has been achieved.

Was I hallucinating about Utopia on my camp-bed in Manzili? At some time, the level of human misery and political cost is going to force realism. I believe, sadly, that greater trauma will be necessary before attitudes and policies change. But, thank God, there are changes already occurring, almost spontaneously, almost by chance, almost everywhere and especially in South Africa. There is recognition by people working at the local level that 'small is beautiful' has special significance and truth in Africa.

A heartening development in the West is the rennaissance of the philosophy of Adam Smith and the decline of faith in Keynes. Friedrich

Hayak in *The Road to Serfdom* (1944), was already warning of the dangers of democratic socialism and suggested that planned and managed economies would create the conditions for new totalitarianisms. He promoted the concept of people at the simplest level creating social stability, prosperity and initiative in a law-abiding and moral society through the accumulated integration of a vast quantity of interacting individual thoughts and deeds. This is how human society evolved until modern governments began planning and controlling with the assumed superior know-how of a few fallible technocrats. This seems particularly obvious and significant in Africa today.

There is a growing groundswell amongst a few African thinkers that a revolutionary idea should be promoted to save the Continent. What is the idea? The idea is that the revival of traditional peasant society must be the basis for African survival.

So perhaps I was not hallucinating in Manzili.

PART FIVE :

THE SAHEL

CHAPTER SEVENTEEN : 'PARIS OF CENTRAL AFRICA'

The lights of the city glide within me
but do not pierce through me with their glitter
deep in me there still persists the black depths
of the black history I hear singing
ATTENTION. Mindelense. [Guinea-Bissau poet]

We were leaving Zaïre. After Manzili, I felt sad, because Zaïre had become an extraordinary experience.

The road continued to be narrow, deserted and ill-maintained to the border. The family kraals and villages were like Manzili and we stopped the night at one. There was one open 'square', a thatched open-sided church with the drum in its little house alongside, a covered assembly and the family huts all about. The people were gentle and friendly, watching us as we set up camp but not intruding. A middle-aged man offered us two chickens for sale and the cooks bartered for them, tying them to one of our tables by the strings attached to their legs. Later a teen-aged boy sidled over to Cathie and she gathered that the chickens were 'his' but his father had sold them, so was sad. This, of course, touched our girls and later, mysteriously, one of the chickens seemed to have escaped. I slept in the church in that village, being careful to instruct my internal clock to wake me before six, when the drum was sounded for morning services. It was magical sleeping in the church, I felt its atmosphere and the accumulated emotion of thousands of people-hours that had been spent under its roof, praying and meditating and singing. In the morning, a friendly, jolly fellow came around with paw-paws, pumpkins, bananas and oranges for sale. Money was scarce, so we bartered plastic bags and bottles.

Later that day we stopped in another village which offered us pineapples, bananas, oranges, tomatoes, manioc and pumpkins. When we ran out of things they needed from us, they threw oranges in the windows of the truck, laughing and ululating. A hunter offered two haunches of venison and a monkey, and we bought the venison for the equivalent of about £1.50. Karen pointed out a number of teenagers and young adults who had the twisted limbs and vacant faces that she had talked to me about earlier.

Trying to start the ferry at Bili River, Zaïre.

I saw that there were children with orange hair, one of the symptoms of protein deficiency. But there was no sense to that as the village was overflowing with food, they were giving away their surplus joyfully. These problems had to be the result of one of the doleful catalogues of parasitical diseases.

The countryside was frequently changing to savannah and back to patches of forest as we approached the geographical border of the Congo Basin, a mirror of the lands we had traversed after Lake Victoria and along the Western Rift Valley. Bamboos in thick, impenetrable thickets caused us to stop and push our way through by manual effort, then they dramatically disappeared. Small, untidy palms began infusing the deciduous bush, then there were tall raffia-leaved palms like those that were common in Malawi. Areas of grass became frequent.

The next day, we came to the Bili River, as it looped through the land, and had to cross it on a ferry. It was not a strong ferry, just four open twenty foot hulls made of sheet metal and bolted to a rusting iron frame. In one of the hulls a shining, three cylinder Lister diesel stood, its original green paint almost polished away. A plate on one of the hulls told that the ferry had been built in Leopoldville in 1956. A pleasant young man in an orange overall welcomed us but explained that the Captain had gone to Bondo, shopping for a few days and had left the engine's starting handle with his wife, who had locked it in his house and gone visiting her family. Who knew when either would return? They usually had only one or two vehicles a week passing through. I sat and admired the river: wide and grey, still without a ripple, thick green forest bounding its banks. It made a great bend just downstream from us and the pictorial composition was very pleasing. I took pictures of a dug-out canoe resting on its own sharp mirror image while Bob, Steve and Charlie wrangled with the *sous-Chef de Bateau*. Bob finally solved the problem, adapting a special tool from the truck and skinning his hands with prodigious effort. For some reason, a small black dog took off in front of us when we had crossed to the other side and ran ahead for about five miles. Bob stopped a couple of times and shouted at it, but it stood in the middle of the road, panting, with its ears cocked. We all remembered that little dog afterwards. It eventually veered off when it reached its home village.

We climbed a bluff standing above Monga which lies on the banks of the broad Bili river and pulled up in a stately avenue of sixty foot high royal palms fronting the simple buildings of a small Norwegian mission to ask for water and permission to stop for lunch. An attractive, blonde mission wife with a baby fussed over us, showing us the water tap, and gave us three loaves of wholemeal bread she had herself baked that morning.

Apart from our familiar Guerba companions, it was the first strange young blonde woman and the first wholemeal bread since Nyamkunde. I don't know which sight was more attractive. From the hill, we could see over the forest, fading into grey misty distance. It was a different experience to look over the great trees instead of crawling along through them. I sat for a long while gazing and thinking.

After lunch, we descended to Monga, another abandoned colonial town; the original streets were covered by knee-high grass so that the brick stores, offices and houses stood about in incongruous rows in silent park-like surroundings, scattered with ornamental trees grown tall and ragged. We had to stop there because it was the last customs post before the border and we had to get the truck's carnet processed. Charlie went off to find a lost official in the ghost town and returned after an hour in a state of controlled fury. The customs official had to check off our currency decla-ration forms and stamp our passports. Fine! But we had no declaration forms; the *Chef* at Bukavu, where we had entered the country, had said that the rules had changed. Therefore, we had now to fill in both entry and exit forms, they would be processed together in order and we could pass through. There was a 'fine' to pay, of course. But we had no Z's left, so with incredible reluctance the official would accommodate us by accepting dollar bills: a hundred dollars would probably cover his inconvenience. "Just fill in whatever you want on the bloody forms," Charlie said, stamping around. "It doesn't matter a shit, he won't even fucking read them." While we wrote up the forms with fictitious amounts of money and cheques imported, cashed and being exported, the *Chef de Douane* strolled among us, joking and smiling, the picture of bonhomie. We had broken the rules, but we were good people and had been chastised gently according to our worth, so all was now well. Zaïre!

That night we slept for the last time in amazing Zaïre. Bob selected the site of an abandoned and overgrown kraal, the mud walls of the huts eaten away by the rainy seasons and the poles honeycombed by termites. An orange tree, heavy with fruit, stood in the centre of the ruins and I found some canna lilies submerged by grass and creepers. In the morning as we milled about in the confined area, packing dew-wet tents and damp clothing, a small group of ill-clothed people stopped in the road twenty yards away. They waited, quietly, watching us and I saw them out of the corner of my eye as I struck my tent. When I had done, I could not bear the silent scrutiny any longer and smiled and waved at them. They instantly came forward, as I knew they would, for they were adhering to time-honoured good manners in not entering our camp until recognised. The oldest man carried a battered plaited-straw hat piled with rather tired

215

and dirty groundnuts which he offered. I called out to our people, but nobody wanted them. The old man knew the answer from the tone of voices before I could try and explain to him. He smiled gravely at me with friendship, nodded his head and led his family away without a backward glance. I stood, watching them go, my heart aching.

The countryside changed finally to sustained grassy savannah with smaller, big-leafed deciduous trees and many palms. The sun shone strongly from a misty blue sky, but the air had a different feel to it, a sort of pleasant cooling balm. At Mbu, the last Zaïrois police check-post, I stood in the shade of the truck watching the feathery palms about us with puzzled interest. Their tops were swaying in a strong breeze and little gusts were penetrating the bush. The balm persisted and in the gusts my skin felt the cooling effect of evaporating sweat, and for a moment I did not understand until suddenly, I realised what it was. It was the dry wind from the Sahara caused by high pressure over the centre of North Africa. The rains were definitely over, and we had travelled into another climatic zone. No more rain; no more mud, dirty clothes, mouldy tents and damp bedding.

"Ted!" I called out. "The Harmattan's blowing! The wind from the Sahara is here."

Later, I stood on the banks of the Oubangui River, about a mile across, in Bangassou in the Central African Republic. The girls were talking about showers and washing clothes. I watched the Zaïre shore with a lump in my throat and sadness in my heart. I had come to love that vast country and its gentle people. Would I ever return? I doubted it, for I would not undertake the journey we had completed in a private vehicle. The worry and dangers of breakdowns were too great a price to pay. In my head I heard the howling of engines at the big holes, the calls of forest creatures in the misty dawns, the rhythms of Zaïrois music in the bar-restaurants at Rutshuru and Isiro, the laughter of women and the screams of the children as we passed by.

We camped that evening in the grounds of an Affie bar in Bangassou after shopping in the small town where a Greek shopkeeper readily changed French francs and U.S. dollars: there was no BM in the CFA hard currency zone of ex-French West Africa. All the smokers bought Benson and Hedges or Rothmans cigarettes, Ted got some whisky and I found Ricard, the cooks lavished money on fresh vegetables and potatoes. I was reminded of Rwanda, all the buildings were occupied and in good repair, the street was tarred, the people were well dressed and prosperous looking. The Greek supermarket was full of imported goods. But in the market there were several permanent stalls manned by very black, tall, thin men with aquiline noses and thin lips wearing white robes and Moslem skull-caps, which showed us dramatically that we were on the way to the Sahel lands.

There were no showers at the bar where we camped so we had to postpone the great clean-up, but we had a party. The owner was a round barrel of a woman, a laughing fat mama, and there were several bar-girls who served us iced beers. One of these was tall and slim with a gentle smile on her pretty face. Most of us boogied with her during the evening. She smelled of Palmolive soap and sandalwood and was very sexy. It was a happy evening and we ate well of the fresh 'European' foods we had bought. Also staying overnight was a mysterious fellow with whom I had a long, involved conversation. He was bearded and looked just like Jonas Savimbi, the Nationalist rebel guerilla leader in the civil war in Angola. He spoke British English and said that he had studied at the Inns of Court in London. We discussed appropriate aid for Africa and talked about Zaïre about which we shared the same enthusiasm. We had an instant rapport and I greatly enjoyed his company, but he would not tell me where he was from or what he was doing, except to say that he was heading for Kinshasa via Douala, the capital of the Cameroon. That was a strange roundabout route and I teased him, accusing him of being a secret agent. He grinned and changed the subject. He knew Angola and Uganda and we reminisced about those sad countries. The next morning when we said good-bye, he embraced me.

The road from Bangassou to Bangui, the capital of the C.A.R., was good and we sped along it. We stopped for lunch off the road on a great terrace of rock overlooking a roaring waterfall on the Kotto River. Above the falls there was a lake and joyfully several people plunged in. I remained cautious about bilharzia so contented myself with emptying buckets full of water over myself, and while I was doing this a local appeared on the scene and warned that a white Overlanding girl had been swept over the falls and drowned a few months ago. Overlanders do die, a trans-Africa safari is not a European coach tour. Ted was still not well, Claire was seriously ill from her infected legs and was running a high fever and Marie was in a strange mental state that day, sitting alone and staring blankly into space. She had insisted on swimming and her body was stripped of all fat, her ribs showing starkly, her normally attractive breasts and buttocks shrunken. I was quite shocked, not having seen her without clothes since Lake Kivu, and I mentioned my concern to Charlie. "I know," he said. "I'm going to have to talk to her and to Claire. They can fly out from Bangui easily enough and with a doctor's certificate our travel insurance will pay. After Bangui there won't be a chance for quite a long while."

Because of Marie and Claire and because we all wanted to get to Bangui without delay, Charlie decided to do a night drive. The road was good, there was little traffic and in those parts there were no security checks, so it was an easy drive. Charlie and Bob alternated as they became sleepy and we dozed off and on as we trundled through the cool blackness. I was reminded of the long night drive through Tanzania to the Indian Ocean coast and how shocked I had been at the ribbon of dreadful shacks seen in the moonlight on the great East African plains. Along this road, the few villages we saw in the erratic beams of our headlights, battered and unfocused from the mudholes of Zaïre, were scattered kraals with huts in traditional Bantu style surrounded by cultivated fields, fruit trees and oil-palms. At first, I noticed a continuation of the Zaïre style of beds of exotic flowers, poinsettia, canna lilies and hibiscus, but it did not persist.

As we approached Bangui shortly after dawn we came to a military check-point, very formal and menacing. The soldiers were smartly dressed and heavily armed and a tough young sergeant ordered us out of the truck with a harsh command. He lined us up by the side of the road and left us there under the eye of a private soldier sporting a machine pistol. "OK, chaps, be careful, no laughing and joking," warned Charlie. We waited, feeling humiliated and foolish, but soon saw that we were being given superior treatment. Two local kombi-taxis were stopped and the fifteen or so passengers were lined up, harangued and their personal possessions prodded and poked about. Two big bundles, neatly tied up with cloth, were ripped open and, with a heave, the contents were scattered across the road which had the owners wailing and crawling about retrieving their belongings. Their papers were examined and a young man had some fault found with his. The sergeant was called over, he took one look and ripped the folder across and flung it into the long grass beside the road, tripped up the offender and kicked him in the stomach as if punting a football to goal as he fell heavily to the ground. He curled up with arms over his head pleading in a high terrified voice. A shudder ran down both lines of watchers, the white Overlanders on one side of the road and the local peasants on the other.

"Keep it cool, everybody," Charlie called in a low voice. Katie was silently crying.

The young man was hauled to his feet and roughly pushed, stumbling, to one side where he squatted miserably. Silently, the rest of them were checked and allowed to return to the kombis which roared off, the drivers relieved to have passed through. The young man then had the sergeant's attention again. He was slapped across the face and as he stood blubbering, he was shouted at for a minute or two until he was given a push in the direction away from town. He walked up the road a few hundred yards then sat on the verge, head in hands, lost in hopeless despair. His worldly goods were on the kombi on the way into the city; his papers, whatever the fault, had been torn up. He was a lost person with nothing but his scruffy shorts and shirt many miles from his home village. It was a small incident in the sergeant's day. It was total disaster for one youngster.

We waited, numbed, until an English-speaking senior officer drove up in a jeep and we were herded, one at a time, to stand before him. He leafed through each passport with exaggerated care, studied our faces and asked us to pronounce our full names before making an appropriate remark and passing us on. "Montgomery is a good soldier's name," he told me gravely. "I would like to test you for marriage," he smilingly approved the stunned Marie.

That was our introduction to Bangui, the 'Paris of Central Africa', where the notorious Emperor Bokassa had reigned in his extravagant palace, supported by President Giscard d'Estaing of France, and kept pieces of the corpses of his political enemies in a deep freeze. It is reported that he ate them.

Bangui had been the French administrative capital of the colony of Ubangi-Shari, situated in lazy mediocrity on the banks of the Oubangui River, one of the Congo's more massive tributaries. It had endured the excesses of its crazy, self-styled Emperor Bokassa, the jumped-up ex-colonial soldier and Francophone counterpart of Idi Amin. The casual viciousness created by the years of fear and personal insecurity of his reign persisted. France had a strong grip on the C.A.R., not only managing its poor and insignificant economy but also overseeing national security. Flights of Mirage and Phantom jets exercised over the city daily, the airport was operated by the French and there was a noticeable presence of fit young men with crew-cut hair and scrubbed pink faces in well-laundered designer jeans and highly polished loafers in the French restaurants and the Novotel Hotel in town. From Bangui, a French enclave, the airforce could sally to Chad and hit Colonel Gaddafi's Libyan army occupying half that war-racked country. The Foreign Legion and other Regular Army units were based near Bangui and in permanent cantonments in Cameroon, nearby. Within the tight ring of security that we had penetrated there was no visible sign of policemen. Urchins repeatedly tried to get into our truck and we had to have two people constantly on guard when we parked in the city centre. It was the only place where our camp was actually burgled, in the evening while we were eating, and the contents of Cathie and Dave's tent removed. In the 'Five Kilometre Market' we were accosted and threatened with knives. It was a wild, rough town, in a state of barely subdued anarchy.

Despite all this, I enjoyed Bangui and it was the last town in Black Africa to make an indelible impression on me. There were many Sahel people about, tall and robed with almost blue-black skin, and the Moslem presence was strong, but it was still clearly a Black African town. The easy-going cheerfulness, the noise and laughter, shouted argument and penetrating calls, the endless boogie music from a hundred competing loudspeakers, the restlessness and constant movement, the complete lack of order, the direct openness and instant personal contact of Black Africa were all there. It was also very hot and very dusty with the pale silver-blue cloudless sky of the Harmattan wind above.

We camped in company with our Guerba Overland friends, whom we had caught up, in the International Red-Cross refugee centre in the middle of the 'Five Kilometre Market'. There was no specific market, the shantytown had grown like a cancer and the market had spread with it so that the whole sprawling township was a market. Different types of produce and hardware stalls could be found anywhere along the long stretch of highway and in the dirty alleyways that spread out into the mass of mud houses with dusty corrugated iron roofs. The bedding sellers were in one area, furniture makers and carpenters in another. Butchers, vegetable pedlars, sandal-makers, cloth sellers, 'pharmacies', appliance dealers, drinking bars, eating houses, discos and brothels, vehicle spare-parts shops; all had their specific areas. One space, about three hundred yards long, was devoted to the 'brochette' and fruit juice stands where you could select your own piece of goat or beef and supervise its grilling on beds of charcoal before choosing your desired mix of fresh oranges, limes, paw-paw and pineapple to be chopped and buzzed in a blender. The delicious smell of charring meat wafted down the road to mix with the permeation of bananas and millet cakes being cooked in palm-oil next door.

Electric boogie was everywhere, twenty-four hours a day, and there were so many sources that it acquired its own music; an extraordinary sound, so complex and infinitely varying in loudness with distance that the percussion sounds did not become a roar but retained split-second integrity. The brass, electronic instruments and voices with unforgettable African timbre rose and fell and mingled.

A great clean out at the Red Cross refugee camp, Bangui, Central African Republic.

Since real people could not possibly produce the background sound of hundreds of individual hi-fis, it was an unearthly and unique experience. After the first day, I was not conscious of it, even at three in the morning. It was like living fifty yards from a waterfall. But there was another sound that was also memorable.

The refugee centre where we camped for several days had been a cinema and recreation complex with ruins of concrete ornamental fountains and the cement borders of flower beds, all surrounded by a twelve foot, broken-glass topped wall. Abutting one side was a mosque whose pale green and cream concrete minaret towered fifty feet in the air above us. Five loudspeakers sprouted from the top of the minaret and one was aimed downwards into our grounds. The mosque had a fine, modern hi-fi system which would have been quite suitable for a rock concert. At five o'clock every morning, and at the appropriate intervals through the day, the muezzin called. The first morning, as the pearly fingers of dawn stretched above the boogie filled air, we were all woken as if by an electric shock by the blast of, "Alla-a-a-a-a-h-a! Ak-k-b-a-a-a-r-r!" Later, I would wake before the muezzin began, alerted I'm sure by his psychic waves at the moment he decided to begin. There was the electric hum as his amplifier was switched on. After a minute, there was the echoing 'tock'-sound as he switched on the microphone. Then, there were moments of breathing as he composed himself and perhaps a giant's cough. I would hold my breath until the praising of Allah began. Thereafter, it was all right and his sonorous voice and the measured cadence of his readings became almost hypnotic, despite the ringing in my ears. I would even go back to sleep and awaken again when he switched off. On Sunday, we heard the distant toll of a church bell in the afternoon and this provoked three hours of dignified reading from the Koran. I could not handle that, I'm afraid, and with several others was driven to the nearby Portorico Bar where we had a noisy party.

That was the evening that Graham would not let me forget. We were cooks and I said that I would buy the ingredients for the best 'native' palm-oil chop ever cooked. Ted and I strolled in the market, relaxed and enjoying it after several beers in the Portorico, watching the people, joking with the market ladies and absorbed by the pastel shades of sunset engulfing and softening the harsh disorder of the township. The Harmattan air was balmy and we were at peace with the world.

We were followed by a tall young man with red eyes, obviously high on drugs, who suddenly grabbed a bottle of palm-oil from Ted's shopping bag. He did not run away with it but used it as a sort of bullfighter's cape, tempting Ted to attack him. Ted, like a terrier, was ready to do this and I shouted loud abuse, hoping that my yells would provoke an end to the confrontation one way or another, because I saw that he carried a long knife like most men on the streets. He darted round the side of a vegetable stand and stood there, grinning stupidly, waving his knife and the palm-oil at Ted. "Let it go, it's just twenty pence worth of oil," I said to Ted, but he would not have it, and my eyes searched for something suitable to club our tormentor. We were saved by a middle-aged lady of very aristocratic bearing who stopped with her two young, nubile companions, lavishly made-up with purple lipstick and eye-shadow and swathed in bright cotton prints. The lady put a restraining hand on Ted's arm and addressed the young tormentor with a stream of abuse. She made a gesture at his face with two fingers and he crumpled, mouth quivering. I had never seen such a strange instant show of abject fear. As she continued to abuse him, he presented the bottle of palm-oil to Ted and slunk away. Turning to us with a faint smile, she told us in excellent French to return to our camp. She looked at me from the corner of her eye as she drew away and handed me a business card, suggesting that we should visit her 'Maison' later. Her two lively young companions giggled.

"Rescued by a whorehouse Madam!" Ted said disgustedly. "We need a beer or two to get over this." We entered the Portorico again and the friendly waiter brought iced beers without being asked. The sun set in a blaze of scarlet.

I asked Graham if he would prepare the vegies and meat and Karen said she would help, so I returned with Bob, Dave, Adie and Cathy to join Ted. Later, concerned about leaving poor Graham to cook on his own, I returned to help. The stew and rice were bubbling, but there did not seem to be enough of it. I looked about in the gloom and saw a bowl of chopped vegetables, so poured the contents into the stew and started to add the packets of spices that I had bought. Graham's face did not look quite right.

"What's the matter?" I asked.

"Well, Den. You've put all the peelings and stalks in. That was the rubbish bin."

I stood, shaken, for a moment and Karen was laughing at the two of us. Then, "Jesus H. Christ!" I bellowed, seeing the solution. "That's all right, Graham, my friend, we'll just cook it for another half hour. That's time enough for a couple more beers!"

It wasn't the fine palm-oil chop I had planned. Ted refused to eat and had to be put to bed. Charlie and several others went off to have a better meal and a party with an Exodus Overland truck that was camped elsewhere, and I went to bed. At about two-thirty in the morning I was

223

having a vivid dream that the French Navy had sent a frigate up the river and it was announcing itself by blowing its siren. I struggled into wakefulness and the ship's siren was still blowing. I poked my fuddled head out of the tent to see a strange Overland truck parked beside the Guerba truck with lights blazing and silhouetted figures dancing about. I heard Charlie's distinctive voice. The truck had magnificent wind horns, which somebody blew again. There was no way I was going to join them, but would I be able to sleep? Squatting, naked, outside my tent for a while, I smoked a cigarette, listening to the ribald shouts and laughter of the party. There were also lost tempers and shouted argument from the Guerba tents where their 'serious' faction had woken up. Against the continuous background boogie noise, suddenly Pink Floyd erupted at maximum volume: the strange Overlanders had their own portable disco machine. I crawled back into my bed and slept off-and-on. At some time there was silence in our compound, then I heard the hum of the amplifier from the minaret.

The 'night of the disco-truck' became another memorable punctuation point in the safari. It was also a strange quirk because the next day our own stereo player finally failed after playing erratically since the big holes in Zaïre. All that rock and pop music that accompanied us through South and East Africa became nostalgic memory and we travelled the rest of our safari without electronic sound.

We spent quite a lot of time in the city centre too, and Ted and I had our second oustandingly memorable meal in the 'La Tropical' Restaurant. For a few hours, the nickname of 'Paris of Central Africa' was true. The 'La Tropical' was air-conditioned and the decor was that of a Parisian brasserie: polished solid wood panelling and furniture, a long bar presided over by a chic French girl from Paris and a plump, white-faced, bald gentleman with a strip of black moustache who appeared from the kitchen occasionally. The waiters were locals, but discreet and well-trained. I wrote their names down, François and Gustave, and they signed a beer mat for me as a souvenir. French airforce men were at the bar, chatting up the barmaid. We had a magnificent lunch of paté de Normandie, a giant rare fillet of beef with pepper sauce, french fries and a crisp salad, washed down with a cooled red Côte du Rhone and followed by ice-cream topped with a chocolate-Benedictine sauce. I had fine coffee with a wine-glass of Calvados and a fat cigar. It took us about three hours of eating and laughter, and Bob joined us at coffee time and had a beer or two, so Malindi memory was present although we were far away in psychic space.

We stayed so long in Bangui because apart from having a break and a 'blow', our American and Antipodean comrades had to get entry documents for Niger, which was not easy. Nigeria had closed its land borders to British tourists which meant that we had to go north-about round Lake Chad, through the unmarked desert, and there were no consulates or tourist-oriented border stations. We British did not need visas for Niger, but the others did. However, Niger did not retain consular facilities in the C. A. R. either, so foreigners had to get a 'letter of recommendation' from their embassy to present at the Niger border which hopefully would permit them to travel to the capital, Niamey, and get properly documented. Katie and Al got on all right at the U.S. Embassy which was mechanically efficient, but Charlie had trouble finding the British Chargé who was looking after Canada and the Antipodes. He was a tall cool chap with a public school accent who luckily knew what to do and said that he would issue a 'chitty'. The 'chitty' had to be typed up nicely by the U.S. Embassy, however, since he operated from a hotel and did not have staff. That delayed us another twenty-four hours.

We said good-bye to Charlie the following day and it wasn't easy. He flew home from Bangui after spending fourteen months in Africa as a tour leader. He was not well, suffering recurrent bouts of dysentery, and badly needed rest in a cold country. He left a hole in our party, and the safari was not the same again.

225

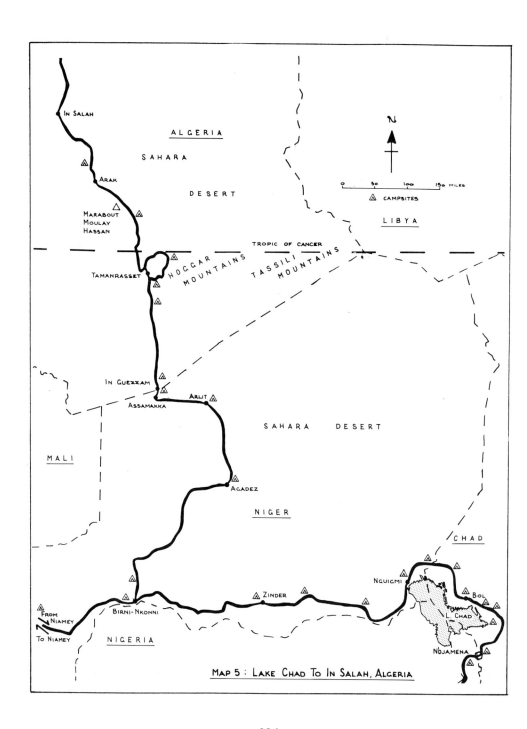

N

IN SALAH

ALGERIA

SAHARA

ARAK

DESERT

MARABOUT
MOULAY
HASSAN

0   50   100   150 MILES

△ CAMPSITES

LIBYA

TROPIC OF CANCER

TAMANRASSET

HOGGAR MOUNTAINS   TASSILI MOUNTAINS

IN GUEZZAM

ASSAMAKKA

ARLIT

SAHARA   DESERT

MALI

AGADEZ

NIGER

CHAD

NGUIGMI

BOL

FROM NIAMEY

ZINDER

L. CHAD

TO NIAMEY

BIRNI-NKONNI

NIGERIA

NDJAMENA

MAP 5 : LAKE CHAD TO IN SALAH, ALGERIA

CHAPTER EIGHTEEN: *THE SOFT SANDS OF CHAD*

There were times we regretted
The summer palaces on slopes, the terraces,
And the silken girls bringing sherbet.
Then the camel men cursing and grumbling
And running away, and wanting their liquor and women,
And the night fires going out, and the lack of shelters,
And the cities hostile and the towns unfriendly
And the villages dirty and charging high prices:
A hard time we had of it.
At the end we preferred to travel all night,
Sleeping in snatches,
With the voices singing in our ears, saying
That this was all folly.

JOURNEY OF THE MAGI. T. S. Eliot

We drove from Bangui, through Cameroon, to Chad in something of a dream. A thousand miles in five days was very fast and there were other changes. Bob was on his own, in authority, with the unspoken commitment from everyone to help where we could. (Steve was a diesel mechanic, and we were all resourceful). But a significant stage of our safari had been completed. We were leaving Black Africa and we were well past the half-way mark in time and space. As Ted put it, lugubriously, "We are on the way down!" But a good result from Bangui was that Marie and Claire were still with us. The rest and the attention of a young French doctor who called at the Red-Cross centre had got them reasonably fit again.

Two thoughts were repeated in my mind in Cameroon. Firstly, I was powerfully aware that this was the originating land of the great Bantu race. Driving along the road, looking at the mud huts of the kraals, with pole-supported thatch roofs which could be Zambian, made it quite clear that I was in the reflected mirror of Africa. It could also be seen in the birds; rollers, fiscal shrikes, cattle egrets, doves and vultures reappeared and there were flame trees and baobabs again. But, secondly, there was the increasing influence of the Arab culture from the north. In Zambia, the interference was that of the White man; in Cameroon, it was that of the trans-Saharan Arab. Half way up the country, the curved thatch walls encompassing each kraal changed to rectangular mud-brick constructions.

It was so sudden that one could have put up a sign: 'Arabs came to here!' Thinking of the origins of the Bantu people and their spread across the face of East-South Africa, I could have stayed there for many weeks, but we had to move on, fast. The unknown difficulties of Chad lay ahead.

The French military was there. A tropically camouflaged helicopter gunship buzzed us on the road and at the small town of Bouar there was an extended, old-fashioned colonial-style military cantonment with white-washed stone walkways and White soldiers standing guard duty. The extra cost of maintaining a regiment or two of an established regular army in Central Africa was not much, but the political value was enormous.

I saw women digging in a dry river bed, looking for water, and was reminded of an identical sight fifteen years ago in Mozambique near the Zambesi. Further on, the bustling town of Garua was particularly exciting for me and I persuaded Bob to slow down as we crossed the long bridge over the Benue so I could take pictures of the warehouses and the quay on the river front. When I was a young man I had worked for The United Africa Company in Nigeria and my first appointment had been as Transport Manager at the Niger Delta port of Warri. It was all new and exciting and I did not know much about the job, but I had been particularly struck by the romance of the barge trade on the river system with stern-wheel push-tow tugs.

Every year, as the Niger River began to rise, fleets of barges heavily laden with cement, salt, beer, flour, corrugated iron sheets, medicines, enamel bowls, printed cottons and all the miscellania of manufactured goods set off from Burutu and Warri. Six months later, the barge trains returned with cotton and groundnuts, the wealth of the Sahel regions of Northern Nigeria and the Cameroons. Some years, if the rivers had not been full enough, the whole of the crops did not get away and the wealth of nations was delayed. The Benue River was the main tributary of the Niger and Garua was the furthest station to the north-east reached by the barges from the sea nine hundred miles away. I had often watched crates and bags being loaded at Warri marked for delivery to Garua and dreamed of the distances and the strange peoples linked to me. Now, travelling in our truck, I finally saw the warehouses of Garua, but the barge-trains and their tugs were long gone, the river was silted beside the quay, the cotton and groundnuts went by road in many hundreds of trucks. I could not believe that the disappearance of the river fleets was an improvement. I presumed that they had stopped running at the time when diesel fuel was much cheaper and trucks are more convenient once the roads were built; but what about the immense increase in capital costs to poor countries?

After Garua, semi-desert began. The acacia thorn trees became smaller and sparser, grass was poorer and bare earth began to show. Succulents appeared with pink and orange flowers. I was reminded of Namibia or the Kalahari in Botswana. During the day it was hot, a dry baking heat, at night it was cool. For the first time since South Africa I was woken up by the cold at night and the stars were magnificent in a sharp, clear sky. At dawn, I saw the Southern Cross. Approaching Lake Chad, the country became flat, obviously the long-dried bed of an older and more vigorous lake.

We stopped at Kousseri to check out from the Cameroon customs and immigration and to buy fuel. This was an extraordinary farce. Bob drove to a very smart BP service station in the town and was nonplussed that it was locked up. About to drive off again, he was accosted by a breathless young man who had pedalled up on his bicycle. He was the BP manager and would take us to get fuel. At his direction, we drove out of town into the middle of an open sandy plain where there was a great square of black plastic sheeting supported by poles that looked like an alien fortress. Inside this construction was a mountain of plastic jerrycans. It was the black market fuel dump. Ordinary trucks smuggled thousands of gallons of diesel and petrol in jerrycans from Nigeria, and it was dispensed by wild-looking entrepreneurs. Young men, drenched in fuel, hauled the jerrycans up onto the roof of our truck and poured the diesel down a thin plastic tube. It took a long time, but Bob said he was saving £100. I wondered why they did not deliver the fuel to the service station and work some fiddle there; after all, the local manager was involved. Oh no! that would not be 'proper', I was told. A police Landrover drove up when we were half-way through and I thought that we were going to be in trouble. But it had merely come to fill up with petrol.

On the other side of the wide Chari River lay N'Djamena, the capital of war-torn Chad. In colonial times it was called Fort Lamy and it was hidden amongst palms, eucalyptus and giant old acacia trees. A massive diesel engine's 'thump-thump-thump' echoed across the river from the water pumping station. There were lines of trucks awaiting the ferry, including Nigerian trucks from Kano loaded with consumer goods, and I tried to chat to the drivers, but they had been driving non-stop and were high on marijuana and amphetamines.

Colonel Gaddafi's army had occupied N'Djamena until the French sent their army up and ordered the Libyans out, so the town centre was battered by tank cannon-shell explosions and many buildings were pock-marked by bullets. The Catholic cathedral church had been destroyed. Since the country remained in a state of civil war, partly occupied by Libya, we spent a long time passing through the various authorities before driving off in the dusk for the Hotel Chadienne where we were to camp. Bob took the direct route along the riverfront and we were held up by an efficient and heavily armed military post. Floodlights blazed and a heavy machine-gun was trained on us. Eventually a colonel drove up in a Landrover and released us. We were unknowingly going to drive past the Presidential Palace, and we could have been a mercenary assassination squad . . . It sounded like a joke, but it was quite real to the colonel.

Our Guerba Overlanding friends were waiting for us together with a Tracks truck and a wild Scotsman who was riding a motorbike home from Gaberones in Botswana. He had been working at the University of Cape Town and had to go to extraordinary lengths to get his papers in order and laundered from any taint of South Africa. He was more canny than the desolate Italian in Malawi and I saw it as a strange quirk of fate to meet him.

Because Nigeria had closed its land borders to the British in feeble retaliation for our refusal to extradite a political refugee whom the Nigerians had tried to smuggle from Stansted airport in a packing case, we had to go around Lake Chad to Niger, and since this was a route that nobody would normally take, there were no roads or marked tracks of any kind. John, the Guerba tour-leader, had good notes since his company had had other vehicles going around Lake Chad, whereas our company had not done it before, so it was agreed that we would travel in convoy for safety. We began to realise that we were undertaking a very dangerous journey. The country was under martial law and at war with Libya, there was no marked route and the authorities had little interest in tourists trekking in the desert to escape a political feud with Nigeria. Bob was worried because our truck was not designed for sustained travel in soft sand. We were not four-wheeled drive like the other Overland vehicles. Bob had not driven the desert that we were facing, and he knew that our safety, and survival, would depend on the sheer physical ability of our people to cope with the endless slog of days of sandmatting. It was very approximately three hundred and fifty miles from N'Djamena to Nguigmi, the first town in Niger, provided we did not get lost. This was not a truly Herculean journey but is a long way in a trackless desert wilderness and I would never think of trying it in an unaccompanied Landrover.

We had a day relaxing in the grounds of the hotel. Some of us went into town in the truck but I stayed behind. For a while I watched organised gangs of teen-age boys going through the garbage tip at the end of the hotel grounds like the baboons of the Kenya game-park camps. There were

230

at least three gangs, and one independent operator with a friend. He lived on a plank with swivel wheels because he had no legs, and he propelled himself around with his hands encased in rough-sewn leather mittens. Bob and Steve changed the rear wheels of the truck, taking off the two ordinary wheels on each side and replacing them with one great wide wheel and special tyres that had been bought for the normal trans-Saharan journey. We filled the water tanks and all our water-bottles and jerrycans. Al was put in charge of the water and it was agreed that we would use no more than ten gallons a day, which gave us a range of about ten days. There would be no washing, water would only be used for drinking, cooking, cleaning infected wounds and teeth brushing.

About thirty miles from N'Djamena on the metalled road to the north, there was a police post where we were checked out as usual. The officer in charge directed us to a dusty track, heading away through the scattered stunted acacia thorn, small palms, prickly pear bushes and a kind of willowy tumbleweed. There was no grass and the earth was grey and finely powdered, obviously the long-dried bed of Lake Chad which had been receding for hundreds of years. Along the first miles of this track there were a few scattered kraals, grey mud huts surrounded by plaited palm frond fences. Dirty children waved to us. The Harmattan wind was blowing steadily and as we went north the sky became a grim yellow-grey in which a dim silver sphere showed where the sun was hiding. It was a depressing commencement to the journey, but that first afternoon we did not get stuck and our spirits began to rise. Maybe it was not going to be so bad. We camped that night in company with the other two trucks and the mad, bike-riding Scot. He came over to talk to us and he spoke and used wit like a Glaswegian TV comic. We were all in stitches.

The sun set, creating an orange and crimson pall in the west, the air was cool and dry, the dust between my toes was like talcum and I felt physically in an excellent state, despite my knee joint, still stiff and sore. Bob insisted that I did not attempt hauling sandmats around and I could do other chores if I felt guilty. The rest of us seemed fit and in high spirits except Ted and Marie, but they were mobile and able to look after themselves. That evening we had a memorably awful meal, poor Aussie Steve had been conned into buying some meat which had to be donkey, it had a particularly strong and unpleasant flavour and was as tough as leather. I lay in my camp-bed, staring at the dust blanketted, black sky and the flicker of dying fires on the scrub nearby. A quiet burst of laughter came from the Tracks truck a hundred yards away where the Scot was telling a joke. The feel of forty Overlanders sleeping or resting around me in the Chad wilderness, in the dark night, was a good one. British,

American, Australian, Canadian, New Zealand, (there should have been South African!), we were all comrades, bound by the same great English-speaking culture, together for a good purpose, linked by the danger and excitement of the journey, but strong and self-sufficient now. We had all come a long way from Johannesburg or Nairobi and had many different experiences on the way. We were all beginning to feel that we were 'on the way down', we had left Black Africa, but we were still on the great adventure.

By lunch time the next day, there was a different feel to it all. The day was hot and the Harmattan continued to fill the sky with gloom. During the morning we had left the grey clay dust of the old Lake floor and had entered the zone of sand dunes, flowing away into the southwest like an ocean lying under the endless beat of the trade winds. We were to struggle in these dunes for a week. They were not high and beautiful like the pictures in films of Lawrence of Arabia or Beau Geste, and if they were, we could not have attempted them. They were low and choppy, riding over very long undulations, just as if they were ocean waves stirred up by a moderate breeze over the great swell of a distant storm. The sand was coarse and clean, beautiful sand, but not good for our truck. Tough old scrub grew in it, twisted and gnarled like ancient olive trees, and every dozen miles or so a wadi crossed our track running towards the Lake where water ran when a storm reached up to these latitudes. Doum palms grew in the wadis and the banks had quite thick scrub growing along the margins.

When we left the level grey clay-dust and met the coarse sand we began to get stuck. The first time we sandmatted it was almost fun: laying the heavy steel mats in a road in front of the wheels, then walking them round to the front after each ten foot advance, like a giant crawling caterpillar. We had listened to so many stories of sandmatting in the desert and here we were doing it, successfully, that it was still all part of the adventure. By that evening we had stuck several times and it wasn't fun, it was hard work and hands were cut and aching. There was stumbling and falling in the sand, and I saw quickly that I would become a liability if I seriously hurt my strained knee again, so I had my own personal routine. We stopped so frequently, that there was no point in trying to stow the mats on their racks welded to the side of the truck each time, so we took them inside and stowed them temporarily in the aisle between the seats. I made it my job to heave them out and restow them after each session. If I was careful I would not strain my knee and it relieved everyone of an awkward task. I became quite skilled at the rhythm of the work and after the first day my shoulders stopped aching.

Late that afternoon, we had a disaster. As the back wheels dug in, the power of our turbo-charged engine could fling the sandmats out and they became bent and twisted. One mat reared up and jammed against the tap of one of the two water tanks, breaking it off. Water gurgled, silver-clean, into the white, greedy sand while we scrambled for half-empty jerrycans, water-bottles, old beer bottles, anything to preserve the water. We gulped our stomachs full, then had to watch the last of the tank splash away. Bob, lying on his back staring at the sky, called out to Al: "You'd better do some calculations, I think." After a while, Al crouched beside him. "If we cut the allowance to one jerrycan a day, we should be all right. That's just over two pints a head a day. No washing, no tooth brushing, just food and drink. There's also quite a lot of tinned vegetables and fruit for emergencies and we better start using them. This is an emergency, we need that liquid inside us."

"Rightie-ho then! That's the rule. John says there's a village half-way to Bol, the only town on the route. That village is supposed to have a very good well so we can get water from them, but we may miss the village. I wouldn't guarantee anything in this country."

"Could we miss Bol, as well?" asked someone, and there was a chill in the air. The deadly seriousness of our position was beginning to penetrate. We had seen no life for hours; no people, no sign of people except wheel tracks we were following.

"Yes, we could miss Bol, I suppose," said Bob, slowly. "Let's not think about that too much yet." He got to his feet. "Anyway, we've got to catch up to the other trucks, so let's get the show on the road."

The other trucks had their four wheel drive and the Tracks truck, which had a worn gear-box, was travelling almost empty with only five people on board, so although when we were running, we could out distance them with our more powerful engine and more convenient gear ratios, we were very much the hare and they were the steady tortoises. We eventually caught them up as dusk was falling and Bob went over for a conference.

He returned after dark when we were eating and sat quietly by himself for a while. When I was putting up my camp-bed, resting its legs on a platform of sandmats, he wandered over.

"Worried, Bobby?" I asked.

"Just a few things," he said. "That water tank is not good, but it's more of a pain in the arse than dangerous. I just hope that nobody knocks over a jerrycan or something stupid. No, the problem is that the other trucks are

233

worried about us keeping up with them. Tracks have a problem with their transmission and they've got to keep going. Their tyres are not too good either, and they haven't got enough people on board to effectively sandmat on their own. They've offered to lend us four good long mats which they can't use, by the way, which we'll pick up in the morning. So Guerba have got to stick with Tracks and they'll keep on at their own steady pace."

"And we'll follow as best we can?"

"That's about the size of it." Bob sighed. "John of Guerba says there're no sandstorms this time of year, so their tracks won't get blown away. If we follow them, we shouldn't get lost. John has good route-notes and he's very experienced. I just don't like being on our own."

"Maybe the sand will improve and we'll keep up."

"No chance, but we'll try of course."

"We can't really get lost," I said. "The Lake is to the south and we can always head for it if the worst comes to the worst."

"If we get too close to the Lake, the sand is heavier, they say. And the wadis are deeper . . ."

I took a little longer to get to sleep that night and the Scotsman's jokes were not so funny. I had a nightmare for the first time in ages. It woke me up and I lay thinking of our isolation and the unique adventure of it.

We were up early and packed as the rosy fingers of dawn caressed high mottled cloud above the veil of dust. At least the Harmattan was dying and the dust was settling so the landscape was not quite so gloomy. I saw a wild donkey and a camel. The morning brought some optimism and we left first, roaring off at thirty miles an hour, bouncing over the small dunes with a crash, engine screaming. We crawled over a couple of high ones and picked up speed on the other side. Gradually, the tension eased; maybe it was not going to be so bad that day. Cruising well with a tail of dust behind us, following some old, half-buried tracks, Bob was suddenly confronted by a row of bushes too heavy to smash through. He had to make an instant decision and swerved to the left. Immediately he was confronted by a slope, jammed on brakes which caused us to lurch heavily, so accelerated again to straighten out. We plunged over the lip, sliding down a thirty foot dune, crashing to rest in a cloud of dust on the floor of a wadi. There was silence.

"Jesus H. Christ," I said quietly to myself.

"We nearly rolled down that slide," said Bob, leaning on the wheel, holding his head and lighting a cigarette. "We'd better see how we get out of here."

It took three hours to find a way. It was a fine wadi with firm grey clay covered with powdered dust and inhabited by doum palms, but the sand escarpments on both sides were soft and steep. We drove up and down looking for a ramp until, amazingly, we saw a man and a boy riding a camel. Nick went over to use his rudimentary Arabic and we watched the gesturing and pointing. What would that man think of this Overland truck deep in this wadi? Nick came back with a smile.

"There's a small village over there somewhere," he said. "If we drive further south there's a harder bank he thinks we can get up, then we must head north till we come to some tracks, then we head west again, following the tracks. He heard vehicles about two hours ago or more."

"That'll be the Tracks and Guerba trucks," said Bob. "We're on our own now, they won't know where we are." I felt gut-anxiety as I saw an image of our truck, alone in that sand sea, the familiar shapes of the other trucks drawing inexorably away. It was the real stuff of nightmares. But the man on the camel was right. We found a gentler slope and steadily sandmatted our way out and stopped on the top for a breather. The dunes, shining hard in the dim sunlight, continued to run away like tropical seas churned by the trade-wind. An hour later, we found the fresh path of our comrades, following old traces. We saw where they had stopped for a bit of sandmatting and gone on. Inevitably we got stuck there and had to sandmat for a distance about three times as far. We stopped for lunch. In six hours we had travelled maybe ten miles along the route, and it was clear that we would not catch up with our friends unless they waited a day for us. My stomach had now begun to feel the constant clutch of tension; not the big fear of death, but fear of minor disasters and a long ordeal without any end in sight.

Later that afternoon, Bob had to choose rapidly again between two alternatives to get around a bigger dune and chose the wrong one. We ended up in a bowl of sand which led into another bowl too soft and too steep to sandmat out of. We all lay around, watching the sun lowering. I did not know how my companions felt. Some were worried and feared the worst I knew, I supposed others were not fully aware of the potential dangers. Bob was obviously exhausted for the moment and it was bad that he had no relief driver. Steve, Nick and Graham could handle the gears on a good road and with time, several of us could have learned the same, but in this sand anyone trying to familiarise themselves with eight gears in two boxes with a twelve ton load would have dug the truck into a grave, or burnt out the clutch. I had noticed that we dug deeply into the sand when we started up each time after getting the sandmats into place and if the mats were spewed out by the wheels or we slid off, then we dug in deeper. A half hour of digging had to follow, and once we were down until the rear of the truck touched the surface before we shuddered free. If we sunk to the point where the whole chassis rested on the sand we would not get away without a tow from a tracked vehicle, of which there were none. This was obvious, but it struck me that the problem was that most of the load apart from the engine and our human bodies was over the rear wheels or behind it. That was where the fuel, water, several spare wheels and tyres, spare springs, canned food, baggage and so on was stowed. When I saw Bob sitting up, smoking, I sat beside him and told him my thoughts.

"Look at it," I said pointing. "You can see the problem."

"The problem is the lack of any regular track and trying to keep up speed on these small dunes without smashing the springs or breaking an axle. I've let the tyres down as far as I dare already."

"With less weight behind the back axle, we will also not crash around so much," I persisted. Dave and Rob were listening and agreed with me.

"Let's have a go then," Bob said.

We all turned to and shifted everything moveable from the back to the centre: wheels on the roof, jerrycans of water, engine oil, spare diesel in cans, boxes of packaged food, spare springs and heavy tools; all were shoved under the seats or piled up in the leg spaces. The cab was filled. The only floor space that was left was the gangway where the sandmats were stowed. It was going to be most uncomfortable, crouched in the seats with no room for legs, and we would all have to cram in together, on top of each other to bring the human weight forward – we ourselves weighed well over a ton without our trappings. The only things we could not move were the ninety gallons of fuel and the remaining tank of thirty five gallons of water. But the truck looked better and next day it definitely felt better; better balanced and not riding through the sand dragging its tail. As the sun began to set we laid the sandmats behind and gingerly tried reversing out of the impossible position we had got into. It worked.

"We'll camp up here and get up at three in the morning," said Bob. "There's a half moon after midnight and there's another trick we can try. The sand is harder when it's cool and maybe a bit of dew on it."

It was a lovely night and there were plenty of chunks of old, bone dry wood about if we scoured the area. The campfire became a roaring blaze with only a small flame to start it. The Harmattan had definitely died for a while and in the dawn I again saw the Southern Cross low on the horizon.

We did quite well that day and Bob quickly noticed the improved weight balance. Al began keeping a record of the length of time between each juddering stop and sometimes we ran for ten minutes or more. It was also easier to get out when we were stuck; the wheels did not dig in so deep. What delayed us was that Bob would have to race on once he was free in order to reach a downward slope, or harder patch, before he could risk stopping, and it could take half an hour for our tired people to follow with the mats and for me to get them stowed safely. Most of us had bloodstained rags wrapped around our hands to guard against the rough steel edges of the mats and there were slashes on bare legs where they had caught. It was all a matter of endurance now, we had learned all the lessons there were to learn. It had become a hard, hard slog under the dry blaze of the sun. We were all filthy and covered by a film of dust turned to mud on faces, necks and armpits. Our baggage was scattered in the turmoil within the truck, no one had clean clothes or could be bothered with them.

Katie, Angie, Cathie or Sarah would often start up a song; I loved to hear them get the others to join in as they staggered along, feet lifted automatically high in learned rhythm to tramp through the sand. After the mats were stowed and the truck was moving again for a while, we all slumped together, on top of each other, legs entangled, in the centre seats, gazing at the passing dunes. Fists would clench and faces tauten as the engine began to labour up a dune, and relax as we crawled over. When we stopped with a despairing growl and a gentle sway as the wheels dug in, there would be silence for some moments and perhaps Al would call out the time we had travelled, with a joke. Al was a good man, and he worried about the water. The only time I saw him lose his temper was when the screw-cap of a jerrycan got knocked into the sand and was lost.

On the third day, we reached the village with the well we had been told about. For miles around the few villages we passed, the scattered scrub was long gone for firewood and the sand was softened by years of movement from goats, camels and people, so Bob would take a long detour around them. But this village looked more prosperous and there were trees growing within it, date palms and a couple of tall eucalyptus, which proved it was old established. "We'll have a go at this one," said Bob. "We'll probably have to mat our way in." We did mat our way in, advancing like a very tired and worn caterpillar, but we were rewarded.

People began gathering to watch and calling to us and when we finally entered the open space within the well-built, solid houses there was quite a crowd.

Village elders north of Lake Chad.

238

Elders in long white gowns came forward to see what we wanted and naked children, covered in dust, ran about screaming in excitement. The women were shrouded in printed cottons with dark red, blue and green designs and wore gold rings in their noses and ears. These were Kanuris, tall and handsome, and they reminded me immediately of the Samburu in Northern Kenya. They treated us kindly and sold us a goat which Nick and Graham arranged to be slaughtered in the Moslem way with prayers facing Mecca and a quick slash of the throat.

In the centre of the village there was a shiny new hand pump set in concrete with a UNICEF stamp on the handle, so we filled every possible container. The people did not mind being photographed so I took quite a few and a naked girl hung on to my thumb and walked around with me. I wondered how such an old-established village survived until I saw that on the far side, as we drove away, there was a large depression with date palms around it, maybe a mile or two across, where the earth was grey and there were the dried stalks of a great field of millet harvested earlier in the year. It was a well-developed oasis.

The village cheered us up and that evening we had stewed goat meat, as much as we wanted to eat, rice with canned Kenyan vegetables, and canned South African peaches a long way from their origins. A sort of dazed ennui set in next day. We had eaten well, filled up with water and had learned how to sandmat economically, so we were going to survive. In the village we were told that we were en route to Bol and that the other trucks had passed two days before, so that was all right too. But the shining dunes still went on like the ocean, endlessly.

We were up at two a.m. one morning and wandered away into the lonely darkness to attend to nature with a cold dry breeze on naked bottoms. Over a cup of tea I watched Bob who was worried, serious and subdued. Gone was the bawdy Bob with the gargantuan laugh of months ago in Zambia or Malawi, and I thought how unfair it was that he had to carry the responsibility of the Chad Desert on his own. Not that he was without support, but we were still his passengers whichever way you looked at it. He was the professional. Having led expeditions and travelled in deserts before, I knew sharply what he was going through. Like him, however, I had not been on the north side of Lake Chad before: not many Overlanders have that experience.

We had some good runs that morning then got stuck badly on a long flat stretch of particularly soft sand. Rob and Nick had a long row about the technique of digging the wheels free to insert the sandmats, a silly stupid argument which achieved nothing and merely raised the general tension. Bob said nothing and when I looked at him he shrugged, by intervening he would make it a bigger incident. We stopped for a late, silent breakfast in sight of a mud-brick village with a clump of palms which could have been seen as a particularly contrived illustration of a desert oasis, like an advertising poster. Camels and donkeys wandered near.

Suddenly round the corner of a dune, there was a flash of blue. A creek was parallelling us on our left hand.

"Lake Chad!" I called out.

Bob grinned over his shoulder at me. "Bol at lunch-time," he replied.

"What's that mean?" Tory asked from over my shoulder.

"Bol is where we stop and go through police-checks. It's a town."

"A town?" She seemed disinterested. Were we so depressed and beaten down by the experience?

A thin covering of sere grass covered the sand with golden fur. The faint truck tracks became a sort of a road, we passed another oasis. There were men on horses, herding camels! Twenty minutes later, under a big acacia tree a giant, bright yellow M.A.N. four-wheel drive ex-German army truck was parked with White people sitting on folding chairs drinking tea. Extraordinarily, tents were pitched around a still smoking fire. The people stood up and waved as we came to a surprised halt. They all looked clean and wore casual clothes, some of the women were wearing skirts, one of the men had a bright bandanna around his neck and an East African safari hat with leopard skin band on his head. On their feet were suede veldskoens and elaborate sandals with pretty coloured socks. I smelt perfume and the expensive aroma of European pipe tobacco. There was a gingham tablecloth on a long table and a shapely girl with well-brushed hair was drying plates with a clean, printed tea-towel . . . Ye Gods!

They were a party of Netherlanders, Belgians and one or two British on a private expedition heading for Kenya where they would cruise the Game Reserves for a few months. Their gear was expensive and new. Their giant truck shone with bright paint and smelled of fresh oil and new engine. Massive lugged tyres seemed to stand as high as a man. They looked us over somewhat disdainfully, I thought, but perhaps that was unfair. They were so well kitted out, like an old-fashioned gentleman's expedition of fifty years ago, and they were in high spirits; confident, laughing, talking loudly. I looked at our truck: broken windows, smashed headlights, scarred paint beneath a thick layer of dust, gear badly stowed on the roof after shifting it about. We ourselves were filthy scarecrows, dusty and stained garments hanging everyway on our dirty bodies, arms and bare legs scratched by sandmats and thorns, hair like wire from dust and dried sweat, the men unshaven. We were not laughing much, we had eyes that were still looking far ahead into the dunes. They

240

made us cups of tea though and told us that they had been on the look-out for us and were glad to see that we had made it safely. They shook their heads when we told them how long we had been on the road from Nairobi. "Much too long!" an elegant fellow pronounced, waving a cigar. "We shall be in Kenya in four weeks only. Of course, we have more than one thousand litres of water and the same of diesel. We can travel better than you." I hope you bust an axle in Zaïre, I said to myself.

Bol was a town on the shore of Lake Chad, a big village of maybe five hundred people. The traditional mud houses straggled along a main street and at the end there was the Chief's little mansion hiding within a mud-walled enclosure with old, shady trees inside. A few modern houses with corrugated iron roofs in a compound proved that it was an 'official' town. Around the open space fronted by the Chief's house were the offices of the *Gendarmerie*, the Military, the Customs, the *Sureté de l'Interieure*, the Administration. We had to be checked out by them all and we had been warned that we faced having the truck stripped down and ourselves body searched with sharp interrogation. More travellers' tales, perhaps, but Bob was apprehensive and it tempered our pleasure at arriving in safety. A soldier greeted us when we stopped under a large tree, agreed to the parking place, said we could make camp there and took Bob away with our passports. We sat around, too bemused to unpack, until Bob returned doing little skips and grinning.

"Listen everyone. If we have nothing to upset them like drugs or guns, we should get away to-morrow. There's plenty of water a little way down there, there's a market with some fresh food and firewood. We can camp where we are. Guerba and Tracks left this morning and told them about us." He paused, looking us over. "And at the end of the street I'm told there's a bar with cold beers in it!" Smiles began appearing on faces. A slow swell of excitement gathered. I could hear somebody calling to Nick to open the baggage locker with his key. There was a clatter as pots and buckets were tumbled out of their lockers. "Where's all this water, Bob?" a girl's voice asked. I sat on a stool and lit a cigarette, thinking of a clean shirt and the feel of an ice-cold glass in my hand. Over the Military offices there was a flag flying and I watched it wave in the gentle breeze. It took a moment for me to realise that it was the French tricolour and I had an extraordinary quiver of déja-vu. Was it now or was it twenty years ago? No, the tricolour still flew, and next to it the flag of the Republic of Chad. It had to be something to do with the civil war and Colonel Gaddafi: a warning not to fire on this place without provoking France. Nevertheless, it was weird looking at that flag, I could hear the particular sound of French military music in my ears and there were goose

241

pimples on my arm.

As dusk approached, feeling reasonably clean after a wash (we could not bath all over in the town square) and wearing clean clothes, I went to find the bar with Graham, Cathie, Adie and Dave. Being a Moslem country it could not advertise itself but we eventually found it and entered a courtyard with a dark mudwalled room opening off it, furnished with rough tables and chairs. There were Skol beer advertising signs on the wall and a calender exhibiting a smiling, naked blonde girl skiing or yachting or something equally improbable. We sat in almost reverent silence while a squat Black man came over to us. Cathie began ordering beers in her passable French but he stopped her with a raised hand.

"I speak English," he said. "Please tell me what you need."

Cathie giggled. "Lots of beer, ice-cold."

He smiled. "That's easy . . . Where do you come from to-day?"

"N'Djamena," said Dave. "But not exactly to-day."

His smile turned to a wide grin. "Then I will put more beer in the freezer!"

I was listening to his voice. "You're Nigerian?"

He turned to me. "Oh yes. I'm from Owerri, in the eastern part."

"My God," I muttered. "French flags, Nigerian barmen, Chad Desert."

"What's that then, Den?" asked Graham. "Do you know his home town?"'

"Yes. I've been there," I took the first gulp from the frosted glass. It was elixir. "I'll talk to him later."

Much later, I did have a long chat. His family had owned the bar in Bol for many years and he and his three brothers took it in turns to exile themselves in this alien, Francophone-Moslem-Arabic community. I asked why they kept it on but did not get a straight answer. We talked about the Nigeria of his home. He told me about his father, who started the family enterprise and was still living in Owerri from where he ruled with stern paternalism. One brother was the manager of their trucking business based on Sapele, another was a trader, they swopped around from time to time. It was clear that they were a wealthy family. They were Ibos, of course; 'the Jews of West Africa' some colonial writer had christened them long ago.

I reflected that the Ibos were often considered to be closely related to the Bantu core stock which had always made sense to me. They had a different tribal structure and culture to the style of other West Africans who had been forced into sophisticated, introverted and complex political kingdoms by the lack of living room, constricted by the Atlantic Ocean and the Sahara, subject to waves of Hamitic invasions from North Africa. I

242

had always felt socially at ease with the Ibos when I lived in Nigeria in contrast to wariness with the complex Yorubas and Binis. The Ibos are an easy-going people but hard-working and ambitious. The Hausas of the North have always hated them and persecuted them. The appalling slaughter of the Biafra War was not so far away. The great West African slave-trade had been possible because of the socio-political structures of the area where rival kingdoms were often keen to sell captives in order to obtain the guns and artifacts that Europeans and Americans brought in exchange. Long contact with the slave societies of Arabic North Africa had created traditions of slavery long before the White man arrived in the 15th century. The first sea-traders seeking gold were offered slaves, and it can be easily argued that West Africa corrupted Western Europe rather than the other way around. The Ibos were not active slavers, they did not have powerful chiefdoms and kingdoms making war on each other. They were agriculturalists and traders and nowadays they were also industrialists, but the fruits of their labour and the oil wealth of their lands had been sucked away by the Hausa and Yoruba dominated Federation of Nigeria. I regarded the Ibo people with high esteem.

I asked my friend about his family business in Sapele and he answered me casually, so I told him I had lived in the Niger Delta for four years which brought bright-eyed interest. "Where did you live?"

"Sapele, Warri and Benin City," I replied.

"So you know Sapele and those outstations: Obiaruku, Abraka, Kwale, Ughelli?"

I smiled: "I even know Ivorogbo and Siluko."

He laughed and held my hand. "You are nearly a Nigerian, from my own country!"

I laughed with him, loving that moment there on the north side of Lake Chad. "But that is the old Mid-West, not your own district."

"True, but it is close. Did you pass Owerri-side?"

"I once spent a long week-end with an Ibo friend in Onitsha and we travelled to Owerri to have a look. A long time ago, in 1962 I think."

He stared at me and made a clucking noise with his tongue. "I was still at school," he said quietly. "Before our terrible war . . . And you lived in Warri-Warri?" I smiled, thinking back to the Ibo truckers and traders I had known when working as Transport Manager in Warri. They always called it Warri-Warri to distinguish it from Owerri.

We both felt the strangeness of our meeting there, and the nostalgia. I do not suppose many Overlanders knew his home territory and I had never expected to meet an Ibo in the remote Sahara. We talked some more as the Harmattan blew softly outside and the voices of my companions echoed in his mud-brick, Arab house.

That night I slept under the stars in the centre of the town square, just for the hell of it. As I went off to sleep, I heard a soldier's rifle rattling as he lit a cigarette. I had a tremendous feeling for Bol.

In the morning, the checking out procedures started as we cleaned the truck desultorily, knowing we had several days of desert still to go. Other Overlanders arrived. There was a squadron of German Landrovers whose oil spattered crew had the hoods up and the wheels off, a very battered British Landrover and a heavily-laden French Mercedes-Benz 280 saloon car. I stared at the Mercedes in disbelief. If the Germans are serious and careful and the British are eccentric, the French have to be mad. A VW Kombi full of a French family arrived later with young children. Although these other Europeans could go through Nigeria, the difficulty of getting visas had made them decide to follow the adventurous 'English' route round Lake Chad. They told us that they would travel in convoy and we told them that we hoped they had plenty of water and good sandmats. I wondered if they would persevere or sensibly turn back after a day or two: they did not seem to have a serious destination. The young English couple in their battered Landrover told a classic story of the Sahara. They had branched away from the marked track in Algeria to spend a couple of days throwing off their clothes and being desert vagabonds. That had been fun until they could not get their vehicle going again. For three days they had struggled, running out of water and becoming desperate. Eventually, they got moving but in their state of dehydration and fear had driven in the wrong direction, becoming lost. They composed themselves very seriously for the possibility of death. Next morning they heard what they thought was a plane and had crawled up a dune to wave. The plane was a big truck driving along the well-used *piste* a half mile away.

We left Bol after lunch and spent two days sandmatting, but it was a different experience. There was a discernible route with many tracks to Bol and our problems occurred when we approached a village where there was always a zone of soft sand stretching for miles around. We could not avoid these few villages, because they all had a military-police post between Bol and the border. It took a couple of hours to sandmat in and out and have our passports checked. But the exhausting effort did not seem to matter so much. We were relieved of the anxiety of travelling an unmarked route and we had acquired confidence in ourselves and our vehicle; nothing could be worse than what we had already accomplished. I sat, scrunched up in my seat with cans and equipment still piled about in the centre of the truck, the sweating bodies of my comrades packed around, and thought that we could conquer the world. If Bob had said, "Let's go back and up through the Sudan and along the Nile to Egypt," I would have been the first to roar approval. We were invincible!

On Christmas Day we rose early, as usual. It was a beautiful dawn with rosy sky and blue-mauve landscape. The Harmattan was chilly and we huddled around the crackling fire while Bob gave out our 'stockings'. Tory had initiated the idea in Bangui and we each received, in one of our own socks, a miniature bottle of whisky, cigarettes or chocolate, a balloon, a ball-pen and sweets. The sight of our little group, desert-dirty again, wrapped in coats and blankets crouched about a blazing fire in the waste of Chad with the pastels of dawn all around is another image that will never be lost. The girls sang a carol or two, the nostalgic sound thin in the empty distance and whistling breeze.

At mid-day, we met a British southbound Overland truck with twenty people, well balanced in ages, styles and sex, and stopped to talk beneath the burning sun on the endless sand plain. They wanted very much to camp up with us and have a rip-roaring party, but we had no booze at all and we felt that we could not share their limited stocks. So we parted after enjoying their strong Moroccan coffee, for we had run out long before.

As the sun set on that strange Christmas, we entered a dusty town not unlike Bol, driving straight out of the desert. But there was an innovation: a tarred road in the centre. And over the police station there was a different flag. We were in Niger.

Christmas morning in the Chad desert.

246

CHAPTER NINETEEN: *THE NIGER RIVER*

Slow-moving, grey, the Niger lies;
African python-river where the Arab trailed for a thousand years.
The coming here and the being here burden my mind and hurt my
soul.

Golden and sere was Samburu and afar – white-cloaked Kenya.
Mist hung, grey-green, heavy air was Kivu.
The howl of engines, the throat wrenching cries of good hard men so
patient,
The blue exhaust in the beams shining crooked at the tall trees –
Zaïre.

Yellow world, sand world, Harmattan wind.
Serpent trails of mechanised tracks
Shadows of ancient moving camel shapes
Fatigue and despair –
Chad.

> *NEW YEAR'S EVE '85, NIAMEY. Denis Montgomery.*
> *Grand Hotel, Niamey, 31/12/1985.*

We had to go to Niamey, capital of Niger, to get visas for the Americans
and the Antipodeans: not visas for another country further on, but visas
for Niger, the country that we had now to traverse for seven hundred and
eighty five miles in order for some of us to officially 'enter' it. It is a vast
country, mostly Saharan desert with a fringe along the bottom which is
lightly-watered Sahel savannah, frequently subject to years of drought
when the desert moves south. Fifteen thousand years ago, at the end of
the last northern Ice-age, there was no barren Sahara desert, it was
grassy savannah plains with acacia trees and palms along the rivers. The
Sahara then was much like the Kalahari (its mirror) to-day and anyone
who wishes to experience the Sahara before it lost its vegetation can go to
Botswana and see it.

The horror of the Kalahari is that people are introducing cattle and
goats over large areas by the use of bore-holes. Recently, I travelled in
the Kalahari and in two traverses saw what had happened in a short
twenty four years of my own lifetime. Driving north from the desolate

village of Mopipi near dried-out Lake Xau we drove through country that was very similar to the Sahara fringes of Chad and Niger: dusty land denuded of most grass, battered scrub with all branches shorn off at the level that a goat can reach. Passing through the fence that protects the Makgadikgadi Game Reserve, the vista turned instantly to a great plain of tall, waving grass with lines of ivory palm and tall trees where underground rivers flow. There were scattered herds of zebras and antelope: springbok, wildebeest, oryx and hartebeest. We saw lions, jackals and bat-eared fox and heard hyenas. The Kalahari was alive within the fence as it had been when the only people there were Neolithic, hunter-gatherer San-Bushmen, before the cattle and goats came. So used the Sahara to be and might have been still to-day.

The other traverse was south from Nata along the great tongue of land that probes sixty miles into the vast Makgadikgadi salt lake. In July 1962, I had spent three weeks camping in this area with an old school friend who had taken a job with the Bechuanaland Administration. At that time, we drove about in his official Landrover accompanied by a Tswana assistant and a teenage San-Bushman tracker-boy, observing the game, the natural waterholes and the thick mopani bush checkered with patches of great old trees, where there was groundwater, and clumps of baobabs. One unforgettable midnight, under a full moon, we had watched a mob of wildebeest and zebra in some lunatic charge thunder past our campsite for a full half an hour. Another night a lone elephant had walked through our camp while we slept under the stars and we found his careful footsteps in the dust between our camp beds when we woke in the morning.

On my recent journey in the same area, camping with friends, the mopani had gone: not just been reduced, it had gone. Many baobabs were dead and rotting hulks and grass was patchy. There was no game. I could not understand it and thought that my memory had played me tricks. But I have photographs to reassure me. What had happened? There were cattle kraals and bore-holes now, and what was saddest was that one of the cattle kraals had already been abandoned, the land reduced in just 24 years. For 20 years some local tribesmen had gained the advantage of thousands of acres of virgin ranch land with the help of government supplied bore-holes, but a generation later they had already begun to abandon it. A sand desert, like the Sahara, could be replacing the Kalahari savannah. Droughts, when no rain falls at all, are increasing in frequency and lasting longer. When rain storms come in the course of mysterious global cycles, insecure top soil is leached away. In Botswana, my heart was heavy at man's folly.

Traversing Niger to get our visas, we saw little grass and we saw moving dunes that were covering trees whose top branches still waved feebly from out of the engulfing sand. We saw abandoned villages and others that struggled with poverty, and we saw yellow dust blowing in plumes across cultivated land with dry stalks of millet and sorghum decaying in the ground. We saw stringy goats and camels ravaging the last of the acacia scrub. The Makgadikgadi in Botswana lies on 20^{0}S latitude and our route across Niger ran along 14^{0}N latitude. How long will it take the sand dunes to move northwards to reach 14^{0}S latitude? If they do, there will be desert north of the Zambesi River engulfing the mopani forests of Zambia.

These thoughts occupied me from time to time as we drove along the magnificent tarred highway in Niger, built with Aid and foreign debt, linking far-apart towns on the ancient trading frontier between the Sahel and the rich coastal lands; Nguigmi, Diffa, Maine-Soroa, Gouré, Zinder, Maradi, Birni-Nkonni, Dogondouchi and Niamey. It was a modern roll-call of medieval West Africa, of camel trains across the Sahara to Cairo, Tunis, Tripoli, Fez and Marrakesch carrying 'Morrocan' leather, many slaves and herded camels, but principally gold which fuelled the Moslem Mediterranean Empire, launched the Crusades and sent Portugal's small ships off around Africa and eventually to India.

The dusty, straggling mud-walled towns that we stopped in, seemingly so similar to each other, were shadows of their former magnificence when the gold of West Africa travelled north and the metal and textile crafts of Arabia and Barbary travelled south. Here was another 'culture vortex' that had affected so much of European history from 900 AD and subsequently changed African, Indian and Far East history. The old Kings and Emirs of the Sahel had fine capital cities, centres of culture and learning, thriving populations and powerful armies dressed in chain mail and mounted on tens of thousands of horses and camels in the Middle Ages. The engine of trans-Sahara trade had helped send the 'Moors' into Spain and Portugal, even into France. The violent reaction to Moslem colonisation had provoked European princes to lead armies to Palestine and Portuguese and Spanish fleets to sail the oceans to the Americas and the Indian Ocean. My own principal historical interest in the eastern side of Africa and the Indian Ocean had its roots in this land that I was travelling through at the end of my exhausting personal safari.

I frequently dozed in the heat and monotony as our truck steadily ate the hundreds of miles along the insidiously encroaching edge of the Sahara. In between the periods of half-consciousness, I was deeply grateful to be there so that I could smell the land, imprint a million images in my subconscious, allow my soul to feel it.

Niger had to be the most organised police-state we had passed through so far. At every far-apart town we had to report to have our passports checked and stamped at roadblocks checking every vehicle. We filled in dozens of personal transit *fiches* that were filed away in some monstrous bureaucratic system. At one checkpoint we were sitting by the side of the tarmac in the shade of the truck, waiting as usual, in company with the contents of some local taxi-kombis, when a World Health Organisation Peugeot station-wagon drew up. It had a smartly uniformed chauffeur and two officials lolled in the back. They glanced about through their sunglasses, lingered momentarily on our motley group, then turned to each other with a laugh and joking remarks which I knew were concerning us. The officer in charge of the roadblock hurried over and sent them on their way with a salute. I watched the locals watching and I could feel the thoughts in their heads. To ordinary people, were there visible differences between the old colonial masters and the new Aid officials?

I remembered the oasis town of Mirriah because there was a green centre to it with doum palms and baobabs, cultivation and well-fed cattle wandering about. I also remembered it because we stopped to food shop and I bought a tin of salted peanuts (10 CFS's - two pence!) from a young lad. He invited me to sit on the bench next to him and when I had enough of the nuts, I gave him back the balance and got up to return to the truck. He walked beside me and held the door open while I climbed in. We smiled gravely at each other.

Zinder was important because it was one of the great ancient caravanserais about which I had long been aware. At the usual road-block, a very jolly policeman came aboard to look us over and practice his English. He asked us if we were enjoying ourselves and received a few muted "yesses". That was not enough so he said, "I can't hear you," like a TV show compere. So we all gave him a roar which he liked. "Where is your rock-music?" he asked. "The player is broken," somebody answered and he made a mock-tragic face. Zinder had a modern industrial suburb with grain silos and some office blocks with air-conditions. A large satellite dish and relay station fed waves to the many TV aerials. Bob dropped us at the Hotel Centrale in a street lined with cassia trees where we had a cold beer in a shaded, gravel-floored courtyard. Curio sellers fenced with us, offered Agadez crosses, finely-worked necklaces, leather-work and camel blankets. They were persistent and sophisticated

250

traders, sitting down with us, offering and taking away, re-offering and changing, each time with different prices, to confuse and intrigue. I had bought a Bornu dagger and worked leather scabbard twenty seven years before from a Hausa trader in Warri which looked like one I was now offered and I had a real blanket at home made from thin, handwoven strips sewn together, which these modern traders told me was not made to-day. I enjoyed them and they were happy to laugh and joke even if we bought little, although Nick found a 'soovie' or two that satisfied him. They called me 'Papa' as so many people did in Francophone Africa.

I was especially pleased to be in Zinder, not only for its historical interest, somewhat smudged by the modern additions, but because it reminded me of the first trans-Africa travellers I met, on 24th May 1958. My wife and I were living in a small company bungalow in Benin City in southern Nigeria and the branch manager had called me in to ask if we would give hospitality to two young travellers whom the company had agreed to help on their way through the country. I had been quite excited and my wife had prepared the spare bedroom with little feminine touches. Late that day a pre-World War II London taxi had driven up, piled high with spare tyres, tool boxes, petrol and water cans. A mountain of dirty clothes and bedding was disgorged which the young couple insisted on washing themselves. They each lay in the bath for hours and they had been strange and shy sitting at our dinner table to eat the four course meal my wife specially prepared. They talked haltingly of crossing the Sahara in their funny old vehicle and had told us how relieved they had been to reach Zinder. They were Alfred and Jokobine Hobbs and wrote in our guest-book: 'We will meet again somewhere – In sh'Allah!' Maybe they planted a germ in me that has not yet been worked out. In Zinder that day, 27th December 1985, I silently drank a toast: "Where are you now Alfred and Jokobine? Are you still together, did you reach South Africa? Do you remember that eager young couple you stayed with in Benin so long ago?"

After Zinder, the Harmattan blew hard again and visibility was reduced to half a mile. It was a dreary journey, especially since we would have turned north at that point had we not been forced to continue westward to Niamey for the visas. The towns, all the same, were dull and lifeless in the heat and dust. From time to time we passed areas where agriculture seemed more prosperous and the villages were larger. All had grain silos made from mud bricks or giant pottery, raised on legs against the attacks of rodents. Some had very elegant shapes, rounded with heavy straw-thatched hats and the shapes changed from area to area. Some were twenty feet across. I did not know any detail of the local tribal divisions, only that the people were generally Hausa and Fulani in those parts. Both these people had commanded great empires in their day and had been nomadic herders. Now the land was degraded and they were settled, trying to live mainly by agriculture. We saw Tuareg and Fulani people from the desert who still wore indigo dyed cloths about their heads, some still herding camels or a few cattle, but most whom we saw were truck drivers and petty traders. Times have surely changed since Alfred and Jakobine passed by in their London taxi with its thin, wire-spoked wheels.

We met a southbound Guerba Overland truck near a small town with an irrigation scheme nearby where rice was growing, which told me that we were nearing the Niger River. The Guerba people told us that we were catching up 'our Guerbas' who had talked of their worry about us in Chad. They also told us that Mali was at war with Haute-Volta (or whatever it's called these days). The two neighbouring countries had bombed each other's towns and shot down a plane or two, but big brother, France, was putting a stop to it. They did not know what the war was about and I don't think they cared.

When we arrived in Niamey, we met the Guerba and Tracks trucks at the Sureté Nationale, checking their visas ready to leave the next day. Forty Overlanders whooped and yelled at each other and formed a fast-talking, laughing mob on the pavement, spilling into the city centre street. It was great.

Niamey lies on the River Niger, about a thousand miles from its delta mouth. It is not as famous as Timbuctoo nor as historically interesting as Kano or Jenne. It had been a minor caravanserai, but the French had made it a regional colonial capital, and so it had acquired modern power. The older parts had square, flat-roofed mud buildings, but most of the city was French colonial or post-colonial featureless concrete. Further out there was that modern African menace, the shantytown, and refuse blew in the Harmattan. Unlike Bangui's cheerful anarchy of the Black man, Niamey had the quietness and greater dignity that went with Arabic culture. There was not the noise of a thousand hi-fi's pounding out boogie music in the townships, but there were the calls of the muezzins.

We camped in an official camping site, quite pleasant with small trees for a bit of shade, ablution blocks with running water and a simple barbed wire fence to keep out the public. Now that we were under Moslem influenced jurisdiction we had practically no worries about theft. We had to stay there several days. It was the New Year holiday week-end and apart from getting their 'entry' visas, our colonial cousins had also to get Algerian visas: there are definite advantages to being British and belonging to the EEC when travelling in North Africa. I did not mind. Ted and I spent a morning 'doing' the commercial centre, drinking a cold Coke from a street stall when we felt like it, walking the cassia-shaded streets and looking in the shops. There seemed to be a fair variety of manufactured goods, groceries and domestic essentials from Nigeria and France, electrical goods from France or Japan. We had omelettes and French fries in a patisserie with Katie and Marguerite, saying farewell to Marguerite as the Guerba truck was leaving that day. It was sad to say good-bye; the 'Guerbas' had been close to us for a long time and we talked of the 'night of the charades' in the Zaïre rain forest and 'the night of the disco-truck' in Bangui . . .

The feeling of change and the beginning of the end was heightened by Karen and Al deciding to leave us in Algeria. Al wanted to chalk up Tunisia, Sicily and Sardinia on his list of countries he had travelled in and Karen decided that she would head for Turkey where she had some Canadian contacts. Our mood was worsened by a confused furore at the banks in town. I kept well out of it by exchanging dollar bills with Karen who wanted US currency for the BM in Tunisia. Bob was badly upset by the money problem, however, since the company had arranged transfer of several people's extra private funds together with running expenses through a local bank which levied a massive exchange commission of about £300. It was hardly Bob's fault, but the anger inevitably rubbed off on him, since he was the company representative, and some of our people were now seriously worried about cash. The whole matter was exascerbated by Algeria requiring that all tourists exchange £75 into non-refundable local currency before being passed through immigration controls. To a package tourist this was a bagatelle, to Overlanders at the end of a five month journey, it was a heavy burden. Marie, Angie, Tory and Nick particularly had problems. A pall of itchy insecurity and 'end of voyage' lethargy began in Niamey. Some began to wish that the safari would end and the great spirit of togetherness that we had for so long, began to dissipate. There were outbreaks of bickering and criticism and Bob became a target, as the leader often does. Bob became taciturn.

New Year's Eve morning began for me with a great laundering and washing, followed by a magnificent breakfast of barbecued steak, fried eggs and tomatoes and fresh French bread with real butter. Ted and I decided that we were going to celebrate New Year to the hilt, rolling all of the festival season and the beginning of the end of our safari into one great day. I had told him how much the Niger River meant to me and had bored him with 'culture vortexes' and trans-Sahara trading systems, so he said that we had better spend the day at the Grand Hotel which we were told overlooked the River on a prominence. Being the only five-star international hotel in fifteen hundred miles between N'Djamena and Ouagadougou, capitals of the neighbouring states of Chad and Burkina Fasso, we could probably get a good lunch and we could probably let our cameras emerge (photography in Niger is totally proscribed without special permits). So we packed up a day bag with swim-suits, towels, cameras and sun-hats as if we were going on a European picnic and asked Bob if he would drop us off and pick us up. It meant a special journey in the truck, but I bribed him with an offer of unlimited beers if the hotel would accept my American Express card. Rob and Sarah, Claire and Adie also thought it a good idea, so Bob agreed.

The Grand Hotel seemed to have been built in the 1950s on a bluff about two hundred feet above the wide, shining Niger River. It had a dark and cool reception lobby surrounded by lounges, a hairdresser and boutiques which led onto a terrace with swimming pool, beds of flowers, some palms, bougainvillaea crawling colourfully on pergolas, and tables and chairs set out under Martini umbrellas. "This will suit us very well," I said to Ted and it did. We ensconced ourselves at a table with a view out over the River and desert beyond and I went to interview the reception clerk, armed with my trusty American Express card.

"I am not staying in the hotel," I explained. "But my friend and I wish to spend the day here, having a good lunch, using the swimming pool, drinking a few nice beers."

"*Certainement, Monsieur.* That is in order. If you have lunch, there will be no charge for the swimming." We beamed at each other. Above his head there was a large tinselled sign saying, *Bonne Année! Bon Chance!*

"In order to pay all our expenses, I would like to have one account when we leave, and I will use my American Express card."

He frowned at that and gestured to me to wait, disappearing into an office. I wandered about the lobby and was accosted by a curio seller and a smooth young man who wanted to know if 'Papa' had the need of any young ladies or boys for the holidays. I gestured to Claire and Adie who were looking at post-cards inside the hotel stationery shop and told him that regrettably I had my own with me. He looked mournfully at the

254

girls, especially Claire who had recovered her good health in Chad and was dressed for the day to the limit of her Overlander's wardrobe.

The clerk returned smiling and it was agreed. An imprint of my card was taken and my passport number recorded. Two waiters were summoned, one from the terrace, one from the restaurant, and I was introduced to them. I was free to order as I wished. We all shook hands with formal dignity and mutual respect. I felt extraordinarily good: I was a Pasha for the day, an Emir from the desert, a Chief from the jungles. I had stayed at the Paris Ritz on a client's unlimited expense account a year before and had not felt nearly so elevated by unrestrained hedonism. It was a great day there on the terrace. The service was impeccable from the terrace waiter, a grizzled elderly Hausa who spoke English pidgin and called me 'Ogha', for he had lived in Sokoto in Nigeria for a while and worked at the European Club there in his youth.

I watched the sun move across the Niger, gradually changing the colour from shiny stippled silver to greasy grey. I followed the dugout canoes as they lazily slipped by; some had sails bellying out from a short mast and they looked satisfyingly Arabic to me. I watched a man tilling his vegetables on a richly silted island opposite us. Ted photographed a traffic jam on the long modern bridge across the River nearby; a camel train got hopelessly entangled when an impatient bus driver hooted at it and was rewarded by a fifteen minute delay while the chaos was sorted out. I admired Claire's lithe young body in a black swimsuit when she swam and then sunbathed at the table she and Adie occupied a little distance away. In that environment which was so strange to us all, my companions, whom I knew so intimately, briefly became pleasant acquaintances met on a fantasy holiday. At lunch time, Sarah and Rob arrived, flushed and happy. Sarah was gushing about things she had seen in the shops and interesting people they had watched. They joined us for drinks instantly supplied by my Hausa friend. (What a pretty girl Sarah was, so English; quite exciting – a little more rounded than Claire, perhaps . . .?)

"You seem well organised, Denis, old chap," observed Rob.

"I'm a pasha today, Rob. Just a simple pasha."

"Marvellous day," murmured Ted. "I'm not leaving till Bob carries my away. Cheers!"

The maitre d'hotel came to announce our lunch table and Rob shook his head in mock admiration. Sarah perched on the arm of my chair and stroked my head.

"Will you let us dine with you, dear pasha?" she whispered in my ear, her breath tickling.

"If you cut my hair tomorrow," I said sternly. She had cut it in Bangui, an aeon ago.

"Is that all you want?" she murmured softly.

I got up, laughing. "My word," I said. "This is getting too like a package tour for comfort. I'm going to have a quick swim and cool my brains."

After a splash in the pool we went in to have lunch in a pavilion overlooking the River. The waiters were enjoying us and laughed and joked as they offered menus. Sarah was vegetarian and the choosing of her meal took a leisurely five minutes or so. There was not much choice, in fact, principally an excellent buffet of imported French patés, cold meats, salmon and tuna, and a lavish collection of local fruits and salads. Ted had a couple of good helpings and I was glad to see him eat so well. The dryness of the desert, fresh food and the physical relaxation of the last few days was curing our ills. We drank a cold white Burgundy, and were very jolly and at ease. We had a ripe Camembert, coffee and Armagnac. We reminisced a bit, but not too heavily for we were aware of the dangers of that. I wrote a poem on a table napkin with a *stilo* borrowed from the waiter. The afternoon slipped away and suddenly there was Bob and Steve come to collect the promised beers. As the sun lowered, the Harmattan-fogged sky turned pink and the far hills changed to mauve. I was glad to hear Bob's laugh roaring out again after several beers had cascaded down his throat. Eventually, the reception clerk came to suggest gently that the day was ending; there was a special dinner that evening with 'official' guests.

"One of the best New Years of my life," said Ted as I went off to sign the slips. (The restaurant bill was £15 for Ted and I.) I will certainly never forget it. Steve drove us back and I found that a special dinner was also being prepared at our camp. We were to have barbecued steak, baked potatoes and salads with puddings to follow. There were no official cooks, volunteers were doing different things.

"I wondered if we should cook some rice, Den. For the sake of old times?" Graham asked when he saw me. "But I think there's enough food for about thirty already."

"We'll rest on our laurels," I agreed. "Come and have a beer in the bar. You've missed out." There was a rough little bar attached to the camping park with cheap, cold beer.

"We've already had a skinful, most of us. But I'll join me old cooking partner anyway."

The food was a disaster with too many celebrating cooks but we had an uproarious time. Aussie Steve had bought some batteries in town and

Dave had fixed someone's portable tape-recorder so we had our music for the first time since Zaïre. I listened to Nick Kershaw, Juluka, Chris de Burgh and the theme from Local Heroes and there were tears on my cheeks. I started to boogie with Angie but Bob's big hand pulled me away. "I'm not going to have you on a crutch to meet your wife in four weeks," he bellowed. "Stay sat down and drink some more beer, you lovely bastard."

Why do such days have to end?

PART SIX:

SAHARA

CHAPTER TWENTY: *LONG TROUSERS DAY*

When those long caravans that cross the plain
With dauntless feet and sound of silver bells
Put forth no more for glory or for gain,
Take no more solace from palm-girt wells;

When the great markets by the sea shut fast
All that calm Sunday that goes on and on;
When even lovers find their peace at last,
And Earth is but a star, that once had shone.
THE GOLDEN JOURNEY TO SAMARKAND. James Elroy
Flecker [1884-1915]

The muezzins were calling across Niamey and fifty yards from my tent, pitched between two whispy pine trees, a camel was roaring. Further away cocks were crowing. I turned over and slept for another half hour before getting up to a breakfast of scrambled eggs, tomatoes, fresh bread, coffee and condensed milk. Luxury!

At last, the Algerian visas were ready after the long New Year celebrations and most went into town on the truck. I stayed behind with Marie, who was not well again, packed up leisurely and did some final laundering. It took an hour for my sleeping sheets, kikoyi and underpants to dry in that marvellous air. I talked to Pieter, a young German who was marooned in the camp site. Something had gone badly wrong with his safari, problems with companions as usual, and he was trying to get home to Dusseldorf. I had suggested that he phone a trusted friend or relative and get them to arrange a pre-paid air ticket. This had not occurred to him and he had been grateful and pleased with me when it had been apparently all arranged two days after the New Year. So I was surprised to see him sitting by our campfire in misery that morning, but he had spent almost his last money taking a taxi early to the airport to discover that he had no seat or ticket after all. He besieged the airline, Air Algerie, to find that a hung-over and exhausted girl, checking the telex machine after the plane had left, discovered that his confirmation and reservation had come through the night before. She had not looked earlier, "because of the holidays".

"Because of schnapps and *boomsin* all night long," Pieter said in disgust.

"What will you do?" I asked him.

"I do not know, Denis. My brain will not work just now. I told the airline that it is their responsibility. But they do not care, and the next plane is in one week."

When the truck returned I had a long talk with Karen who had spent time in the last few days with a Fulani family whom she had befriended. They were in desperate straits because they had been persuaded by the authorities to put all their resources into groundnuts which had failed in the severe droughts of the last few years. They had lost the family cattle herd and were destitute. The head of the family was trying to learn French, because it was essential for commerce or administration, but could not pass the academic grades without expensive private tuition. The wife and elder children were trying to make money by home weaving of tourist articles, but there was not enough demand for quality handmade goods and there was plenty of competition so they were being exploited by shopkeepers. Karen was deeply upset about her friends.

To most people, the journey we were facing as we left Niamey might have been the pinnacle of their life's experience. We were heading, from the banks of the Niger River, across the world's largest and most romantic desert to the shores of the Mediterranean Sea. Even the mid-winter journey from Gibraltar to England with worn-out African safari clothes in a truck designed for the tropics and little money would be a startling adventure for many. The distance from Niamey to Ceuta where we were to cross to Spain was about two thousand eight hundred miles, two thirds of which was in the Sahara. We were to pass through Niger, Algeria and Morocco. Niger is an impoverished client to France, Algeria is oil-rich Arab-socialist and Morocco is a traditional ancient Kingdom: fascinating countries. Historically, the journey would touch upon archaeological relics that were more than five thousand years old, we would pass along trading tracks and through oases that had been used by diverse people for thousands of years, from the days when horse-drawn chariots crossed the Sahara, through the great age of the camel caravans to the present when snorting articulated trucks pounded through with comet trails of dust. We would see Berber forts and the granary of the Roman Empire. We would follow in the trail of slave trains under the whip of Arab and Turkish slave-masters who were still plying their trade in the 1920s.

However, our truck had to be serviced and renovated in her home workshops after the rigours of Zaïre and Chad and Bob had to get some rest in England before heading off to India and Katmandu. Other Overlanders were waiting for our faithful truck that had been our home for so long, getting ready for their own great experience, building up their excitement. And we were leaving the banks of the Niger, a couple of weeks late. "It's going to be tough," Bob confided in me. "And I know that I'm going to take a lot of stick from everyone. But what can you do . . .?" So we were going to race through North Africa and that caused the magic of the safari to begin to fade for me. An air of anticipation of the 'real' world began to seep through everyone. I heard two of the girls discussing the problems of decent bedsits in London. Karen and Al spent much time talking about their route through Algeria to Tunis. Money became a constant worry to some. The 'colonials' talked about work permits and renewing visas to stay in England.

I began thinking about this book. I had seen the places that had been my priorities, I was surfeited with images and experiences, my brain and soul seemed exhausted. I found difficulty remembering simple everyday things like names of life-long close friends and forgot my own home post-code. I could not remember sequences of events as short a distance away as Cameroon. Johannesburg was definitely on another planet. It was temporary, of course, an overloading of the circuits and I understood exactly what was happening and why. It could be said that I was suffering from a minor nervous breakdown. We all were to some extent, and that was not surprising. I felt some kinship with the old explorers sailing new seas on little ships, trudging mopani wilderness on their feet, riding sand deserts on their camels. They felt the same. So I was grateful for the mental and psychic experience that I had embarked on the safari to obtain: that's why I was there! I had no responsibility except for myself and my relationships with my comrades and friends, so I could relax and let it all happen.

But, nobody can totally abdicate. For example, there was the day when I looked at the sun and realised that it was in the wrong direction and when I questioned Bob, he woke out of his own private daze to find that we were driving south-west into nowhere when we should have been driving north-east towards the wide desert trail . . .

Many of us had picked up stomach infections in Naimey and Katie was suffering badly. We had to stop frequently along the road north to let desperate people off to head behind a dune or clump of scrub with the shovel. I was all right because I had not eaten anything not freshly cooked except for the excellent lunch in the Grand Hotel. Bob was suspicious of the badly cooked meal and poorly prepared salads of the celebration dinner in camp on New Year's Eve. I had dined on beer, so escaped that. Halfway to Agadez we drove alongside surface water for several miles. There were clusters of temporary shacks and intensive cultivation of vegetables, millet and maize. The intensity of the green against the grey sand of the surrounding desert almost hurt the eyes. There had been good rains in parts of the Sahara that year and what we saw was an example of how underground rivers come to the surface when the watertable is raised. All over the Sahara there are oases and rivers which rise and sink according to a mysterious swell of the global weather. In millenia gone by, the ground cover and scrub bush acted as a stabilising influence on the surface soils, smoothing the harshness of the cycles, but with the vegetation gone from over-grazing and the land covered by raw, porous sand, the occasional rainstorm is rapidly lost below ground. That is the way the Kalahari and Masai steppes may go.

We saw Agadez from afar, floating above the skyline in an extensive mirage. It is a Taureg town, an old trading caravanserai dependant for its existence on a long wadi with good groundwater that occasionally floods. It is a town of flat-topped, brown mud buildings sprouting TV aerials. The famous mud minaret of its principal mosque stands tall, a shaped structure with a flat top prickled all over by the ends of the logs used to construct its framework. It looked like a giant brown cactus fruit with its top sliced off.

We stopped at an official campsite which boasted a sort of swimming pool fed by a petrol-driven pump from a well. The pump was broken and the water scummy so nobody swam, but I could imagine the screams of delight in the hot season when Overlanders reached there from the north. The toilets were a filthy disgrace. Rejecting them for the clean sands beyond the confines of the camp I tried to remember when I had last seen such disgusting toilets and after some memory dredging, which was a useful exercise for my lethargic brain, I thought of the unconnected W.C.'s in the fairground at Mwanza on the shores of Lake Victoria.

European tourists were sharing the campsite. There were parties in smart Range Rovers and Toyota Landcruisers and one spectacular Unimog, all with gas stoves, fridges and lights, deck chairs and elaborate tents and folding awnings. There were children and pet dogs and tape recorders playing British rock or German and French pop songs. I fancied that I heard the strains of Brahms at one moment. I watched the stars through the fronds of a date palm and sensed myself in a popular yacht harbour in the Med, lying on the deck of an old ocean-going schooner that had sailed from the Cape of Good Hope, surrounded by shining fibreglass craft with chromed sheet winches and seldom unfurled, pretty-coloured sails. The Sahara has become a yachting lake, I said to myself. That's it, a yachting lake for the Yuppies and wealthy middle-aged middle-classes who want to do something really spectacular for their annual holiday, something that was not as hazardous or expensive as ocean cruising but which could still sound more glamorous. (*"Where did you go this year, Jonathan?" Deidre asked. "Oh! We popped across the Sahara to Agadez: charming old Taureg slave-caravanserai. Juliet bought some superb trinkets there, Maria Theresa crosses and semi-precious stones. A bit hairy in parts of course, but the Range Rover did it splendidly." "How super!" Deidre exclaimed, eyes shining.*) I grinned at my own snobbery, but guessed that it was going that way. The very trendy Paris-Dakar rally was due any day, we had been told. It was a beautiful night with the stars sharp, no wind and balmy air. I watched several shooting stars and Al pointed out a satellite.

We were definitely leaving the real safari.

At Arlit, the last town in Niger, we were deep into the Sahara. It was a new town whose existence depended on a vast uranium mine a few miles north at the foot of a flat mountain of tailings on the endless gravel plain. After dark, the mercury lights of the mine and its compound looked like a grounded space battleship from Star Wars. There was an official campsite in the desert away from the town with baby palms growing in irrigated ditches and a huge sign in red saying, *'Photographie Interdit'.* The nights started getting cold there, we were crossing lines of latitude fast.

There were several parties of Sahara 'yachtsmen' in camp and the lack of contact seemed strongly noticeable. Not since the zebra-striped tourist kombis of Kenya had there been such an invisible wall between us and other travellers, or people of any kind. No wonder other races dislike Europeans so much. I had always known that White people are thought to be arrogant and unfriendly in Africa, and I knew that this was not a pose, it was just the way we are at home. I was seeing my fellow Europeans with African eyes. I was fascinated.

Adie was standing next to me, following my gaze, "You'd think they would at least greet us or even look at us, wouldn't you?" she said, clearly puzzled. Our nearest neighbours were producing delicious aromas from their portable gas-fired barbecue, drinking Pina Coladas and laughing loudly at their jokes: having a pleasant evening on their annual camping holiday.

"No," I replied. "We're an old trading schooner and they are yachtsmen."

"You all right, Denis?" Adie's straight blue eyes looked me over.

"Sure," I grinned and squeezed her arm. "You're seeing them like an African. 'Snotty little shits those White people aren't they?'"

She nodded slowly. "I see what you mean. We're so used to Africans staring and waving and smiling . . ."

"Five months ago you were complaining about it."

She nodded again. "You're quite right."

MY DIARY: 7/1/1986, 10 kms S. of Assamakka to 20 kms N. of In-Guezzam: 'LONG-TROUSERS DAY'.

Woke at 05.11. Last quarter moon with full earthlight just risen. Southern Cross still just above horizon. Cooking. Waited in warm sleeping bag then crawled out at 05.30. Cold wind so started petrol stove inside truck to heat baked beans and coffee. Graham cutting and buttering bread with teeth chattering. Finally broke down and got out long trousers in honour of cold and Algeria – they don't like shorts. Haven't worn long trousers while travelling since leaving Jo'burg, so this is historic and symbolic event of last part of the safari.

Off at 07.30, quick run to border post – a few bushes on a rocky ridge, three white prefab huts, a couple of wrecked minibuses. That's it. Pile of refuse with black ravens on it. Strong, dry wind blowing. We wait the pleasure of border guards, Bob playing it cool. Other travellers hanging around the huts, some French 'yachtsmen' arguing with hands going. After fifteen minutes, a guard strolls over to us and walks around the truck with Bob following politely. He takes our passports away and an hour later they are returned. We drive off, leaving the tourists sitting disconsolately by their Landies. Bob's laid-back technique is the proper way. Patience gets you through fast.

Sped along hard ridge until we met a ten mile spur of soft sand between rocky hills. At one point, the dreaded sandmats came out. Good old times? But everybody quite cheerful. Soon got through bad spot of 500m as our rhythm and routine is so automatic. Also stuck are Swiss party of two motor bikes, short-wheelbase Landie and a Landcruiser with extraordinary, extravagant 'house' built into the back, decorated with pop-art undersea scenes. The 'house' had built-in battery-powered fridge-freezer, heating and air-conditioning. Deeply stuck and no sandmats. One young man digging desultorily, another dives into engine when I approach to look them over. Their tyres are rock-hard and the back axle is on the ground. "You have a pump for tyres?" I ask. I get a wary nod. "Then you must let your tyres down. Go down to one BAR pressure or even less. When you get out of this sand, pump up again." They look at me as if I am an idiot. "You understand English?" "Yes, of course." I shrug and walk away. In the small Landie there is a woman alone, about 35: slim, freckled face, auburn hair, nice worried eyes. I like her. I tell her about the tyres. She says that the men will decide. They have been stuck for several hours, since dawn. Her 'nerves' are very bad. The 'piste' from Tamanrasset is terrible. She has 'bad fears' . I tell her again about the tyres and hold her hand for a moment.

Drove to end of sand onto gravel and stopped to stow sandmats. Watched two big French registered Mercedes articulated trucks loaded with smaller truck chassis and crated engines, towing Peugeot saloon cars, roar past. Both get stuck near Swiss party and they have no sandmats. Dear, oh dear.

Later we pass first Paris-Dakar rally cars and supporters, covered with sponsorship stickers, driving fast and so seriously. At In-Guezzam border post there is chaos of rally cars, supporters and tourists. A long queue. Bob laid-back again and it works. We are promised passage after lunch. Our people chat to southbound Encounter Overland truck. I meet nice little group from Germany, travelling in Mercedes bakery van with tiny wheels. They took five days from Tamanrasset – we expect one day. They ran out of food and water after three days, their children sick; other tourists did not stop although they waved them all down. Incredible! The Encounter Overland truck saved them. Party is German man and ex-Biafran army officer returning from exile with young German wife and two children. Had long chat to the Nigerian fellow: very pleasant, comes originally from Ikot Ekpene, which I know. His town still war-damaged, schools and hospitals still closed by Federal Government. Eastern Nigeria in bad state with brigandage, corruption and poverty. He lives in Europe but needs to return to see his old parents. Because of the seriousness of their experience in the Sahara, they will ship van back and fly home, selling all things possible to raise cash. They are very anxious about sand

266

on the way to Assamakka and I suggested they talked to the leader of the Encounter Overland truck, he might lend them sandmats if they go together; maybe some of the passengers would help them. Talked to Bob who said Encounter driver confirmed story and would look out for them all the way to Arlit where the tar starts. Encounter Overlanders were appalled at attitude of the tourists to the bakery van party. It makes me sick in my stomach. Ignorant, soulless bastards!

Convoy of rally supporters and tourists set out southwards soon after lunch and we passed through northwards an hour later. One customs officer wanted to get all our bags out for a search, but the Chef said: "Enough. Let them go."

There is a whole Algerian army division (15,000 men) camped alongside the town, because of Mali/Burkino Fasso conflict we are told. (Or the long-running dispute with Morocco?) Amazing sight of couple of thousand khaki tents in immaculate serried ranks, many trucks in park, Russian tanks and armoured gun-carriers.

Sun is beginning to set early, we are moving north and it is dead of winter. Spun along open sand 'piste' for 20 kms, then drove off to rocky ridge a mile away from nearest tracks and camped.

The next evening we camped just short of Tamanrasset because we preferred the open desert to the campsites full of tourists, dirty toilets and fly-infested refuse. The run that day had been superb, across a great sand plain dotted with the hulks of lost dreams. We did not need the tall iron post trail-markers every kilometre in this area, the route was better marked by the shells of VW kombis, Ford and Fiat saloons, even old-fashioned looking buses. You could tell how old the wrecks were by the colour: if they still had paint they were a season or two old, if they were a dull silver-grey they were older, all paint sand-blasted away. Many had cheeky slogans painted on them like 'Vive la Liberté', 'Rolling Stones' or 'This was Painted by Enrico' and some had been hoisted up on each other by bored travellers looking for macho exercise.

Early on, I realised that I had not one picture of a camel in the desert and asked Bob to stop if he saw one. Not five minutes later the truck slowed and Bob grinned over his shoulder at me: "At your service, Denis." Half buried in the sand was the fur-clad skeleton of a camel. We all got out to photograph it and it was a powerful image: the pathetic, dried corpse was strung out in the pale sand against a background that flowed immaculately to the horizon where a solitary ship-like rocky mountain stood out.

A victim of the Sahara desert.

We were passed by more rally cars, many were 4X4 turbo-charged Peugeots and Audi Quattros racing on that sand sea at over 100 miles an hour. They sounded like aeroplanes and they looked like speedboats with a curved, sharply defined plume of dust trailing.

Approaching Tamanrasset, mid-point of the Sahara, we nosed our way up a long wadi that the route follows through one of the well-separated escarpments that make the Sahara seem to be a series of enormous shallow steps leading to the folded range of the Atlas Mountains, which is the desert's northern boundary. Each escarpment is several hundred miles apart and the flat plains between have their own distinctive character. That to the south of Tamanrasset is beautiful coarse sand, and at our campsite towards the head of the wadi, sheltered from the route by a spur of rocky hillside, I packed a plastic bag full of that sand. We ate dehydrated food which I abhor but Bob made the day end well for me with a good slug of J & B in my coffee.

Next morning, we took definitive group photographs of ourselves, posing before the truck behind a fence of sandmats.

CHAPTER TWENTY ONE: *HOGGAR*

Afar in the desert I love to ride,
With the silent Bush-boy along by my side:
When the sorrows of life the soul o'ercast,
And, sick of the Present, I cling to the Past:
    AFAR IN THE DESERT. Thomas Pringle [South African
                                        poet]

We had to hang about in Tamanrasset, no matter whether Bob wished to move on or not. Northbound, this was the first town where we could change the obligatory 1,000 dinars [£75] of hard currency and we had to show proof to the police before we could leave again. We arrived to find the banks had just shut and they would not open again until after the Arab week-end, Saturday to us. There was a wail of frustration from our party and angry words.

I wandered with Ted, Rob and Sarah along the main street, lined by white-washed shops and small houses built in the colonial era. Some had been converted into smart boutiques which were open though the banks were closed, adding to our group's anguish. The street was shaded by giant eucalyptus trees, decades old, and leafy cassias with white-washed boles. I liked the style of Tamanrasset. We walked into the old souk in the centre of town where there were several stalls selling a range of brightly coloured rugs, embroidered blouses and thick camel-wool djellabas (the long, cowled monk-like garment that North Africans universally wear). "That's what I have to buy when we have money," I said to Ted, pointing to a rack of djellabas. "I'll not survive the cold from here to England otherwise." Ted wanted a multi-coloured blanket for the same purpose, a djellaba was not his style. Walking back to the truck, we passed the official government travel agency, ONAN, and stared in the window. They were advertising trips into the Hoggar and Tassili mountains, areas of outstanding mountain scenery and many relics of the Neolithic period.

"*In sh'Allah!*", I said, gesturing with a shrug.

Like a genie from a bottle, a large man with magnificent beard popped out of the office. "Tourists!" he announced with a smile and a mental rubbing of his hands.

"No good," said Rob. "We have no money, we arrived too late for the banks."

The bearded giant studied us, his eyes flicking over our worn and dirty clothes. "You come from the South, eh? From the very far south on a truck, yes?" We nodded. "And you have to change money before you leave town, not until Saturday, yes?" We nodded again.

Teeth showed through the black hair. We were perfect prey. "Come inside, sit down. All will be well! I understand everything. Have some coffee. Now, how many are you?"

In sh'Allah, I thought and let it all happen. Within fifteen minutes three Landcruisers had been engaged, a route agreed upon, departure first thing in the morning arranged. We would pay on Saturday, we were trusted, I roused myself to ask an important question: "Will we see ancient rock-paintings, I will not go otherwise?" Mr Didin reassured me. An air of expectation filled our camp that evening as we ate dehydrated spaghetti bolognese bought in Johannesburg for the fourth night running. Because of the closed banks, the cooks could not buy fresh food.

The Landcruiser station wagons arrived on time, each with a driver and already loaded with food, blankets and foam mattresses perched on the roof. We were to sleep at Assakrem, in a hermitage built by an extraordinarily eccentric Frenchman, Charles de Foucauld. Quentin Crewe describes de Foucauld and other French Sahara eccentrics in his book, *In Search of the Sahara*. De Foucauld was a minor aristocrat who had a military education and served in regiments posted to the colonies. He was indolent and extravagant, a habitual glutton, and merited discharge from the service on several occasions, but influence and mysterious charm saved his career. He was not without ability and energy when his interest was aroused however, and he travelled widely in Morocco in disguise as a spy, producing one of the first accurate geographies of remote parts of the territory. He had intriguing love affairs. Later he had a dramatic change of heart and founded Christian hospices in Algeria after spending years in the Holy Land, one of which was the hermitage high in the Hoggar at Assakrem. He settled in the Tamanrasset area in 1905 and was accidentally killed by rebels who wished to take him hostage during a Sennoussi uprising in 1916.

I travelled with Rob and Sarah with the cooking gear and our cook. The men wore slacks and pale-coloured djellabas with black cloths wrapped around their heads. They did not like to be photographed, but they stopped frequently to point out views that they considered photogenic. The Hoggar is an area of massive volcanic activity. It is a great jumble of varying types of ancient volcanoes whose hard igneous pipes and dykes have been exposed over millions of years by the erosion of the softer sandstones and other sedimentary layers, so that the cores of these volcanic structures tower into the sky in all their stripped glory. The first that we came to was a classical pipe, rearing up several thousand feet above the plain like a huge bunch of macaroni all cemented together, the dusky, crystalline rods shining in the sharp sunlight. Our driver stopped twice so that we could photograph it from different angles and I saw it in my memory as a travel poster advertising Algeria in some airline office somewhere. It was awesome in the still afternoon in the middle of that great desert and I would have liked to gaze at it quietly. The faint black dots of ravens circled its summit.

Nearby we visited the dry bed of a once great river and the site of an ancient waterfall with an empty pool at its foot perhaps a hundred yards across and a hundred feet deep. We imagined the foaming mountain water roaring over that fall, filling the gorge with spray, ten thousand years ago, with Neolithic men camped by the side of the pool, cooking a hunted antelope. The marks of modern fires showed where electronic age men had camped and there were graffiti all over the cliffs.

"Amazing, isn't it?" Rob remarked pointing to the names and slogans painted in rainbow colours.

"Do you suppose that people go off cruising the Sahara and say, 'Don't forget the graffiti paint, chaps,' before they leave?" I asked. "Actually, I can't totally disapprove. It's no good admiring and protecting the graffiti of Stone-age people and then sneering at the same thing done by modern man."

"That's an interesting point of view," said Rob.

"I just wish that modern graffiti were remotely as fine as the ancient ones," said Sarah.

"With that I have to agree," I said.

All afternoon we climbed steadily into the mountains, sliding around sharp bends and over switchbacks. Just driving in a small, powerful four wheel drive vehicle with a driver fully familiar with his route was a novel experience for us and it was plain that our truck would never have made it without crawling for miles and reversing back and forth. The mountains kept changing their profiles and composition: some had the extruded macaroni look of the first monster, others were like gigantic, smooth slices of bronze ice-cream, still others were a mass of pinnacles and jagged spikes. The land was covered by sun-cured black shards of rock, sharp and rough. At one place we stopped and walked about and the sound of stone on stone echoed like a mound of cast iron chunks. It was similar to an area of the Namib Desert in Namibia that I had travelled long ago, but on a far grander scale. I saw some wild goats and donkeys half way up one mountain, how could they possibly survive?

As the sun lowered, it became cold as we steadily climbed, and our driver reassured us that we were getting close. At the foot of a series of hairpin bends that seemed to go up forever, he pointed up and said that the hermitage was at the top. Suddenly, he exclaimed to his companion and the two of them chattered excitedly. We slithered around another two bends then came to a halt, perched on the edge of the abyss. A sad sight awaited. A well-equipped back-up truck for one of the Paris-Dakar rally teams had skidded to the edge and tipped over, spilling its contents down the cliff face: shiny new tool-kits, numerous spare parts, many sealed in their plastic bags and polystyrene boxes, were spewed out amongst the rocks. The crew of the truck, one with a bloody bandage round his head, were camped gloomy and cold by the side of the road, faced with the task of trying to guard their expensive gear. A hundred yards further on there was the wreck of a German TV company's helicopter, its tail rotor smashed.

At the hermitage, a hundred or more tourists and rally enthusiasts milled about and the small carpark was filled with foreign four wheel drives and kombis. Our driver clucked in disapproval at this and angrily manoeuvred about in low range, climbing a bank, until he had settled in a strategic position near the back door. We were the last to arrive, and the sun was setting.

I grabbed my cameras and a blanket and limped up the hillside above the strange fort-like building and found a place to sit and watch the glorious scenery. We were at an altitude of about 9,000 feet and the air was iced champagne. There was no wind and the sky above was a deep navy blue, already studded with stars. In the south-west, the golden ball of the sun was falling towards the splintered black silhouettes of the Hoggar and the last of its light gilded the rocky towers to the east. The thin air diluted the sounds of humanity below and I was far above all the problems and joys of our safari. In the heart of the incredible Sahara, I was further isolated in the rarity of this aerie. It was the opposite extreme to the green wilderness of the Congo forest that I had stared down at from the escarpment above Beni. I smoked a cigarette, ignoring the cold eating into me, and tried to absorb every sight and hushed sound as the sun became a red ball and then disappeared, leaving a scarlet slash across the horizon. The sky at the zenith turned instantly black, the rocky pinnacles nearby became purple shapes whose distance could not be determined. A wild donkey brayed suddenly, the sound echoing back and forth towards silence. I sat on, smoking another cigarette with freezing fingers, unable to leave.

Golden light spilled sparingly through the slit windows of the hermitage below and the metallic clatter of shifting stones came up towards me.

"That you up there, Denis?" It was Ted, looking for me and I joined him, my knee stiff and sore. "Come on, we've got a hell of a scrum down there and you'd better grab a sleeping place. Adie is trying to hang on for us all."

Inside the hermitage there were three small rooms already taken up by parties of tourists, and one large room with about fifty people in it, talking in five or six languages, some eating, others sitting in circles talking, and our people lined against one wall with a pile of the foam mattresses from the Landcruisers. I suggested that we lay our mattresses down so that we had sleeping space, relax and see what would happen, which we did. We had not been in such close contact with total strangers of our own culture for months, since leaving the Youth Hostel in Nairobi, and we all felt strange. There were a number of French people and Germans who were easy to distinguish. Slowly, I identified other nationalities; a party of Spaniards, an Italian family, some Scandinavians and around the corner somewhere a loud Dutch voice. We were the only English-speaking group. As we sat, talking tiredly with each other waiting for whatever meal would be served us, a party of a dozen Moroccans came in with expensive camping gear and looked about with obvious displeasure. They had picnic hampers and were dressed fashionably; one of the women was wearing a fur coat. I grinned at their growing horror, this was not the light-hearted escapade into the desert mountains that I was sure they had expected. Their leader, a big man with sleek black hair and a knee-length suede leather coat suddenly laughed and gave orders to his friends. They set up their camping table and chairs in a corner, asking those around to give some room and proceeded to make the best of it, opening bottles of wine and black olives. The young woman with the fur coat sliced French bread sticks and a large cheese. I gave them full marks for amiability.

Our drivers served us dinner and it was especially delicious, for we were not only very hungry but starving for fresh food. There was vegetable soup with a generous helping of olive oil in it, plenty of French bread, a lump of well-braised goat meat with spaghetti and a delicious sauce made with the meat juice, tomato purée, sugar, salt and a spice that I could not define: simple food but as good as any banquet to us then. The Moroccans brought in pieces of an old packing case and lit a fire in the six-foot wide stone fire-place and the room became warmer and smokier. Gradually, all the floor space was taken up, there were mattresses, bed-rolls and camp-beds spread over all the surface: wall-to-wall people. I watched the unselfconscious manoeuvrings for territory, like a text-book exercise, that went on before my eyes, with great interest – we really are simple animals when confronted with simple, natural problems. No more could have crammed in that night. The lamps were put out and voices grew quieter and gradually died away as the people snuggled down. I lay for a while watching the flickering of the fire-light, thinking of this strange, wonderful experience, in that place high up in the frozen night.

I woke at seven in the morning as Graham stirred near me and I rolled over to meet Rob's smile. The Moroccans were quietly making up the fire and there was a murmur in French from the party in the opposite corner. A young German with his arm in a sling came in from the outside bringing freezing air with him. He was dressed in skiing clothes but looked ill with exposure and I guessed he was from the wrecked rally support truck. He crouched silently by the fire. The drivers brought us hot coffee and bread with the word that we must leave as soon as we were ready.

We stopped several times on the way back by a different route to the one we had ascended. The first time was to inspect a rally car that had crashed and burnt out. The body and engine block had been built of aluminium and all that was left were the steel pistons and sleeves, valves, gear box, transmission shafts and an assortment of nuts, bolts and wires. The rest was white powder. I thought of the insanity of building Royal Naval warships out of the same metal and what those sailors must have suffered at the Falkland Islands when their metal frigates burned. Nelson's men were better off in their open-decked wooden ships, cleared for action. I picked up a partly melted and distorted pair of binoculars and kept them as a macabre 'soovie'.

Another stop was for the promised Neolithic rock paintings. We had been told that the authorities were sensitive about tourists and rock art because some Germans had been apprehended in the Tassili chiselling out a whole panel of fine paintings with pneumatic drills, hence my anxiety that we may not be shown any. However, we were taken to two sites close to each other in a small wadi with jumbled, rocky walls. Some of the slabs of rock and giant boulders had slipped and crashed down during centuries of erosion and there were several old paintings amongst the chaos of stone. They were unimportant sites and much damaged by nature, therefore suitable to show casual tourists. Nevertheless, I was enchanted.

Crude but unmistakable outline drawings in pale, aged ochre illustrated elephants, ostriches and birds which I was satisfied were kori bustards. I examined them carefully and took photographs. The style and the animals were identical to other Neolithic paintings I had seen and photographed in the desert mountains of Namibia, especially at Twyfelfontein and in the Erongo. The rock art of Namibia lies about 20°S. latitude, that of the Hoggar is almost on the Tropic of Cancer, 23°N. latitude: that African mirror quirkily asserts itself constantly. In the Tassili, about three hundred miles east of the Hoggar, there are elaborate paintings, depicting a complex society and that style is also mirrored in Namibia, particularly in the 'White Lady' paintings of the Brandberg.

This extraordinary coincidence of style, 43° of latitude apart, equidistant from the great geographical barrier of the Congo rain forests, has puzzled and intrigued experts for decades. Distinguished academics have speculated about ancient migrations and Stone-age African empires to rival the Assyrians or Macedonians. My own view, reduced to greatest simplicity for the sake of brevity, is that there was a common African Neolithic culture linking north and south via the core population of East Africa. As each Ice-age of the past million years pulsed, man retreated back to and advanced outwards from the harmonious tropics of Africa. Each challenging pulse created advances in technology and social complexity. Populations were left behind in parts of Eurasia each time and either expired, such as Peking man, or survived on a slightly divergent cultural and genetic path, such as the Neanderthals. However, the core people provided the next surge forward at the end of each icily debilitating period. Very roughly, around 20,000 years ago, the most recent outsurge occurred in both directions, hence the rock paintings of the Namib and the Sahara. Those in the van of the northern expansion, merged with tough survivors they found in isolated pockets and, fired by the latest challenge, initiated agriculture and what we call Civilisation. The core populations of East-Central Africa steadily maintained their presence and in their tropical environment pursued their own steady development until civilised peoples returned at the beginning of the modern era.

The existence of similar rock art, equidistant from the Kenya Highlands and the Great Rift Valleys of Central Africa, is the great golden key to this idea; a theory that would show that not only is tropical Africa the genetic source of mankind, but that in much more recent time, tropical Africa is the source of human culture and the spring board for the exponential development of modern, civilised man. Africa is maybe the true mother of all mankind, modern as well as ancient. What is happening to-day, is therefore a second wave of cultural re-invasion which commenced only 100 years ago in the days of Livingstone and Stanley: an invasion which is now physically endangering the core-people.

We went hurriedly shopping the next morning after the banks opened. I bought my djellaba which was to be invaluable and Ted bought his blanket, Cathie bought some clothes to replace those that had been stolen from her tent in Bangui. We had problems with Mr Didin of the travel agency because of a misunderstanding over the quoted price for our tour, but patience and slow negotiation, almost on a level with the extrication of terrorist hostages, finally enabled us to reach a compromise.

I will never forget the Hoggar: the mysterious solitude of the high hermitage and the excitement of seeing the rock-paintings which I had been anticipating for many years. But I was now most definitely on the way home. The journey became an endurance test as we trundled through the vastnesses of the endless Sahara plains where the sky was the biggest I have ever seen, bigger than any ocean sky. For hours I was mentally switched off and my diary has an undelined remark written across it in giant capitals:

"I MUST REMEMBER THE IMPOSSIBLE IMMENSITY OF THIS DESERT"

North of Tamanrasset there were three large oasis towns before reaching the foothills of the Atlas Mountains: In Salah, El Golea and Ghardaia, increasing in prosperity and historical interest, and decreasing in distance apart. From Tamanrasset to In Salah there was about four hundred miles of rough desert travelling, from In Salah the tarred road was under construction so we spent most of the two hundred miles to El Golea driving alongside it. After Ghardaia, the road was good all the way to Zeebrugge on the Belgian coast.

In Salah was a bad town, dirty and dusty, the old quarter partly deserted and a new government 'council estate' raw and unattractive. The shops had little to offer and there were no cigarettes, so I dished out some of my horde of Nigerian Three Rings to desperate smokers. Ted and I wandered about and got temporarily lost in narrow, refuse strewn alleyways. To our astonishment we found several young women sleeping in the blazing sun in the dirt of the street, with flies crawling on their faces and goats nosing about. What were they, prostitutes shut out of their establishment, abandoned errant wives, destitute drop-outs from the socialist system? The cooks had found bread and tomatoes, but the *Gendarmerie* chased us out of town when they saw them cutting sandwiches on one of our folding tables in the market 'car park'. *"Pas de manger, ici!"* shouted a belligerent policeman, fingering his holstered pistol. "And fuck you, too, mate," muttered Dave, packing up.

The road to El Golea was unusable, so for many hours we raced across a dark brown stony plain, the largest flat plain I have ever seen. The stones were fist sized, many of them, not much fun to try and sleep on, so Bob became increasingly worried about finding a place to camp comfortably. We continued to avoid official town campsites like the plague. Suddenly, like a God-given gift, as the red ball of the sun was resting on the ruler straight horizon, there was a perfect circle of white sand directly in our track. It was about twenty yards across, just big enough for a circle of tents, and it was quite natural. What was it, we saw nothing like it anywhere else?

El Golea was surrounded by extensive, ancient date palm groves which sheltered irrigated crops of wheat, vegetables and maize. The town centre was unmistakably French colonial with a formal garden and a handsome Prefecture. The market was excellent. You could buy anything in it from second-hand door knobs and old brass bathtaps to aromatic spices, aluminium pots and pans and cast-off clothing. The food section had celery and cabbages, tomatoes and onions, carrots and oranges, turnips and cauliflowers. Dominating the town was a 9th century Berber fort, well-preserved, and we ate lunch at the foot of it and were not disturbed. I struggled up its ramparts afterwards and got fine pictures of the giant green eye of the oasis surrounded by the blinding white sands of the Grand Erg Occidental.

Ghardaia was a strange conglomeration of five communities and I would like to have spent days there in a sharper and more receptive state of mind. It is old and I saw clearly how each community had established itself along the length of a deep wadi, the architectural styles changing instantly from one cultural zone to the next. I admired the narrow three and four storied houses that clung to one hill, painted in pastel colours. We stopped to shop and refuel and some of us had lunch in what I suppose a guide book would have called a 'typical local Berber restaurant'. It was good to eat a well-cooked meal, but I found the food bland and uninteresting. More interesting was an antique shop owned by a strange old man with a short square body, wearing a fez covering whispy grey hairs. He spoke good English and allowed me to potter about his disordered shop despite my warning that I was not going to buy (I had spent my £75!). The room was piled high with artifacts of all kinds; guns and pistols, musical instruments, jewellery of several cultures, hand-woven cloth, traditional cooking utensils and Stone-age flints from the Hoggar and Tassili. I would like to go back to Ghardaia one day, with time and a fresh soul. *In sh'Allah!*

PART SEVEN:

THE MEDITERRANEAN

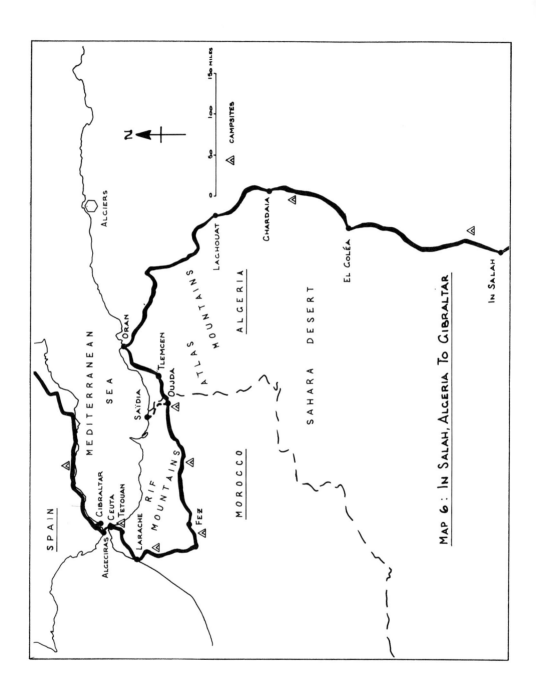

MAP 6: IN SALAH, ALGERIA TO GIBRALTAR

CHAPTER TWENTY TWO: *TLEMCEN AND OUJDA*

MY DIARY: 28 JUNE 1965

Left Melilla around noon and crossed back into Morocco. Very hot, breathless with heat. We are still not acclimatised. Passed through Berkane and Oujda – both rather zoomy towns. Bad time at Algerian border with long hold-up. Some local political troubles? Many military and police roadblocks on Algerian side near border. Into Tlemcen and had coffees at café in main street under trees. Poor compared to Morocco, workless men in faded blue clothes sitting in lines against walls. But this is nice old city. Fine medieval fortress ruins about and long wall (13th Century) around original town. Drove up into hills behind and camped in a field with olive trees and next to a clean fresh-water stream. A shepherd came to greet us, dressed like somebody from the Bible in striped camel hair robe. We slept well in the Landie.

Bob had decided, quite rightly, but to our disadvantage, to make a night-drive from the foothills of the Atlas on the Sahara side to the Moroccan border. Rightly, because he was increasingly haunted by his company's deadline and in winter it was not suitable to camp above 6,000 feet altitude. To our disadvantage, because this was a fine and magnificent piece of African scenery – the only great folded mountain range in Africa apart from those at the Cape of Good Hope, the mirror on the other side of the Equator. We had a scrappy dinner beside a wadi near the town of Laghouat where there were thick banks of tall reeds and stands of old eucalyptus and pine trees. Carrying the refuse bucket, the old chores still held, I penetrated the reeds to dispose of its contents and to relieve myself. I had moments of private calm and communion, listening to the filtered distant voices of my companions. Were we at the end of it all? Yes, we were. Above all, I heard the faint rumble-noise of cars and buses on the main road close to Laghouat town where people were commuting home from work, in the capsuled style of Europe. I stood, holding the familiar handle of the orange refuse bucket, purchased by Charlie in Pietersburg, South Africa, in the middle of a reed thicket on the northern fringe of the Sahara, and was lost in thought.

"Hallo! Denis!! Coo-eee!" Bob's voice penetrated my reverie. I stumbled back to the truck, shouting my acknowledgement.

I huddled in my djelleba as we climbed through the night over the Atlas, dozing, dreaming both asleep and awake. Towards dawn we passed through modern cities and sometimes I saw international road signs to Oran or Algiers, like a subliminal flash. There were traffic lights and ordinary city commuting buses. As dawn broke and we all began to take notice with bleary, red eyes, we entered Tlemcen, just another city to the others, but suddenly terribly important to me. I woke fully, sharply, heart running faster. I kept looking at Steve, who was navigating, and wanted to talk to him but feared disrupting a mood. Finally, I called to him.

"Steve! Are we stopping at all?" I asked.

"Yeah. Bob thinks we should have a blow. Have breakfast and a piss or whatever."

"Got any plans?"

"Not really, I'm looking at the map now. We don't want to stop in town." Steve's glasses glinted as he flourished his map.

"I know a good place to stop, will you follow my directions after we get to the other side of the city?" I asked.

"Your place is going to be better than something picked off a map, Den," Bob said. "Fire away."

I looked out through the front windscreen as we drove through Tlemcen. It was a prosperous, mature town with school buses picking up children and people going to work in conventional city clothes. Then we were through and passed under a red clay-brick, seven hundred year old arch with crenallated top. I saw a turn off to the left that my brain automatically registered. "Up that road!" I called to Bob, and he took it, the truck swaying. After a couple of miles into the hills, there was a large, open parking area that looked down on the wide plain with the city in the centre. The Berber walls stood below us. A French colonial watering place was close by, where a mountain stream had been diverted to a tank and spouts gushed onto a disused communal laundry. The cold, damp winter breeze moaned in the pine trees.

"All right?" I asked Bob.

"It's all righty – all righty! Been here before, have you?"

"Twenty years ago," I said.

I had completed a personal loop in time and space. In June 1965, I had camped in a field in the hills not far above our breakfast picnic place. It had been the first camp that Barbie and I had set up in the open country in North Africa and had a certain magic for us which was enhanced by a herd of goats coming past in the dusk, being taken home by a herdsman

284

who could have walked out of the pages of an illustrated Bible. In the morning, two women, covered in black cloth had come to watch us shyly, standing at a distance and waving in return for our greeting. We had not known that the country was in turmoil with a coup at the top levels of government and we had been somewhat concerned at the number of military about. But we had been treated with courtesy and consideration despite the fact that the Algerian War was still a sharp memory for all the people.

We had gone on from Tlemcen to camp on the beach at Wadi Bou Cheral, near the ancient Cartheginian and Roman seaport of Ténès, in the company of a road gang led by a hero of the Algerian liberation forces and a Communist technical foreman who had been trained in East Germany. They had been good to us and we had spent a week with them. Their womenfolk had made us a traditional *cous-cous* and we had cooked a meat stew and spiced sauce to go with it. That evening, particularly, had been hilarious fun for us all and I had benefitted enormously from the experience of living for a short time with those people. Standing on that terrace, twenty years later, looking down on Tlemcen and on to the hills to the north beyond which the sea lay, it came back to me, sharply. I could see the road workers in my mind and watch the simple evening gatherings we had together, so unsophisticated and lacking in pretensions. I could smell the sea and the pine trees and the diesel exhaust of their temperamental bulldozer which was scraping up gravel from the shingle beach to use for road beds. Back in the truck, I decided that I preferred the Algeria of twenty years before, which was true of most places I had revisited on the present safari, I thought with sudden insight.

It was not far to the Moroccan border at Oujda and we were there by lunchtime, passing through green fields of winter wheat with old olive trees dotted about. The road was lined with avenues of eucalyptus and poplars. Other French relics appeared as we neared the border: abandoned small farmsteads and I thought momentarily of Zaïre. On the Algerian side there seemed to be a zone which had been cleared of all permanent habitation. We passed through the last military checkpoints of the safari.

But we were not finished with the hazards of bureaucracy. The smiling, relaxed Moroccan officials checked us through immigration with the minimum of fuss, but then came a Catch 22. Bob was asked, almost casually, for his 'guarantee' for the truck. He knew nothing of any such document, and it was explained that vehicles crossing the Algeria-Morocco border had to have a special paper from the British Embassy in

Rabat, that the normal Carnet de Passage that had sufficed all the way from Johannesburg was insufficient. Horror! There was no way around it. We were free to travel as we wished, but the truck was impounded at the border. And, could we believe it, it was Friday and Morocco, unlike Algeria, worked normal European week-ends, so the British Embassy would not be able to do anything for us until Tuesday or Wednesday the next week. Bob spoke to a helpful woman on the phone who knew all about the problem and there was a routine, but the machinery could not start running until Monday . . .

We sat around the truck in gloom until a southbound Africa-Access Overland truck arrived and camped up for the night, planning to go through the border the next morning. Their leader was a jolly extrovert from Lancashire who was ready to cheer us up and he had considerable sympathy for Bob. We had no Moroccan cash, of course, and no way of getting to shops in Oujda, some miles from the border post so we were invited to eat dinner with them if we could supply spaghetti, which we could, and he would see what they could do. Their group was just beginning the Africa experience and they were full of questions. They were crowded, twenty four of them in the Bedford truck, but seemed a good group, about half British and half Antipodeans and Americans, a standard mix. I chatted to an earnest young man from California who planned to get a job in a restaurant in Durban or Cape Town in six months time and to a rather strange American woman in her forties. Their leader suggested that we go off to Fez or Marrakesch by train or bus, which was cheap, and rendezvous on Wednesday. He would take us in to Oujda in their truck in the morning. It was a very friendly gesture and we applauded his kindness. We had cheered up substantially before walking back to our poor, marooned truck, parked in no man's land between the two border posts. There was a coating of hoar-frost on our tents that night.

I did not remember Oujda from my previous visit, except that it had been a large and prosperous town. It was still large and prosperous and I was glad to see that it did not appear to have been overwhelmed by new buildings. We were dropped off at the tourist office by our Overlanding friends and trooped in to see what could be done. A powerfully built man with curly grizzled hair and a theatrical pseudo-American accent took us in charge with competent ease, instantly recognising our problems and organising us. An officially-registered money-changer was sent for, bus and train timetables were produced and lists of cheap hotels in the main centres. He separated us into three groups: those who wanted to go to Fez, those for Marrakesch and those who wanted to stay where we were, for the moment at least.

Ted and I fell into the last category and we were directed to a simple hotel nearby, the Hotel de Nice, overlooking the main town square with date palms and ornamental trees and flower beds. I was given a large double room with its washbasin and a balcony reached through tall French windows. It was clean and neat, and simple. It was perfect for me, and it cost an incredible £1.50 a night. Ted, Aussie Steve, Adie and Angie checked in as well. I lay on the bed and decided I was not going anywhere, I would wait till the truck passed through and go with it to Fez. Bob had agreed to meet us for lunch after we had all cleaned up.

So began a strange interlude. Oujda was off the tourist route and there were few foreigners in town. The tourist office was there like a friendly big brother whenever we wanted advice. There were modern shops, dozens of cafés, a central market and the sprawling old Medina where we wandered for hours. That first day, at the direction of the tourist office we lunched in the Restaurant de Paris, the last memorable restaurant meal of the safari. The food was excellent French cuisine and the service was friendly and impeccable. We ate their four course table d'hôte menu and they served it as slowly as we wished. We spent all afternoon in the restaurant and it was dark when we emerged. Morocco was better than I remembered it twenty years before.

One day, I went with our 'Oujda group' by local bus to Saïdia on the Mediterranean. The conductor gave us oranges to eat and I gave him cigarettes. Saïdia was an unpretentious seaside resort of small villas in established gardens and a few private hotels, closed for the winter. What was important was the sea. I sat on the beach for an hour watching the flat, milky blue calmness stretching to the pale pastel of the cloudless winter sky. We had crossed from the Indian Ocean at Malindi to this local resort on the edge of this ancient sea. A crumbled fort nearby reminded me of olden days and there were fishing boats pulled up on the beach.

Four days later we were by the sea again, at a winter-deserted holiday campsite close to Tetouan at the foot of the Rif mountains. The geography was a perfect mirror of the Cape of Good Hope and not far away was the yellow bulk of Monte Hacho, the end of Africa.

The following day, I stood with Ted on a stone bulwark, alongside "The Hundred Ton Gun', looking south at Monte Hacho from Gibraltar. We were in Europe, fifteen thousand miles on the road from Johannesburg.

Bibliography

I acknowledge my indebtedness to the following for the use of their writings:

Ardrey, Robert. *Hunting Hypothesis*. Fontana/Collins (1979). *Territorial Imperative*. Fontana (1970).

Bleek, W.H.I. *Hottentot Fables and Tales: Animal Songs – Elephant*. The Penguin Book of South African Verse, edited by Jack Cope and Uys Krige (1968).

Bosman, Herman Charles. *Seed*. The Penguin Book of South African Verse, edited by Jack Cope and Uys Krige (1968).

Brennan, Garry. *The Daily News* of Durban. 1 August 1986.

Camoes, Luis de. *Os Lusiadas – Canto 1: 103 pub. 1572*. Centaur Press Ltd. (1963).

Caputo, Robert. *Journey up the Nile*. National Geographic Magazine, May 1985.

Cowper, W. *The Solitude of Alexander Selkirk*. Palgrave's Golden Treasury. Oxford University Press (1952).

Crewe, Quentin. *In Search of the Sahara*. Michael Joseph. (1983).

Dangor, Achmat. *The Voices that are Dead*. A Century of South African Poetry, edited by Michael Chapman. Ad Donker (Pty) Ltd. (1981).

Davidson, Basil. *The Story of Africa*. Mitchell Beazley, 1984.

Delius, Anthony. *Distance*. The Penguin Book of South African Verse, edited by Jack Cope and Uys Krige (1968).

Eglington, Charles. *The Lowveld*. The Penguin Book of South African Verse, edited by Jack Cope and Uys Krige (1968).

Eliot, T.S. *Journey of the Magi*. Oxford Book of Modern Verse. OUP. (1966).

Flecker, James Elroy. *The Golden Journey to Samarkand*. Palgrave's Golden Treasury. OUP. (1952).

Fossey, Dian. *The Imperiled Mountain Gorilla*. National Geographic Magazine, April 1981.

Hayak, Friederich. *The Road To Serfdom.* (1944).

Heyerdal, Thor. *Fatu-Hiva: Back to Nature*. Allen and Unwin. (1974).

Hoare, Mike. *Mercenary*. Corgi. (1978).

Humphrey, Nicholas. *The Inner Eye*. Faber and Faber (1986).

Kassam, Jusuf O. *Maji Maji*. Poems of Black Africa, edited by Wole Soyinka. Heinemann. (1975).

Livingstone, Douglas. *Locus*. A Century of South African Poetry, edited by Michael Chapman. Ad Donker (Pty) Ltd. (1981).

Longfellow, H.W. *The Slave's Dream*. Palgrave's Golden Treasury. OUP. (1952).

Marais, Eugene. *My friends the Baboons*. Human and Rousseau. (1971).

McLaren, Angus. *Reproductive Rituals*. Methuen. (1984).

Menkiti, Ifeanyi. *Heart of the Matter*. Poems of Black Africa, edited by Wole Soyinka. Heinemann. (1975).

Mindelense. *Attention*. Poems of Black Africa, edited by Wole Soyinka. Heinemann. (1975).

Moorehead, Alan. *The White Nile*. Hamish Hamilton. 1961.

Morgan, Eliane. *The Descent of Woman*. Corgi. (1972).

Morris, Desmond. *Naked Ape*. Corgi. (1967).

Mtshali, Oswald. *Weep not for a warrior*. A Century of South African Poetry, edited by Michael Chapman. Ad Donker (Pty) Ltd. (1981).

Nichol, Mike. *Livingstone*. A Century of South African Poetry, edited by Michael Chapman. Ad Donker (Pty) Ltd. (1981).

Ofeimun, Odia. *How can I sing?* Poems of Black Africa, edited by Wole Soyinka. Heinemann. (1975).

Pringle, Thomas. *Afar in the Desert*. A Century of South African Poetry, edited by Michael Chapman. Ad Donker (Pty) Ltd. (1981).

Ransford, Oliver. *David Livingstone: The Dark Interior*. John Murray. (1978).

Tardios, George. *The Sunday Telegraph*. 30 March 1986.

Watson, Lyall. *Lifetide*. Coronet Books. (1979).

p. 155